# Visions of Faith

A book of photography and quotations
to inspire conscious contact with a higher power

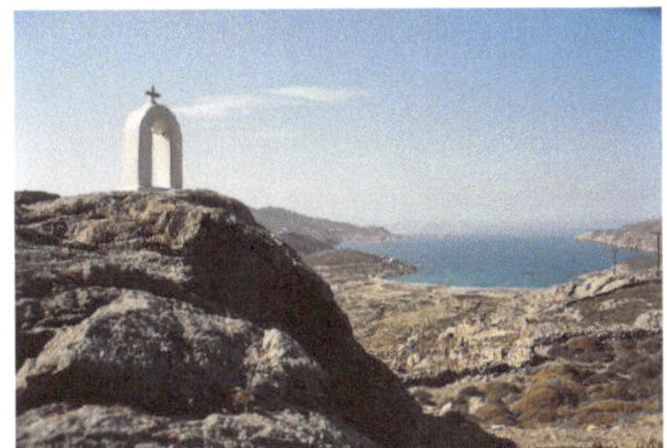

 Visit www.viewfromthepier.com

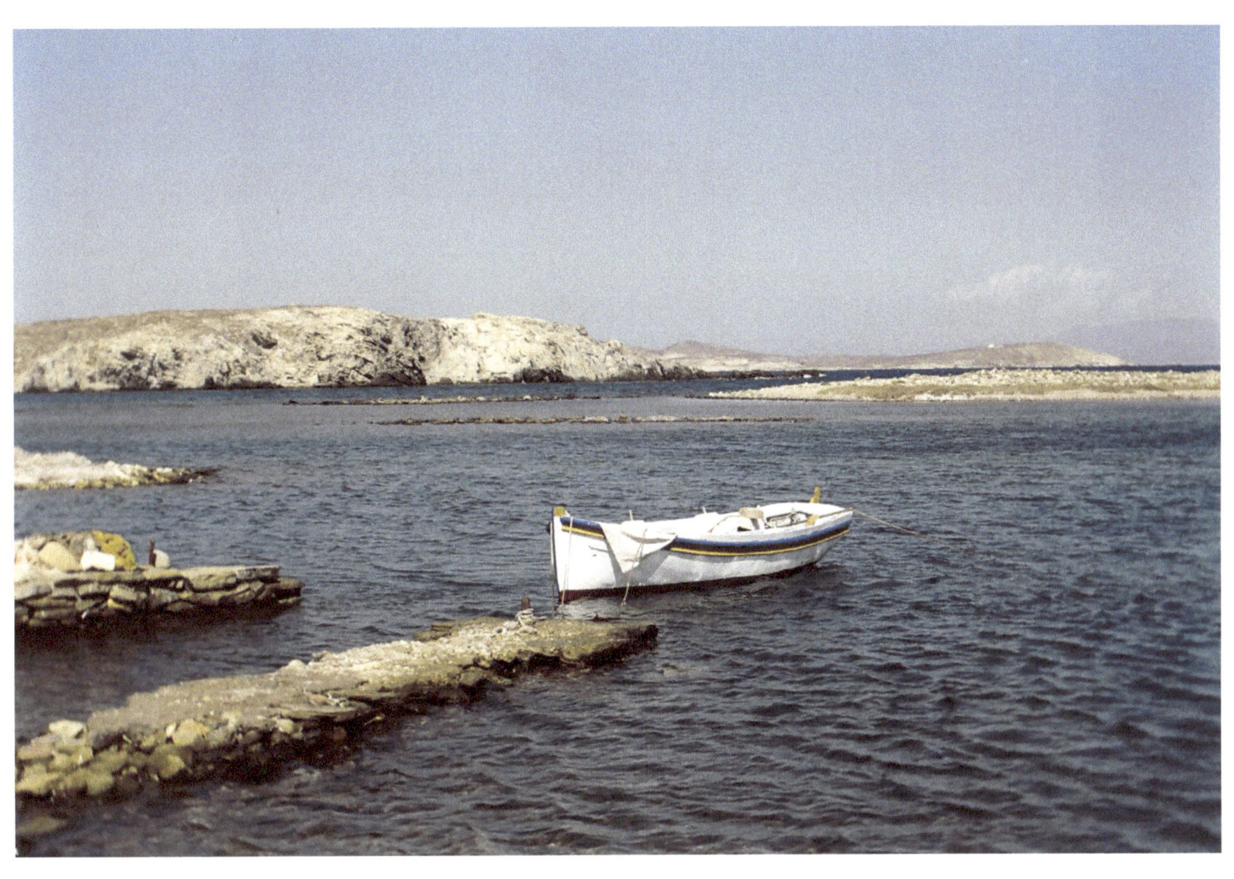

Delos, Greece

Cast all your cares on God; that anchor holds.

--Alfred Lord Tennyson, 1809-1892

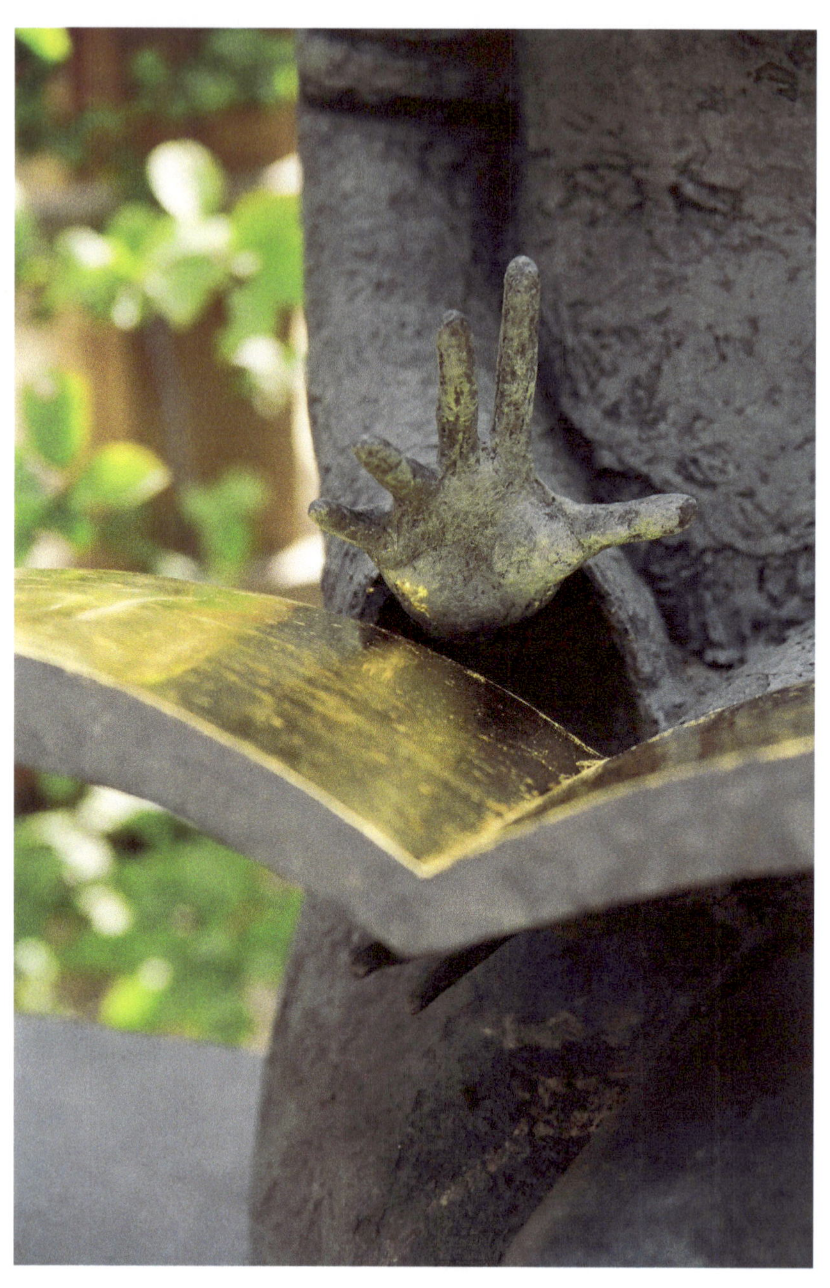

Arundel, England

Life is God's novel. Let him write it.

--Isaac Bashevis Singer, 1902-1991

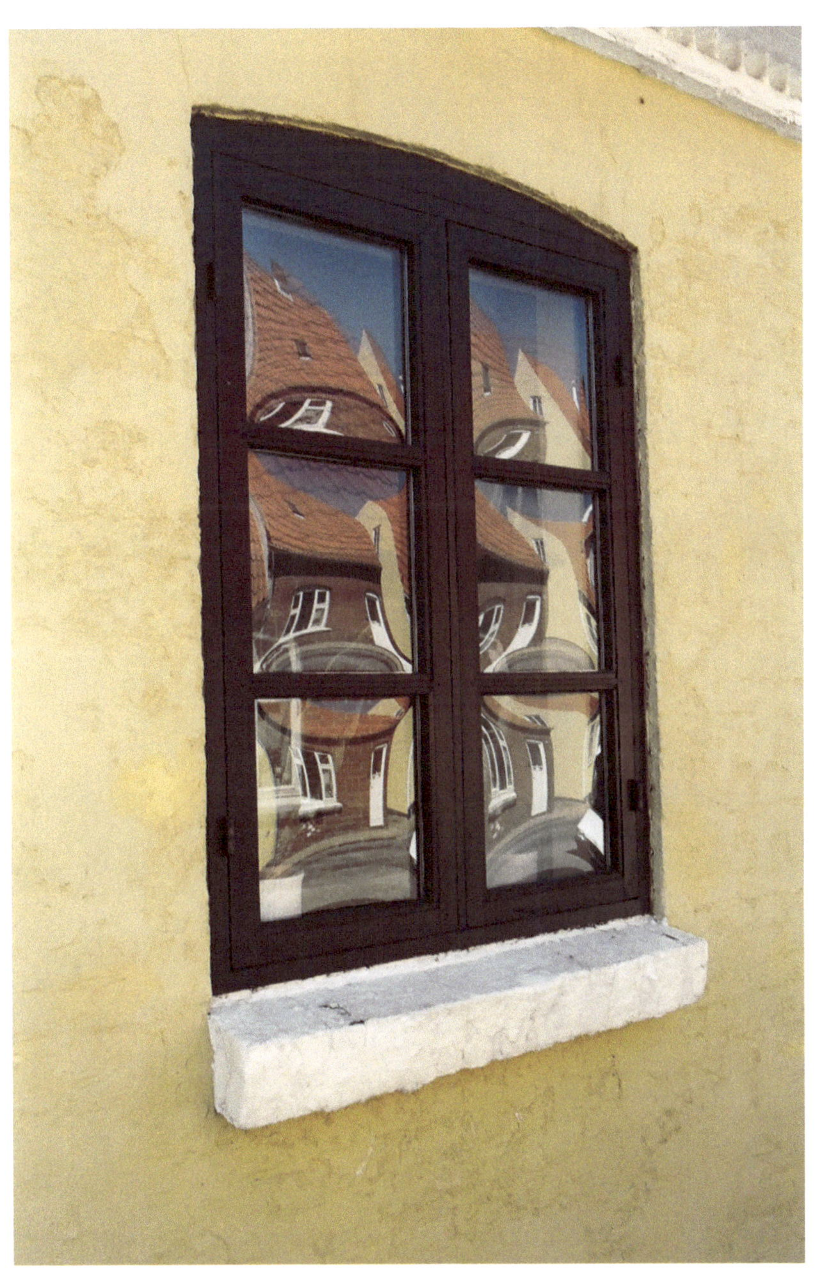

Copenhagen, Denmark

God is like a mirror.
The mirror never changes, but everybody who looks at it
sees something different.
--Rabbi Harold Kushner, 1935-

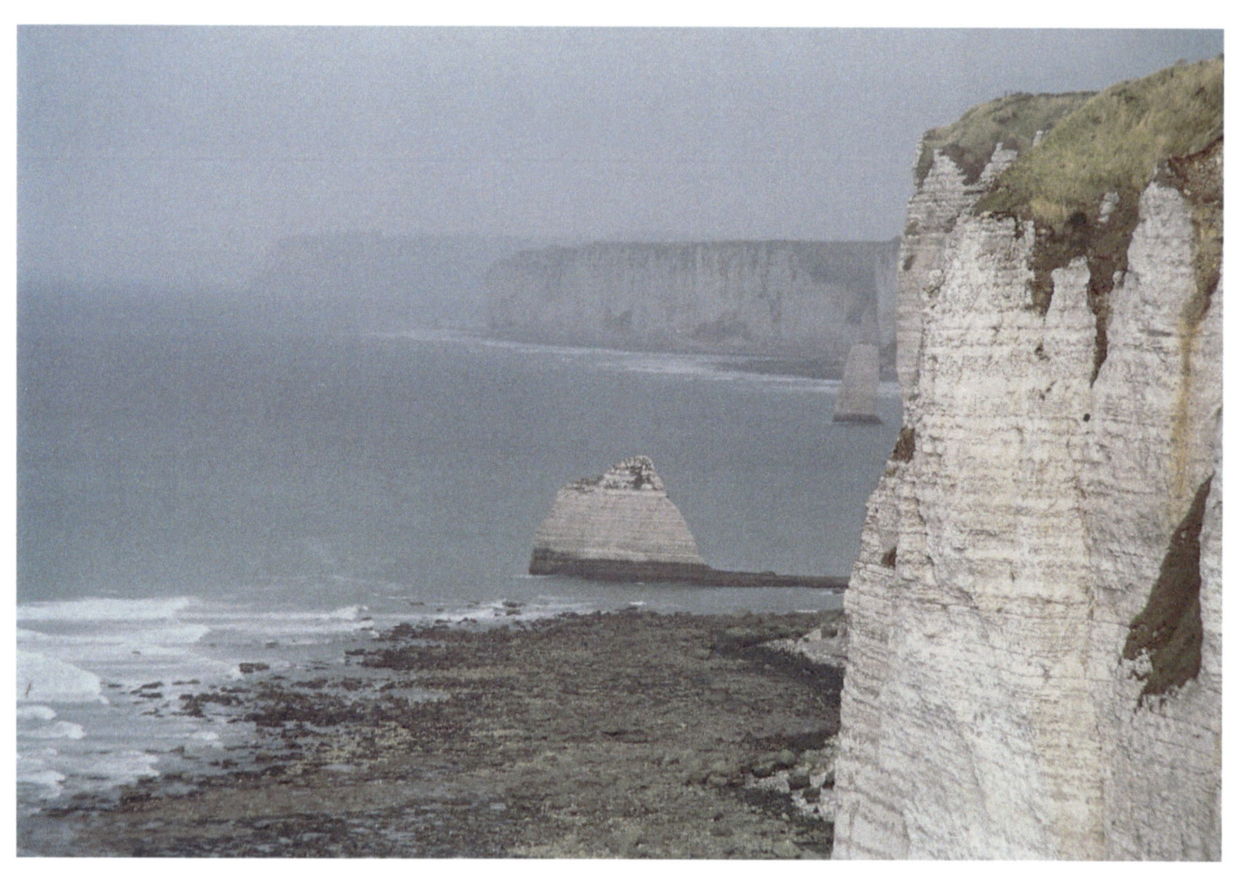

Etretat, France

Faith is the soul's adventure.

--William Bridges

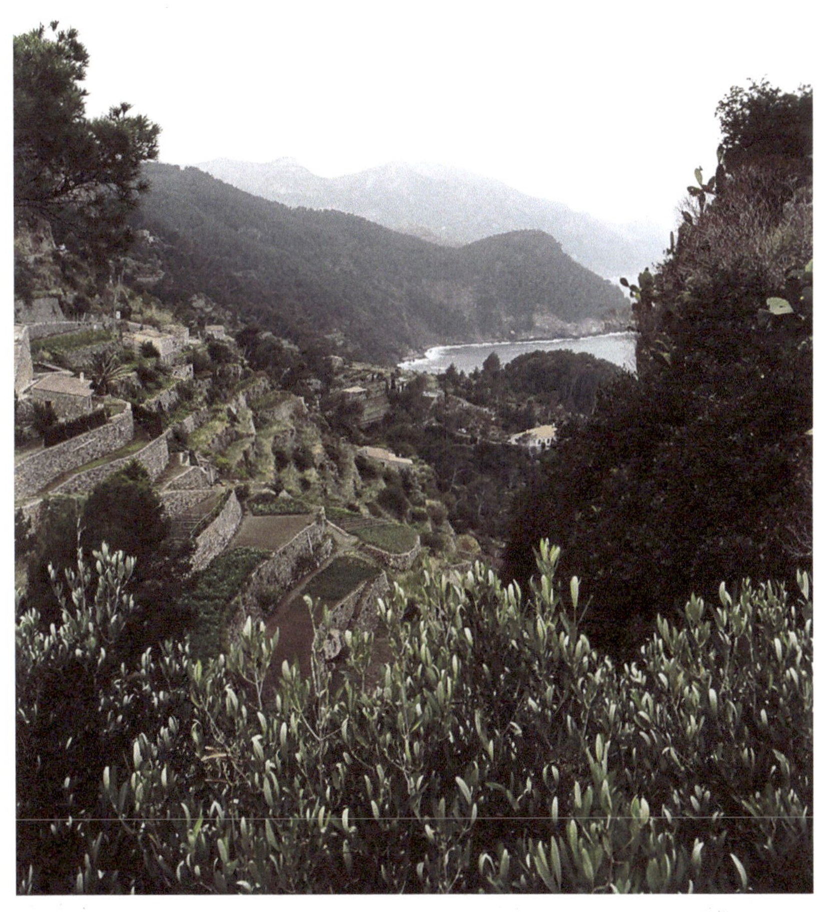

Madeira, Portugal

The hillside's dew-pearled; the lark's on the wing; the snail's on the thorn;

God's in His Heaven--All's right with the world.

--Robert Browning, 1812-1889

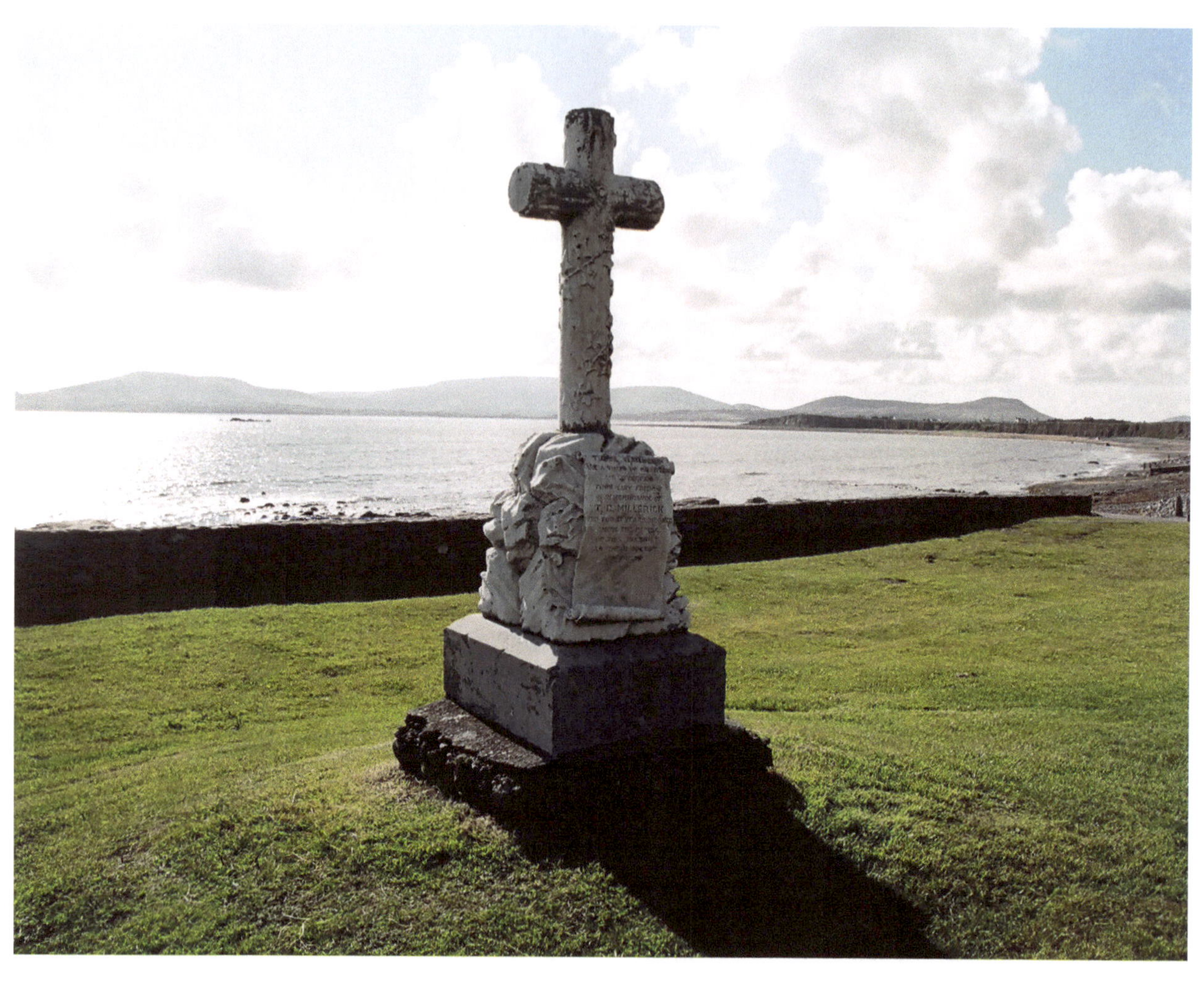

Waterville, Ireland

God is more truly imagined than expressed,
and He exists more truly than He is imagined.
--Saint Augustine, 354 - 450 A.D.

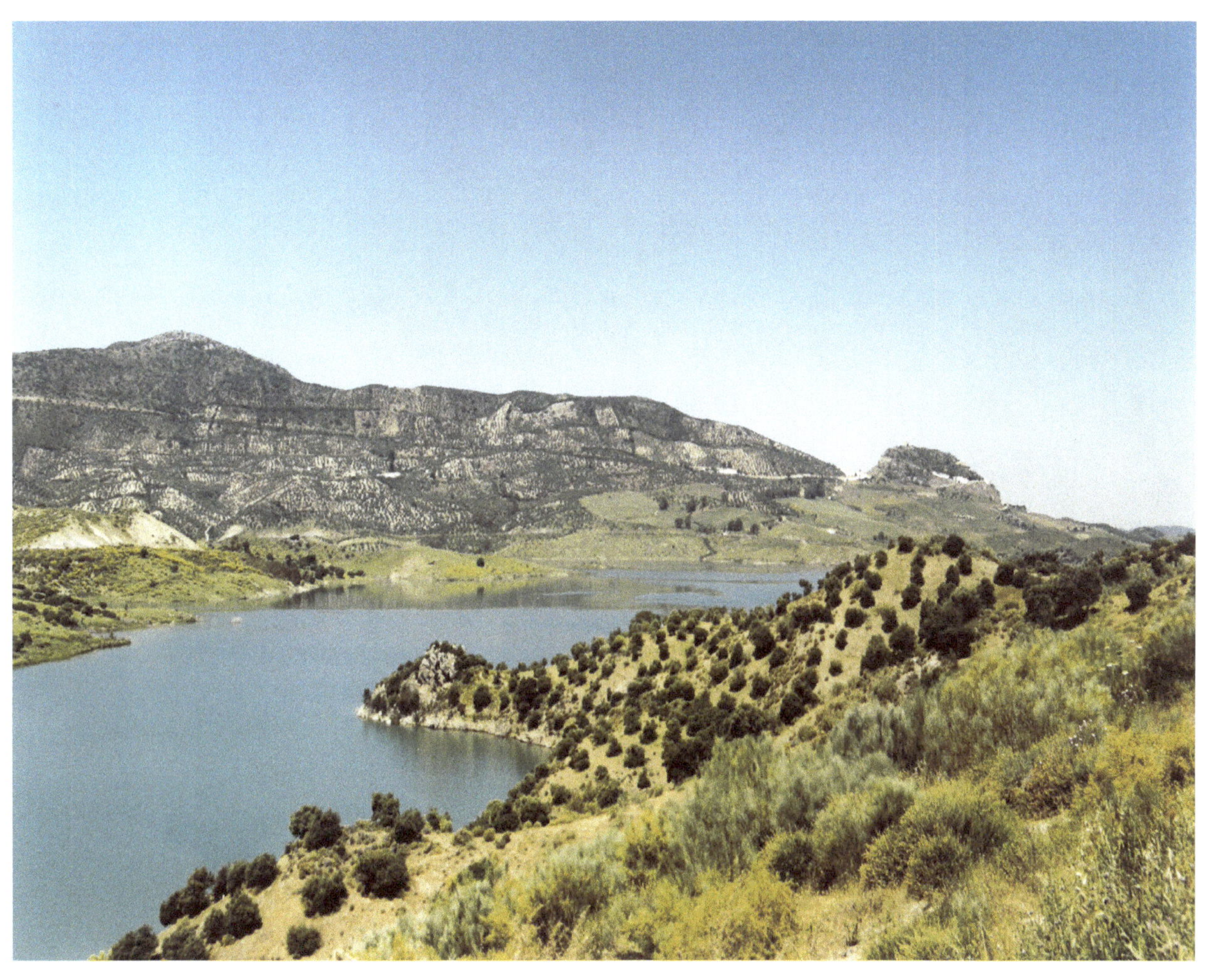

Ronda environs, Spain

Life is so full of meaning and of purpose, so full of beauty--beneath its covering--
that you will find that earth but cloaks your heaven.

--Fra Giovanni Giocondo, c. 1435-1515

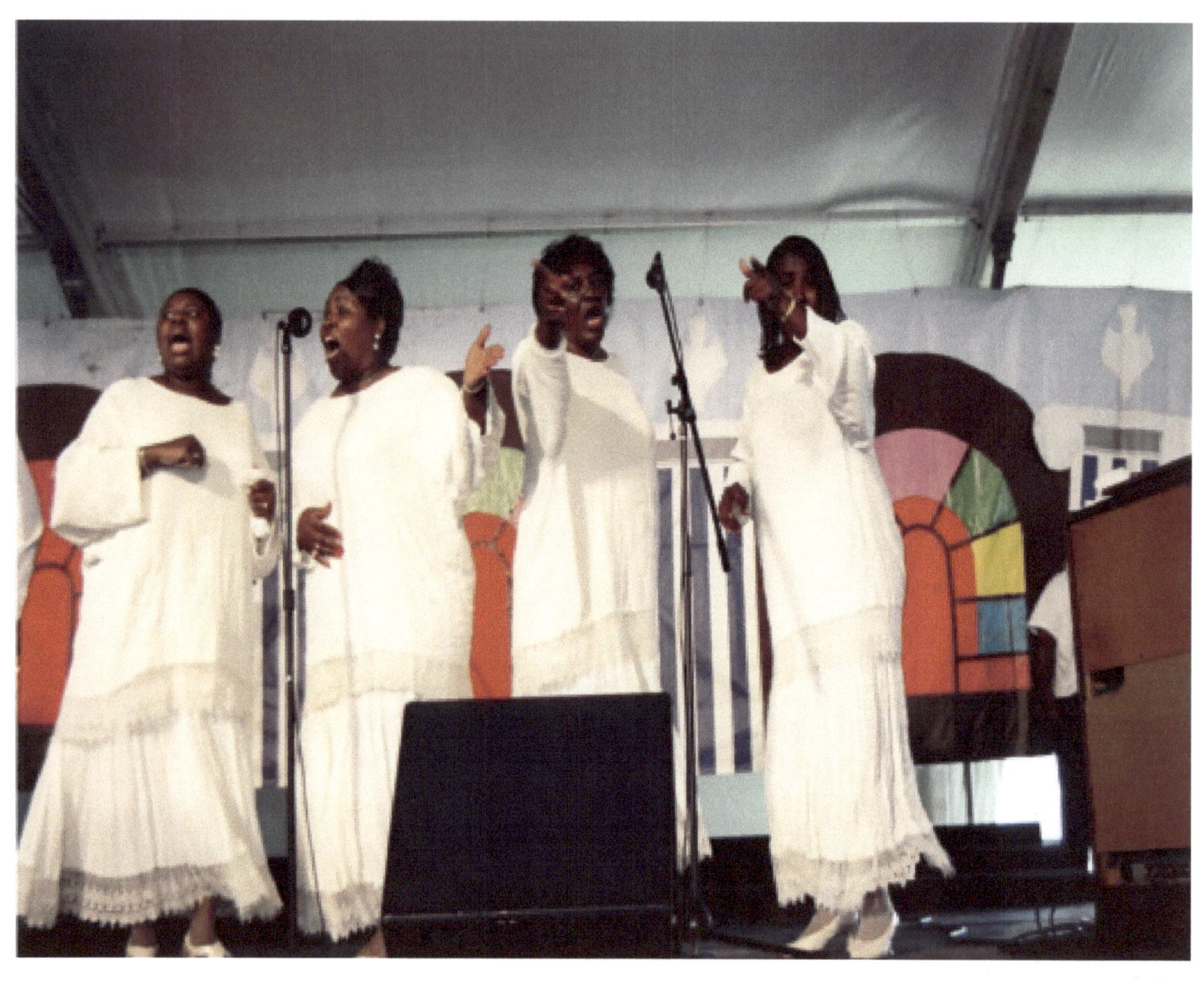

New Orleans, Louisiana

God is a verb.

--R. Buckminster Fuller, 1895-1983

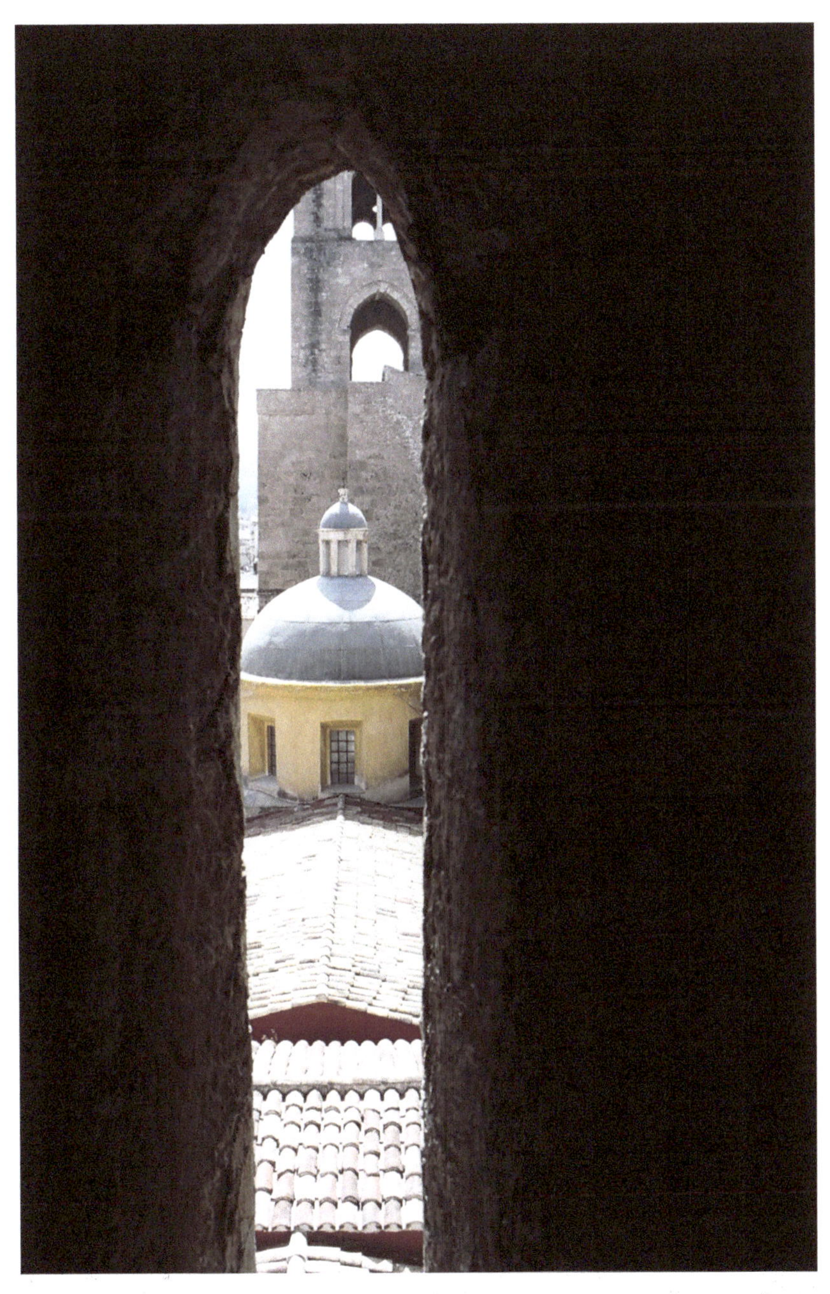

Monreale, Sicily

I do not believe...I know.

--Carl Gustav Jung, 1875-1961

Tikal, Guatemala

Prayer is the contemplation of the facts of life from the highest point of view.
--Ralph Waldo Emerson, 1803-1882

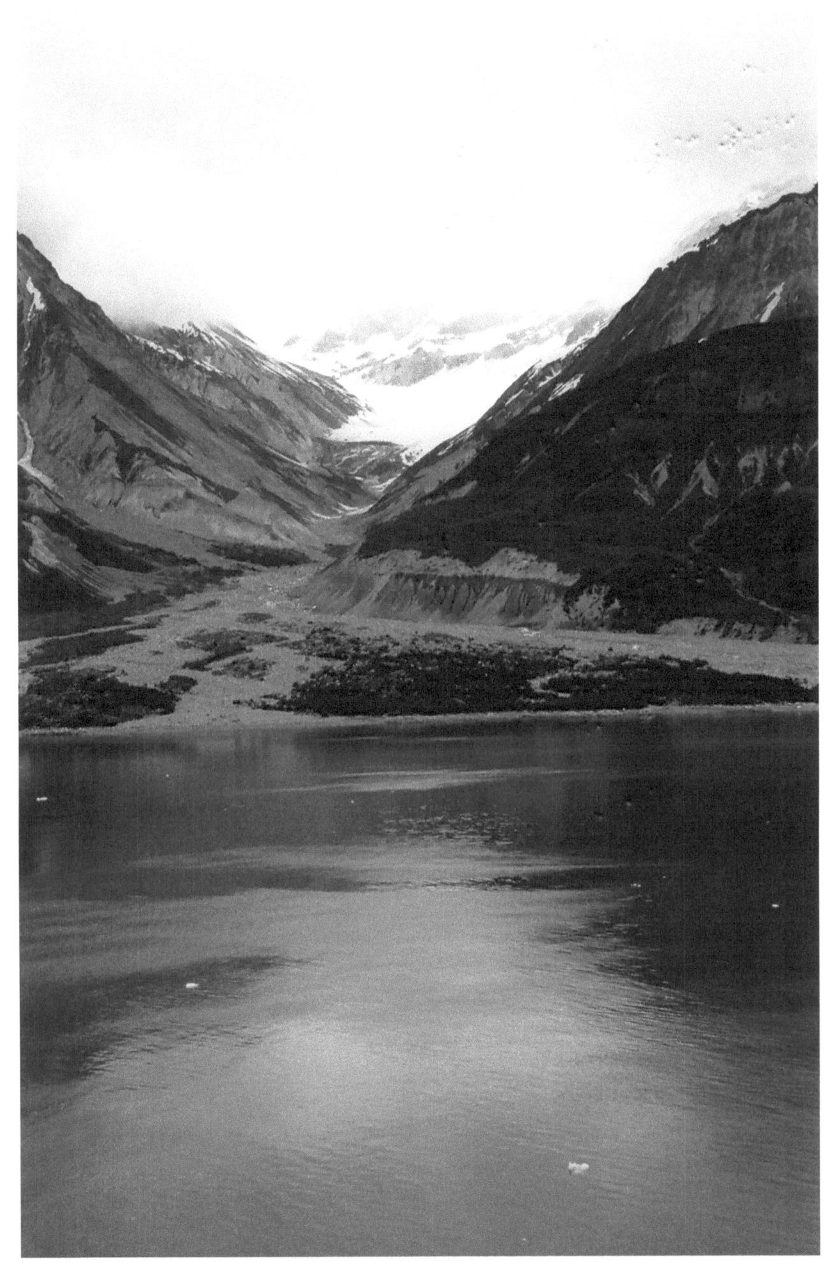

Glacier Bay, Alaska

Prayer is essentially man standing before his God in wonder, awe, and humility.

--George Appleton, 1902-1993

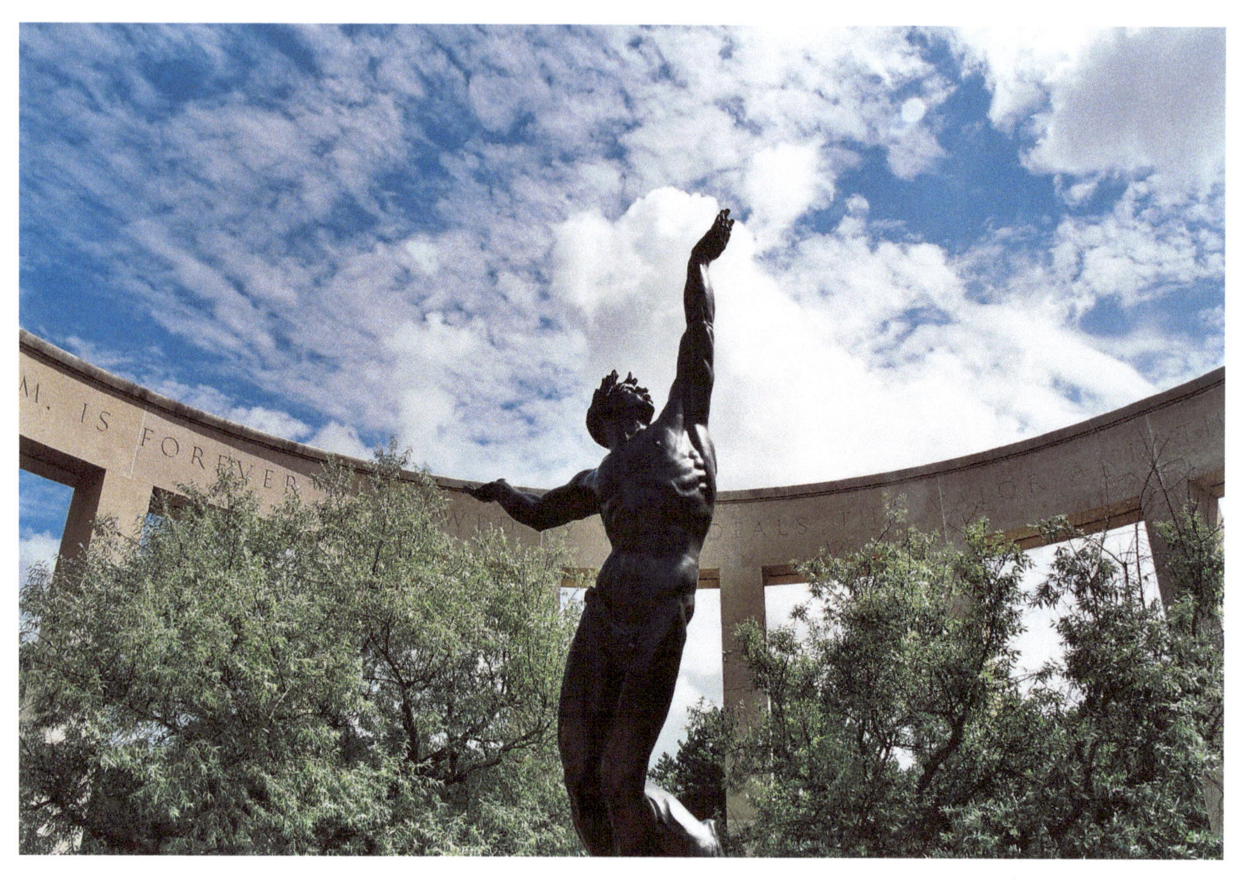

Normandy American Cemetery, France

God knows no distance.

– Charleszetta Waddles, 1912-2001

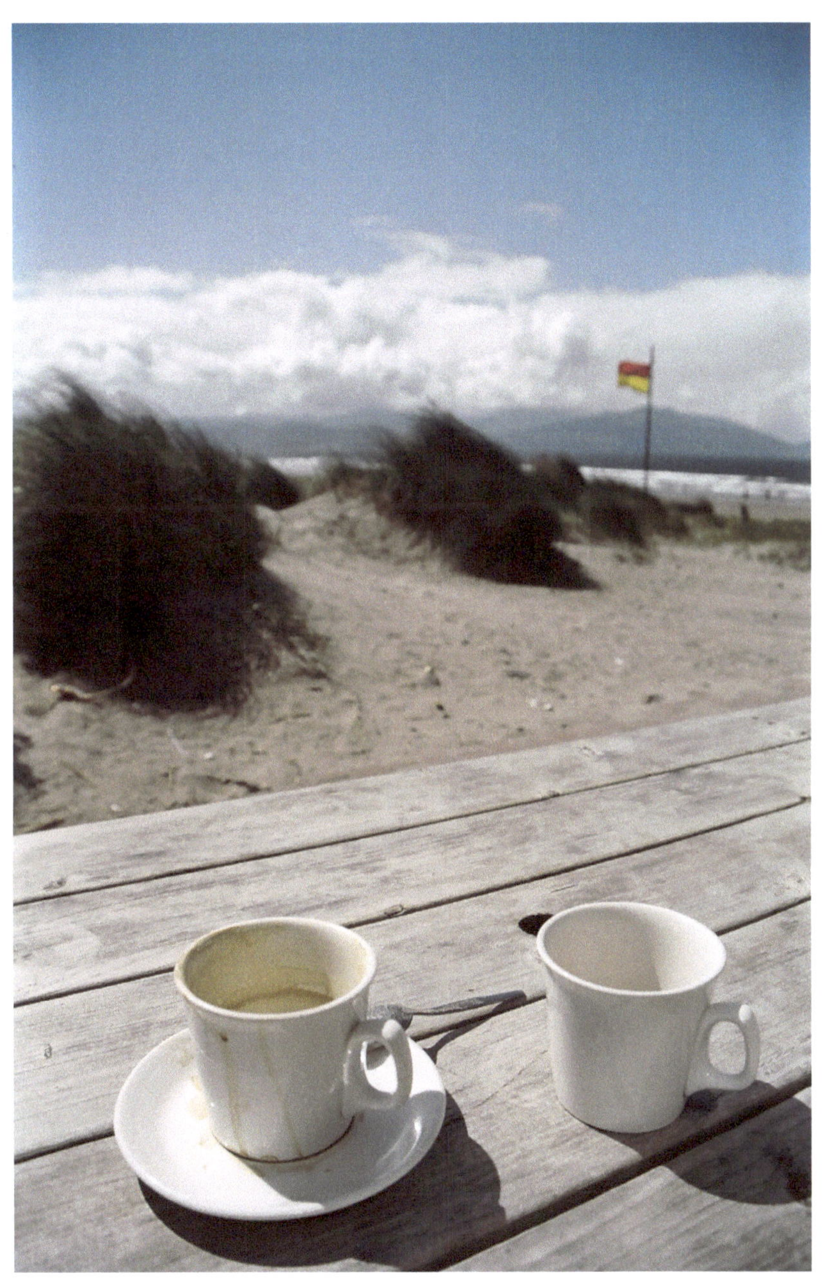

Inch Strand, Ireland

It is necessary for us to withdraw at regular intervals
and enable our souls to attain that quietude and inward composure
which are essential if we would hear the voice of God.
–O. Hallesby

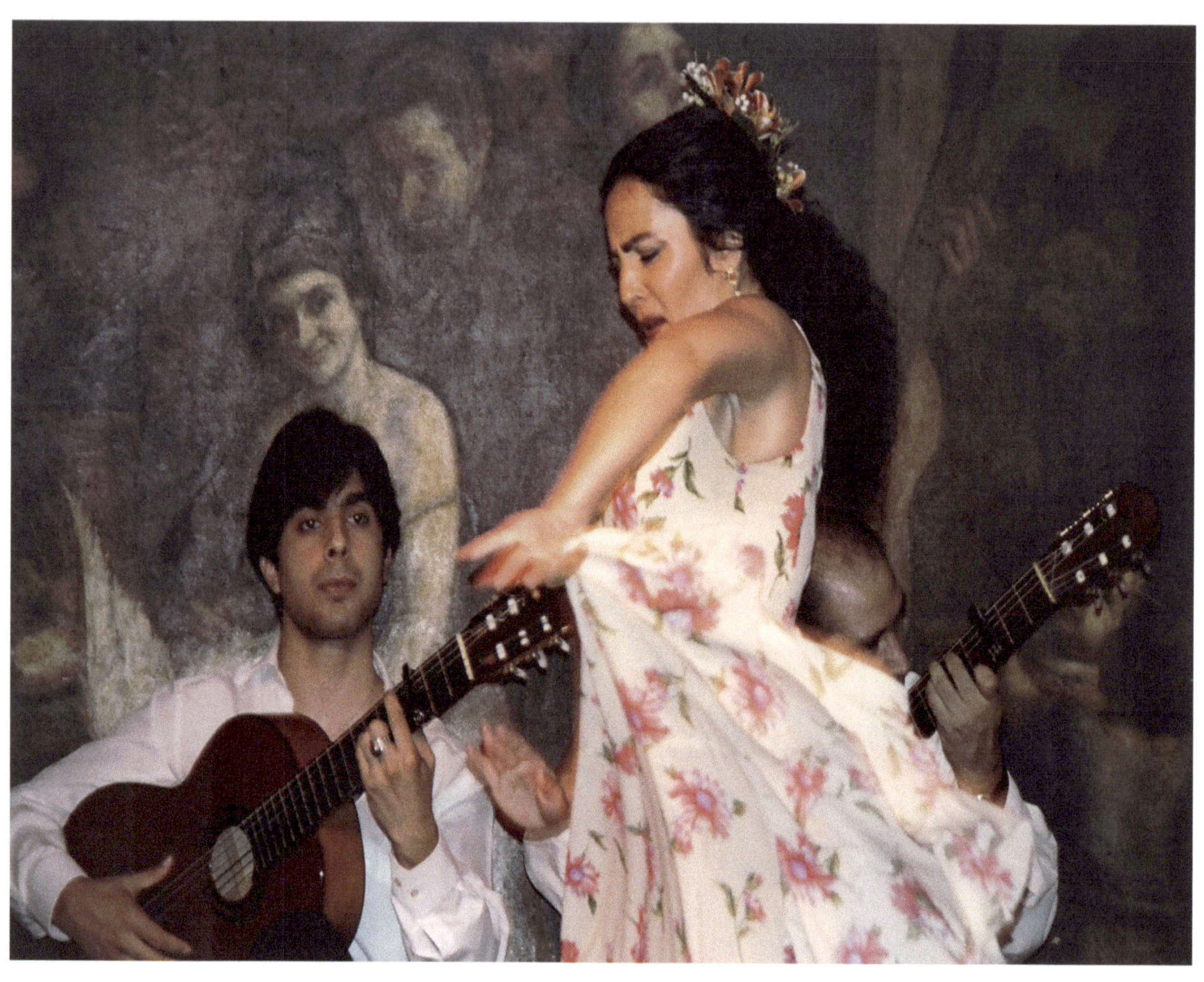

Madrid, Spain

Human beings, vegetables, or cosmic dust--we all dance to a mysterious tune, intoned in the distance by an invisible piper.

--Albert Einstein, 1879-1955

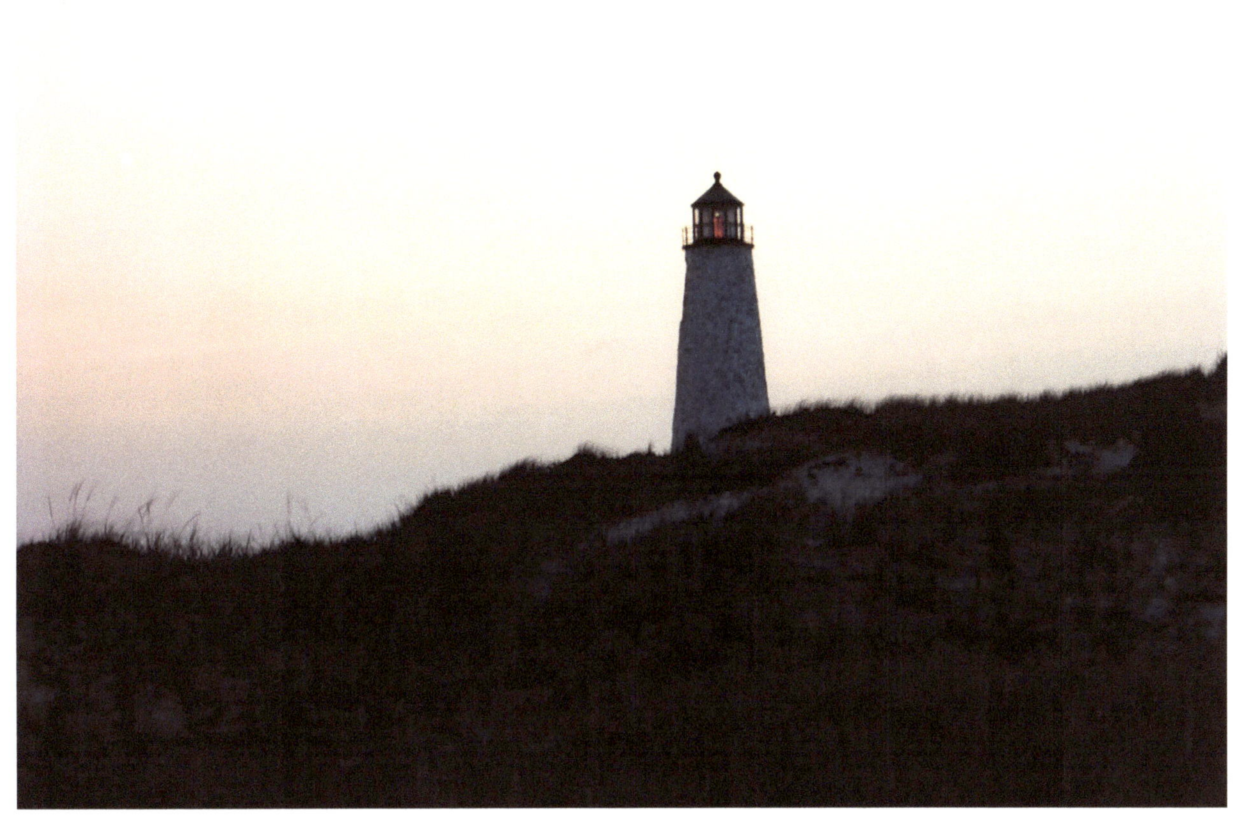

Nantucket, Massachusetts

Faith is the substance of things hoped for;
the evidence of things not seen.
--New Testament, St. Paul, Hebrews 11:1

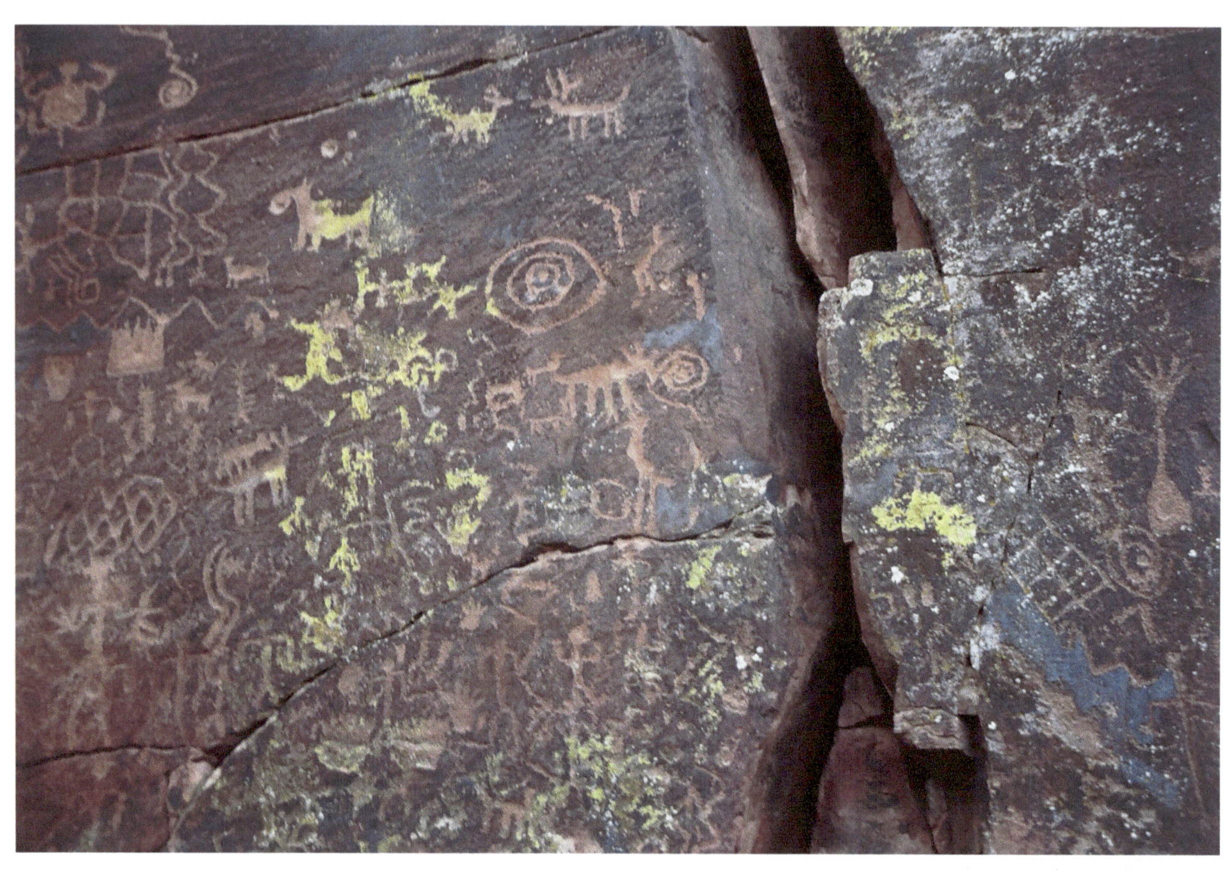

V-Bar-V Heritage Site, Arizona

If you look through all the different cultures,
right from the earliest, earliest days with the animistic religions,
we have sought some kind of explanation for our life, for our being,
that is outside of our humanity.

--Jane Goodall, 1934-

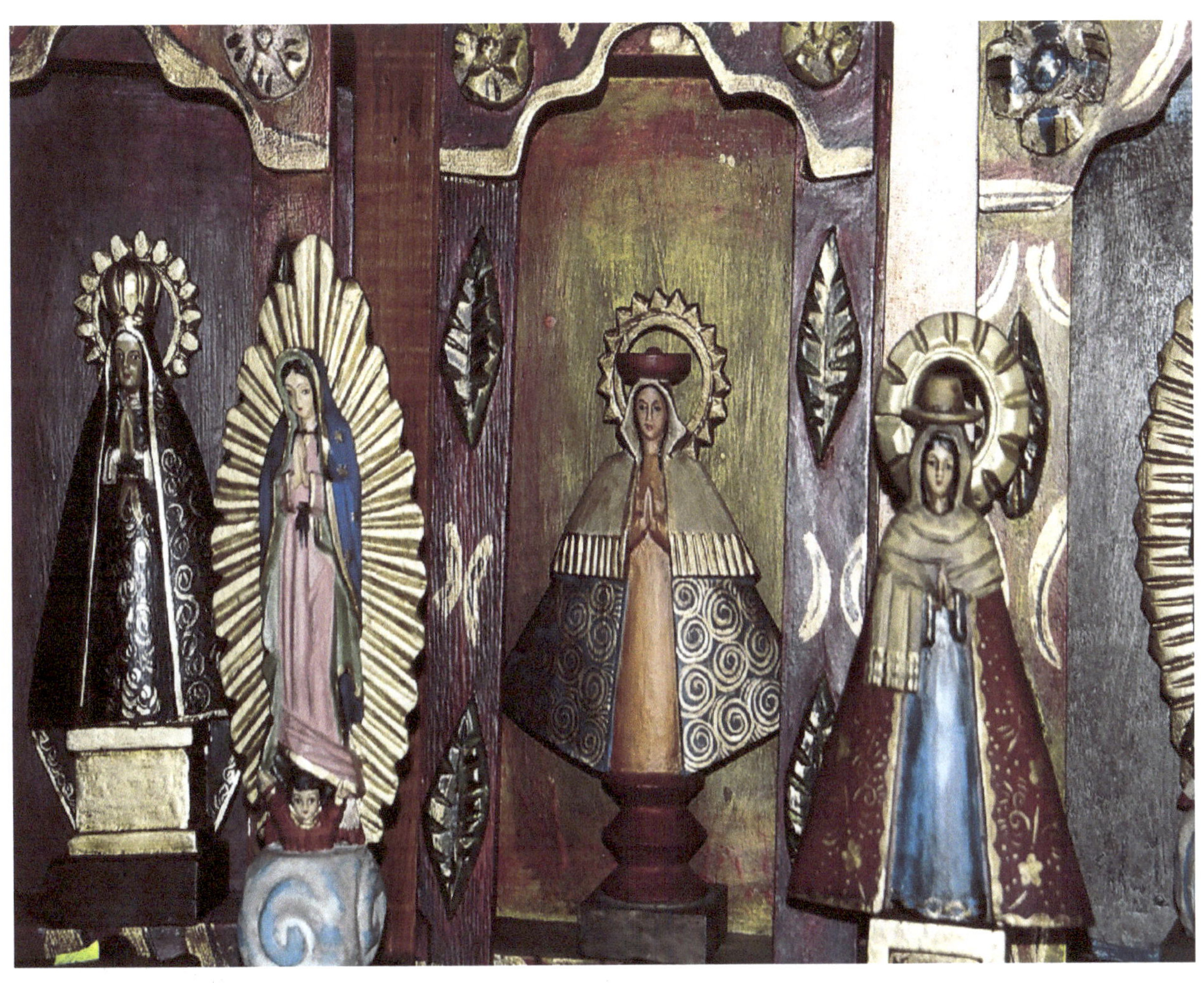

Ixtapa, Mexico

Prayer does not change God,

but changes him who prays.

--Soren Kierkegaard, 1813-1855

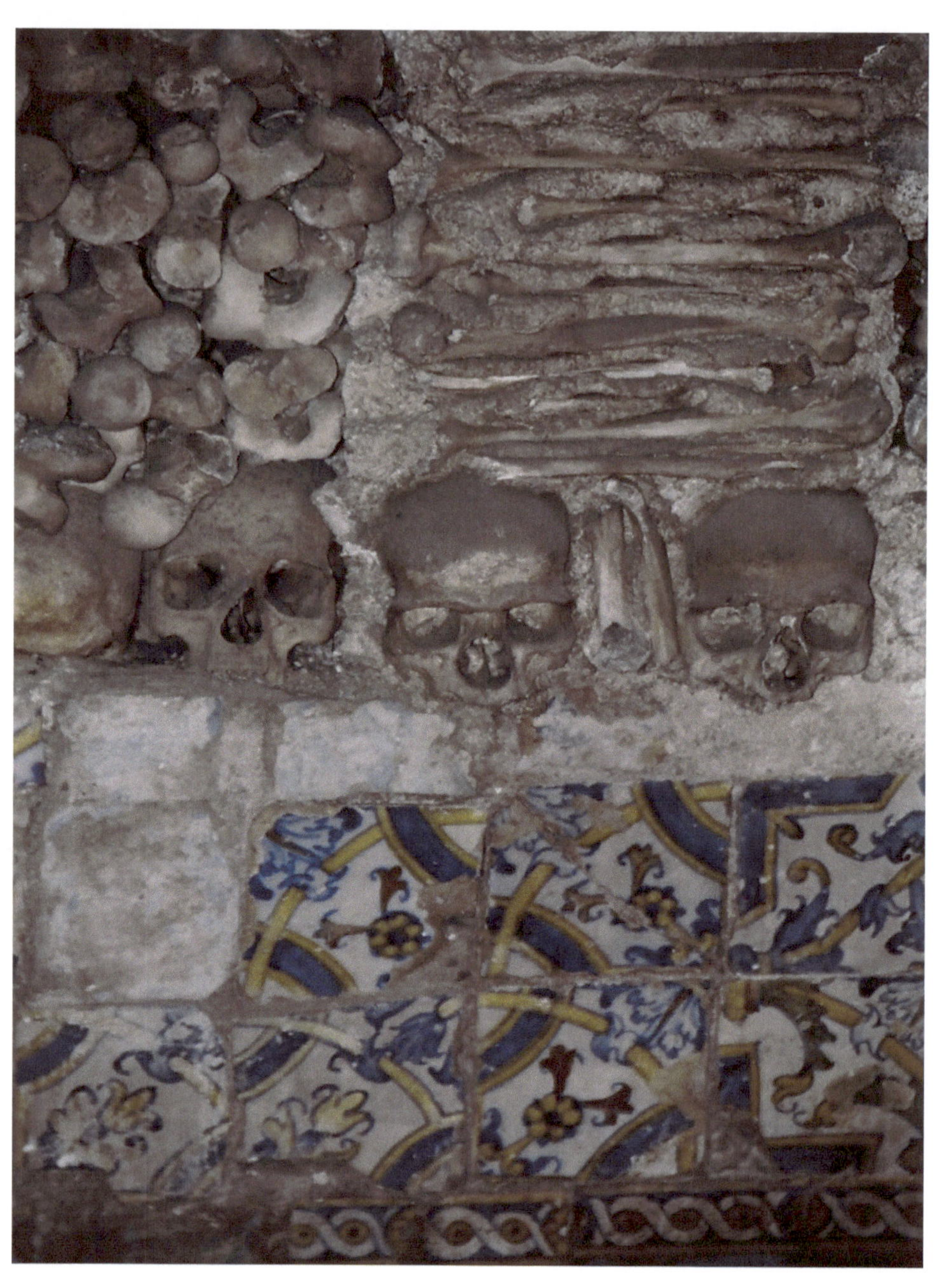

Evora, Portugal

I would rather believe that God did not exist
than believe that He was indifferent.
--George Sand, 1804-1876

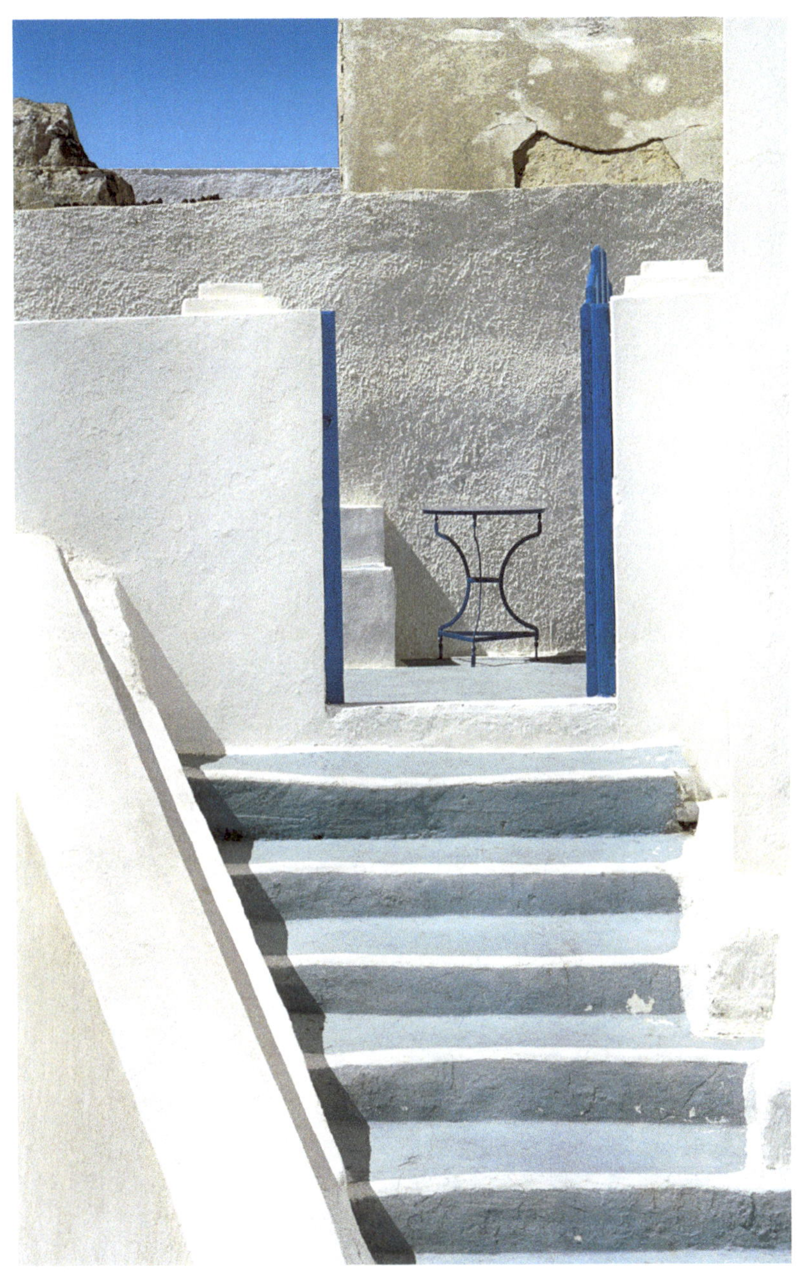

Santorini, Greece

When man takes one step toward God, God takes more steps toward that man than there are sands in the worlds of time.

--The Work of the Chariot

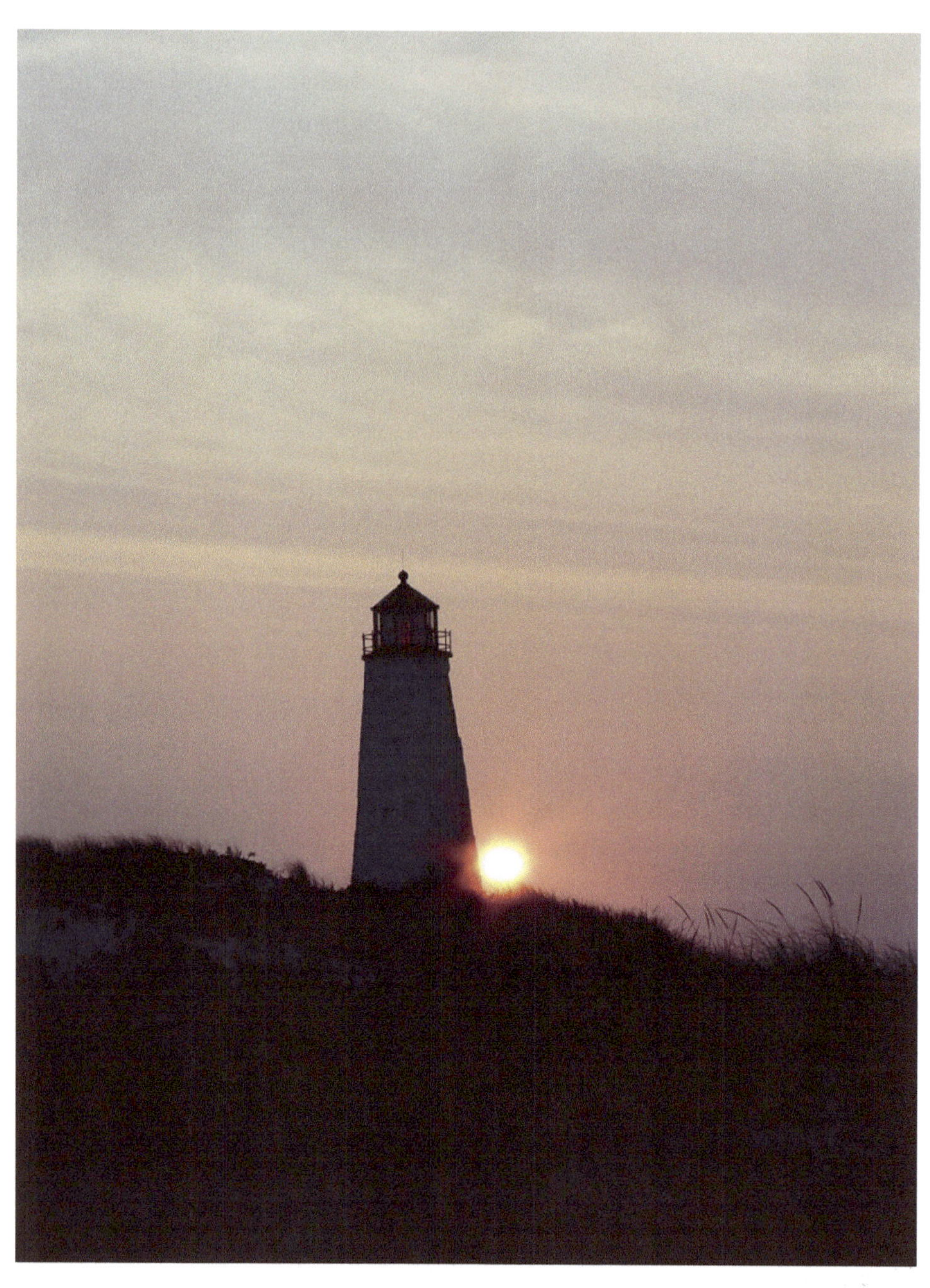

Nantucket, Massachusetts

And o'er them the lighthouse looked lovely as hope,
That star of life's tremulous ocean.
--Paul Moon James, 1780-1854

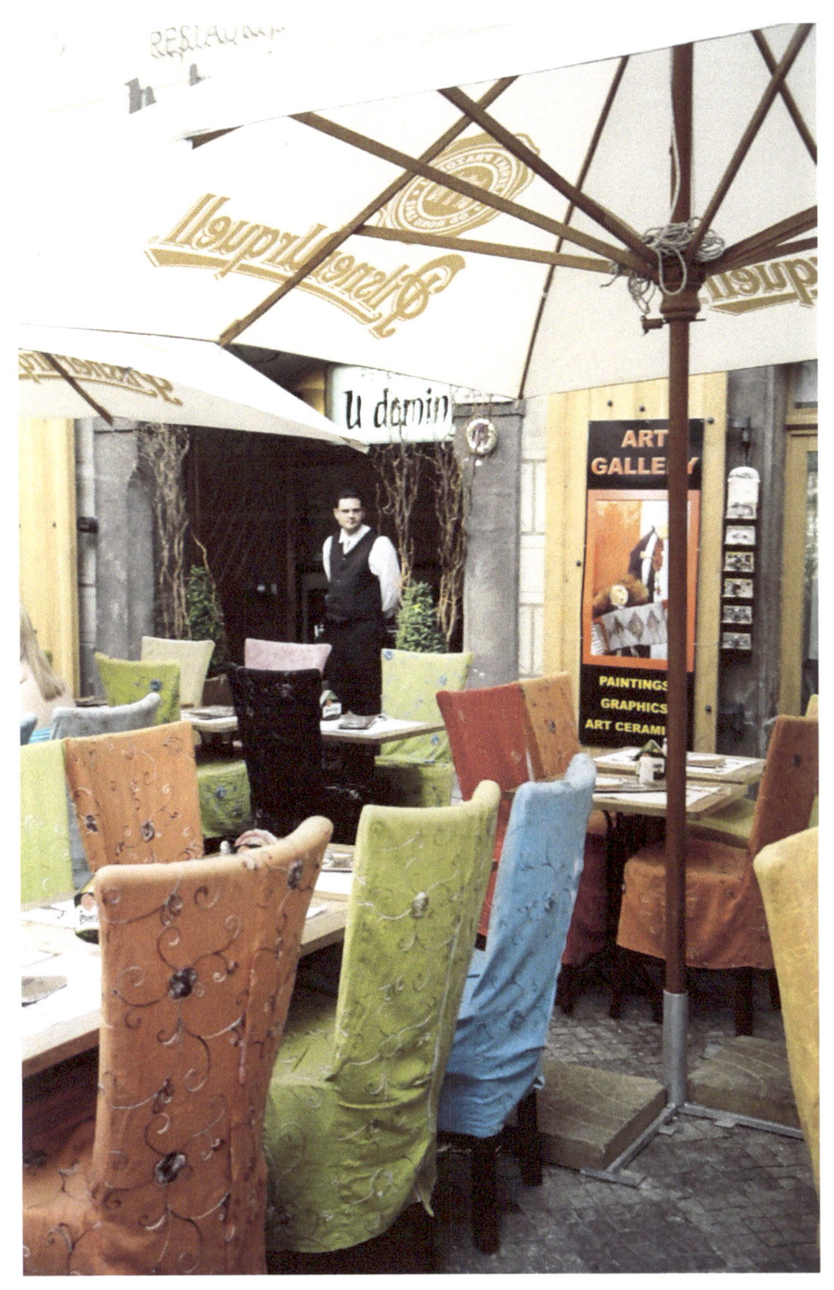


Prague, Czech Republic

God is not a cosmic bellboy for whom we can press a button to get things done.

--Henry Emerson Fosdick, 1878-1969

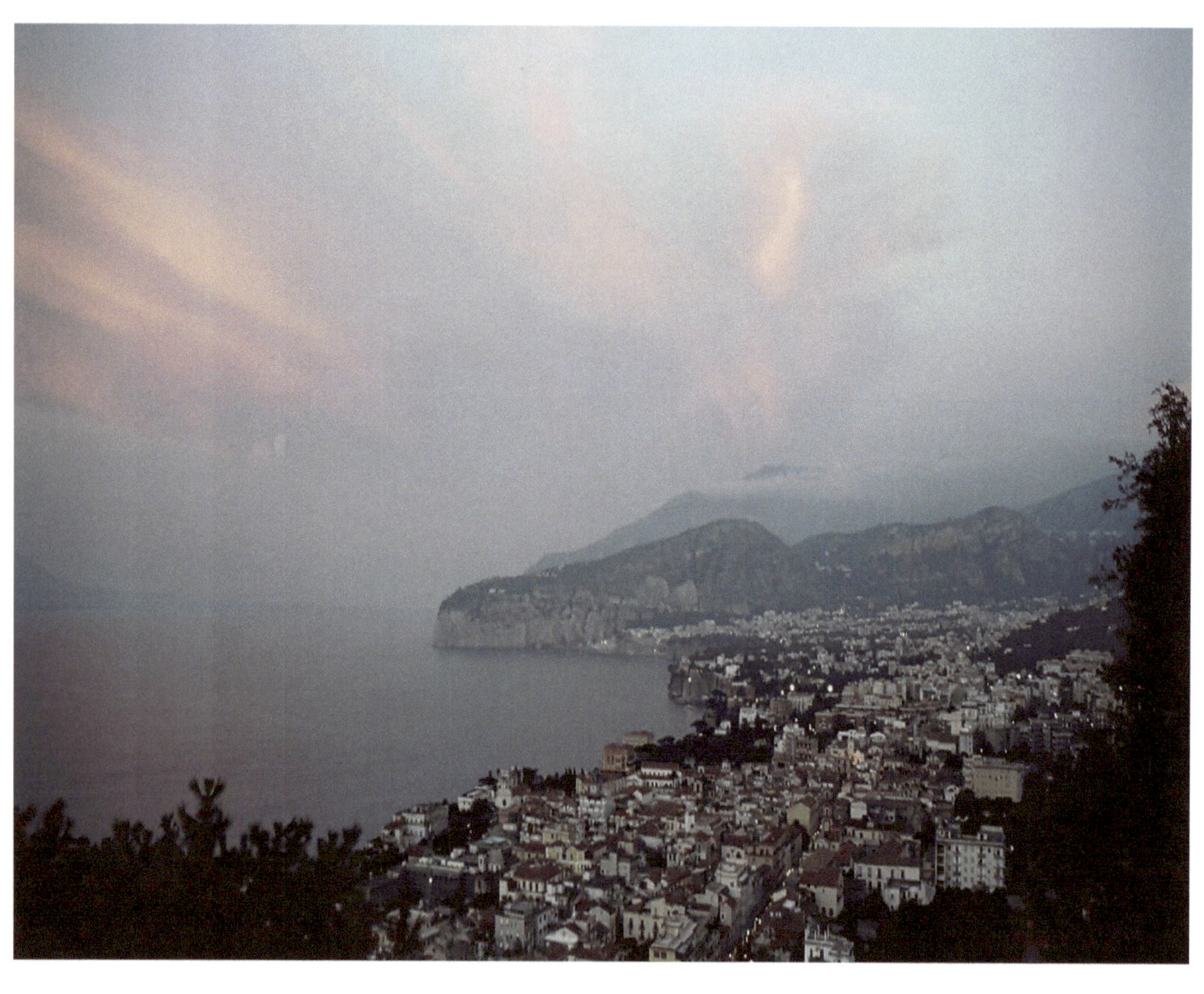

Bay of Naples, Italy

The universe is one of God's thoughts.

--Johann von Schiller, 1759-1805

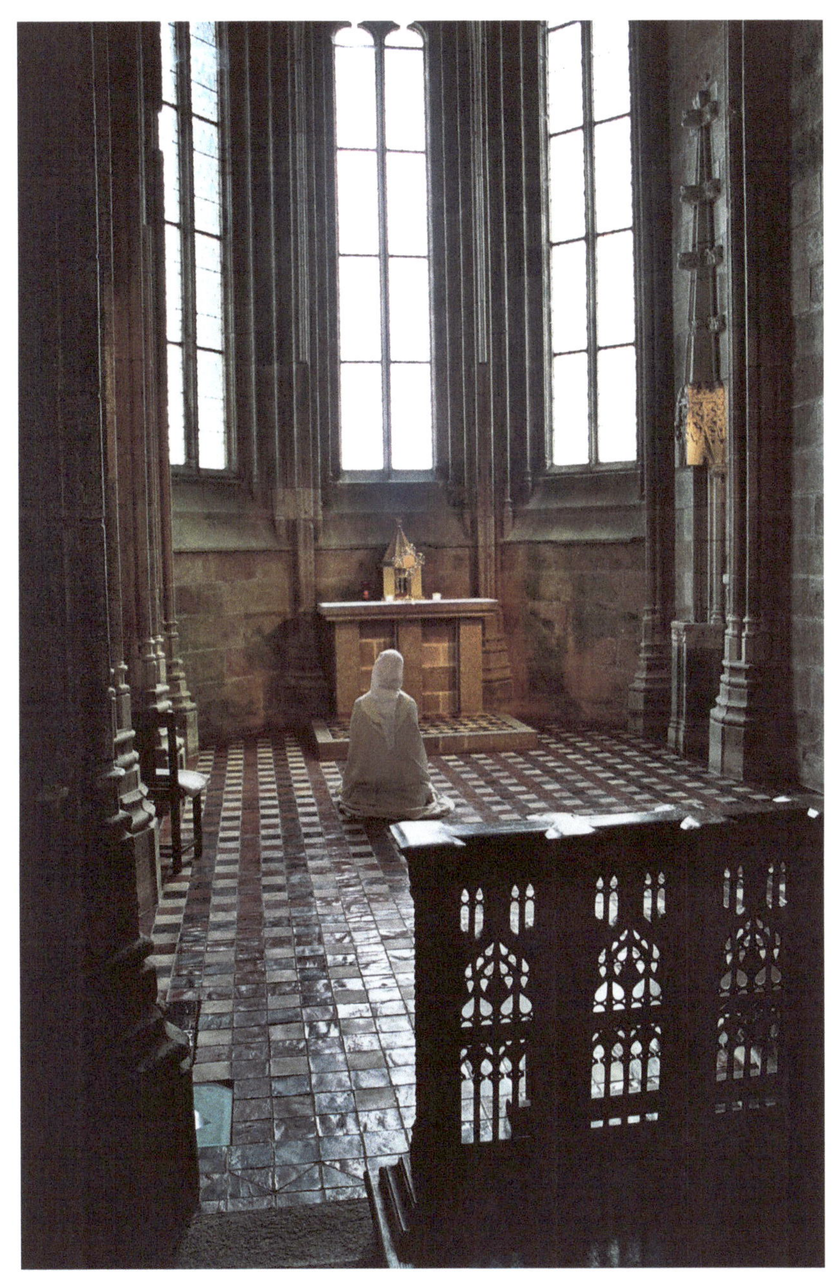

Mont Saint-Michel, France

Grant that we may not so much seek to be understood as to understand.

--Saint Francis of Assisi, 1181-1226

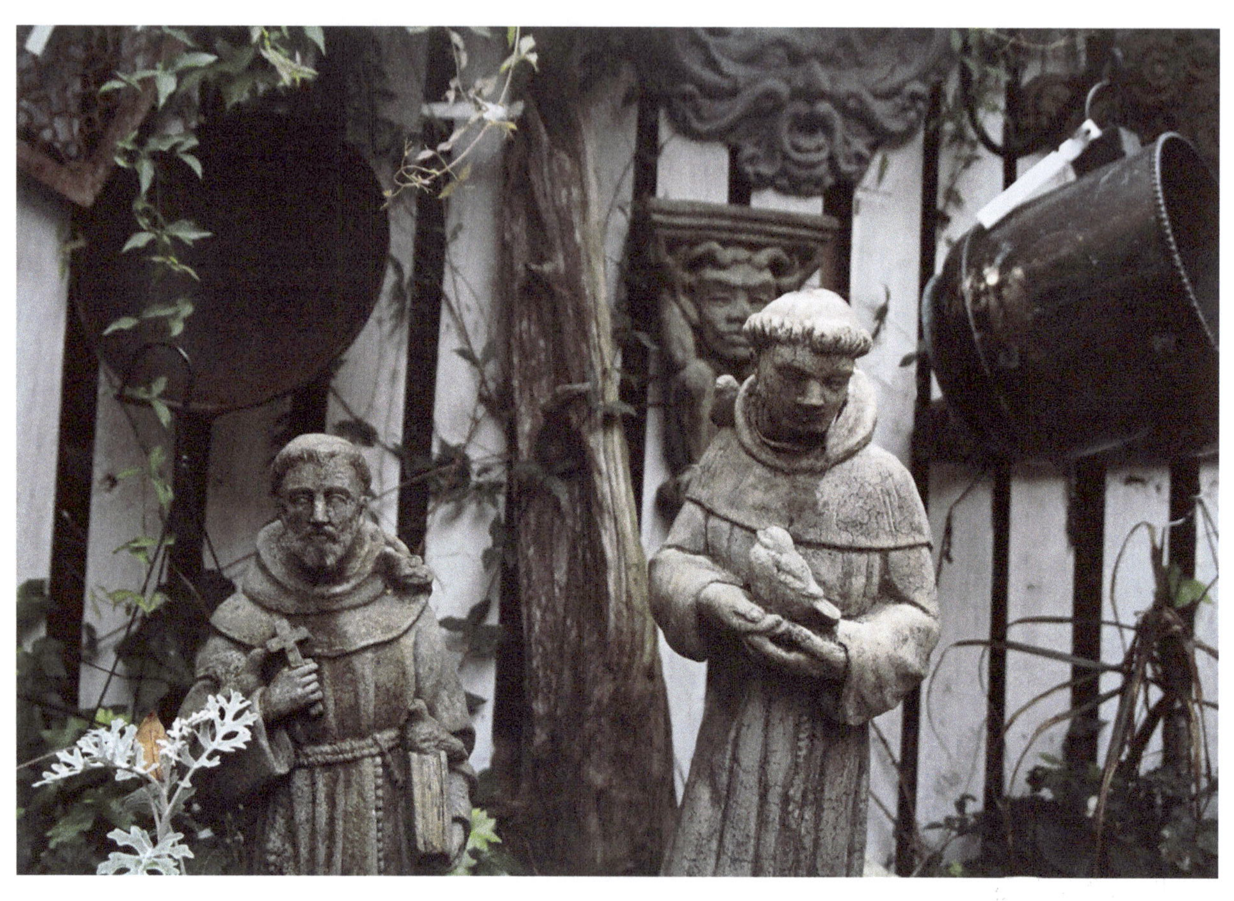

Charleston, South Carolina

Those who always pray are necessary to those who never pray.

--Victor Hugo, 1802-1885

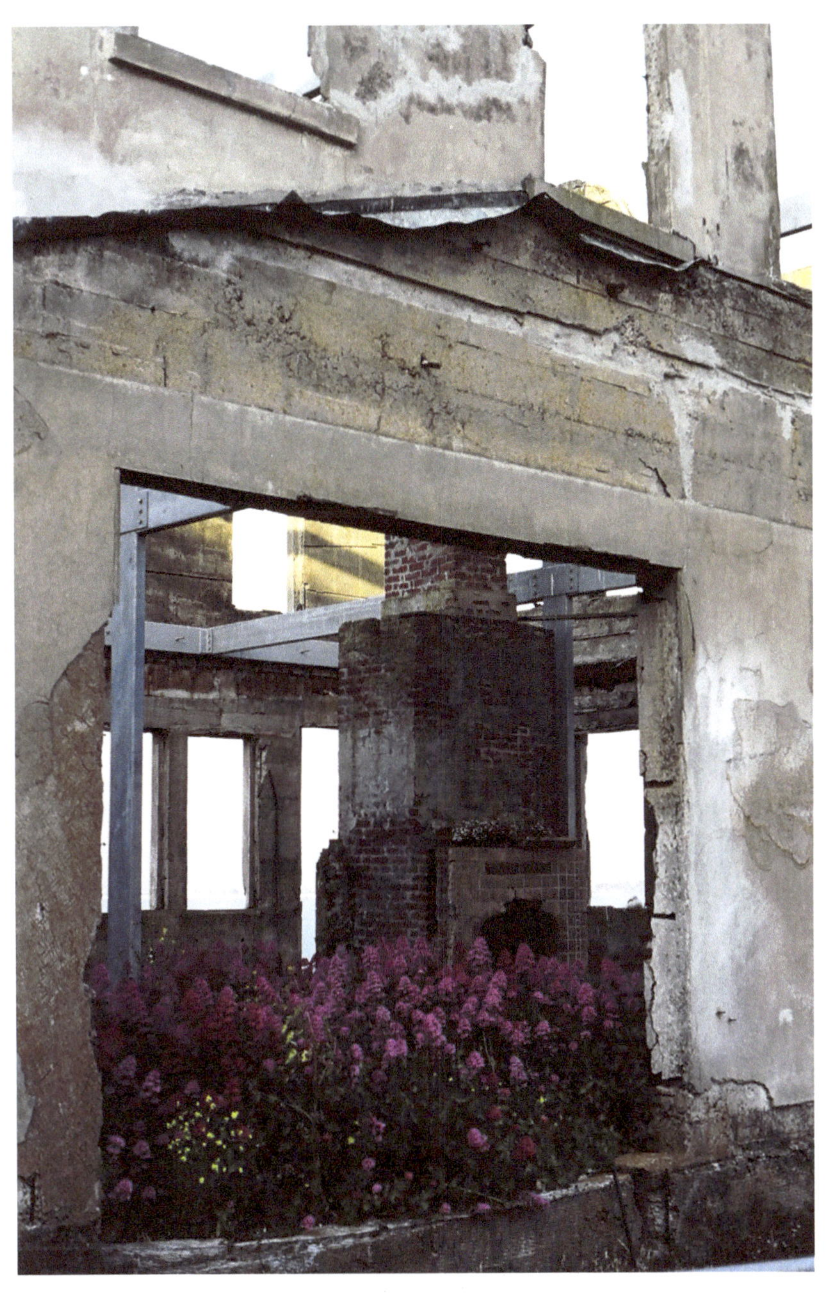

Alcatraz, California

Out of the wreck I rise.

--Robert Browning, 1812-1889

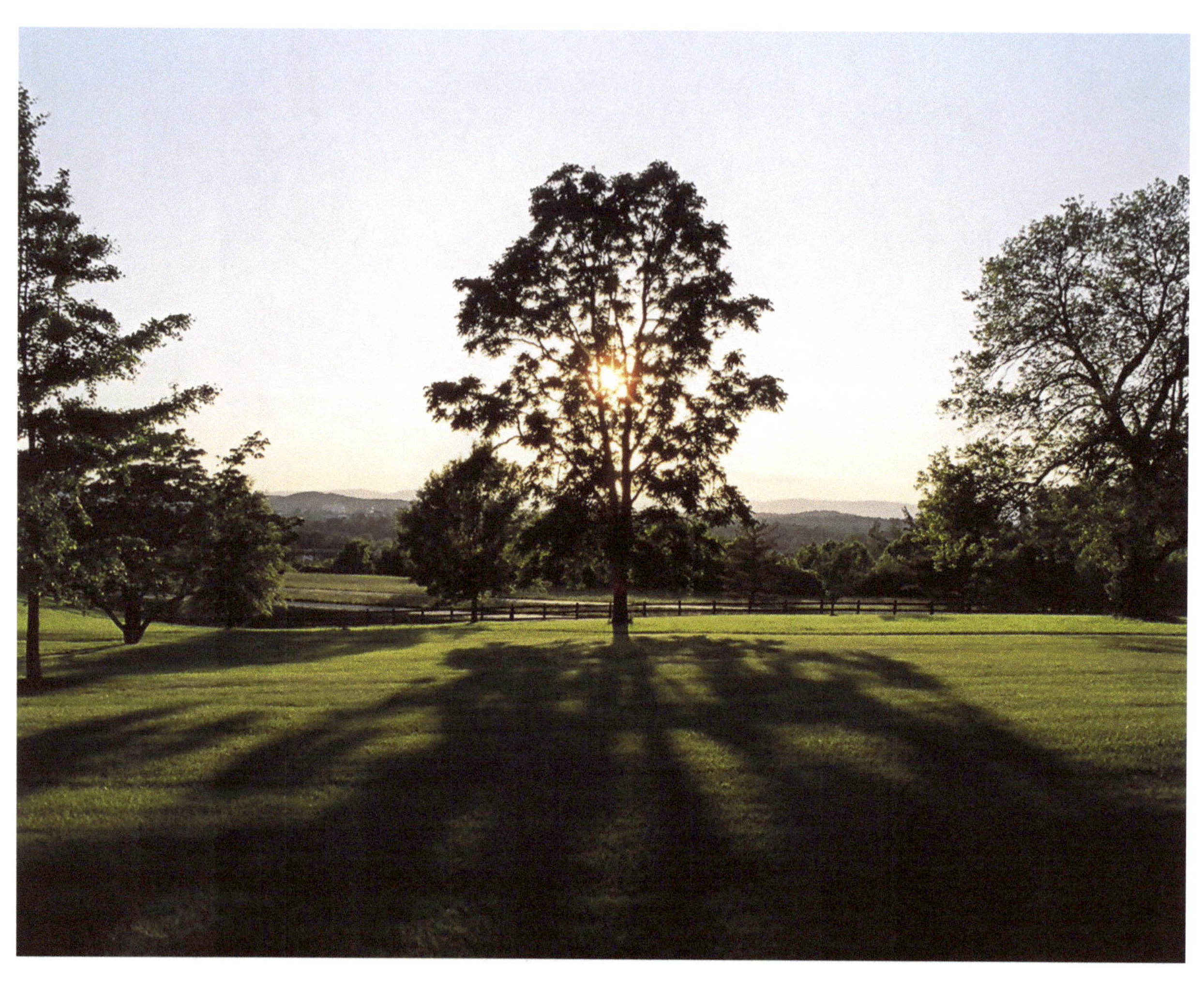

Charlottesville, Virginia

Intuition appears to be the extrasensory perception of reality.

--Alexis Carrel, 1873-1944

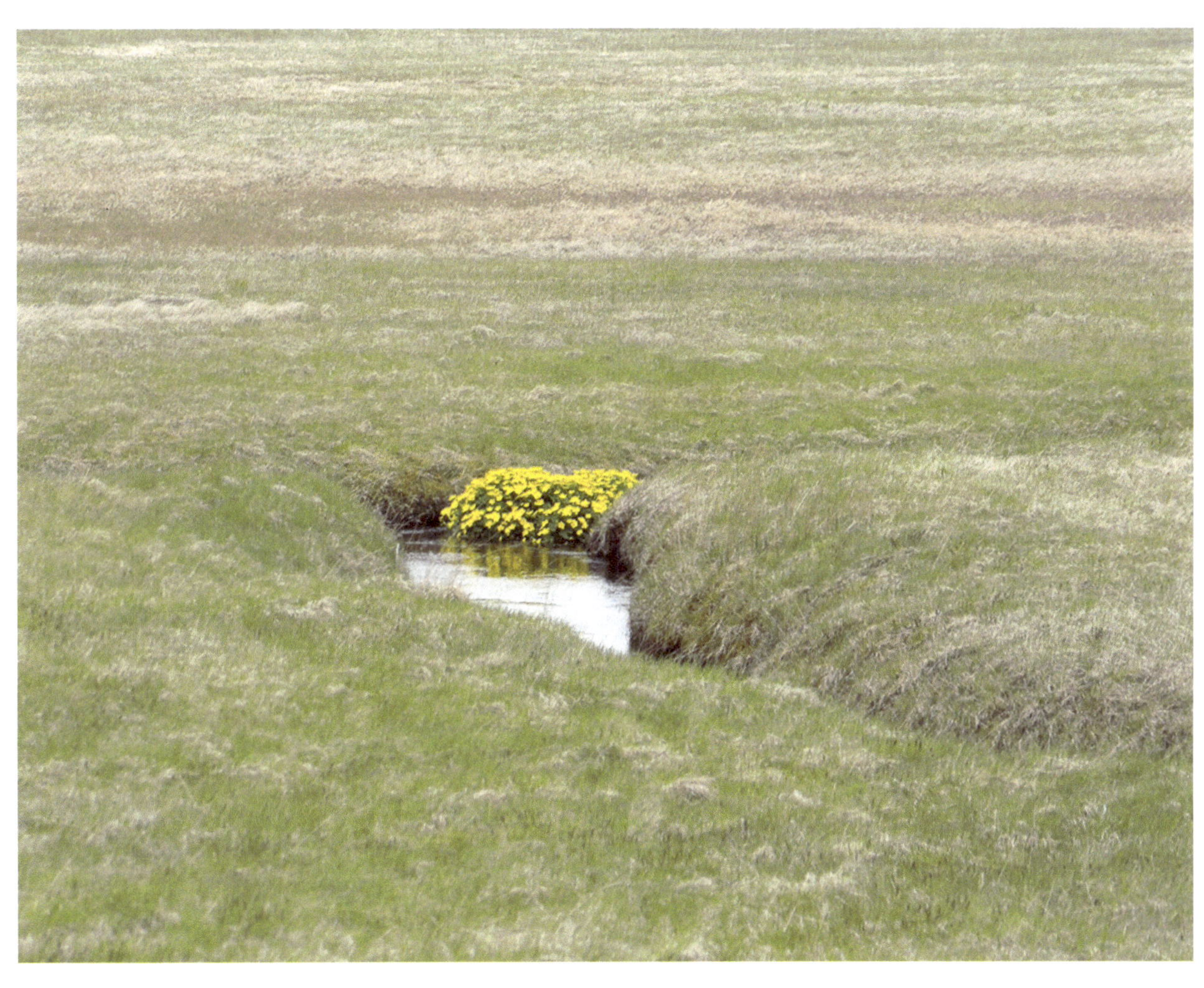

Seljalandsfoss, Iceland

Men talk of "finding God," but no wonder it is difficult;

He is hidden in that darkest hiding-place, your heart. You yourself are a part of Him.

--Christopher Morley, 1890-1957

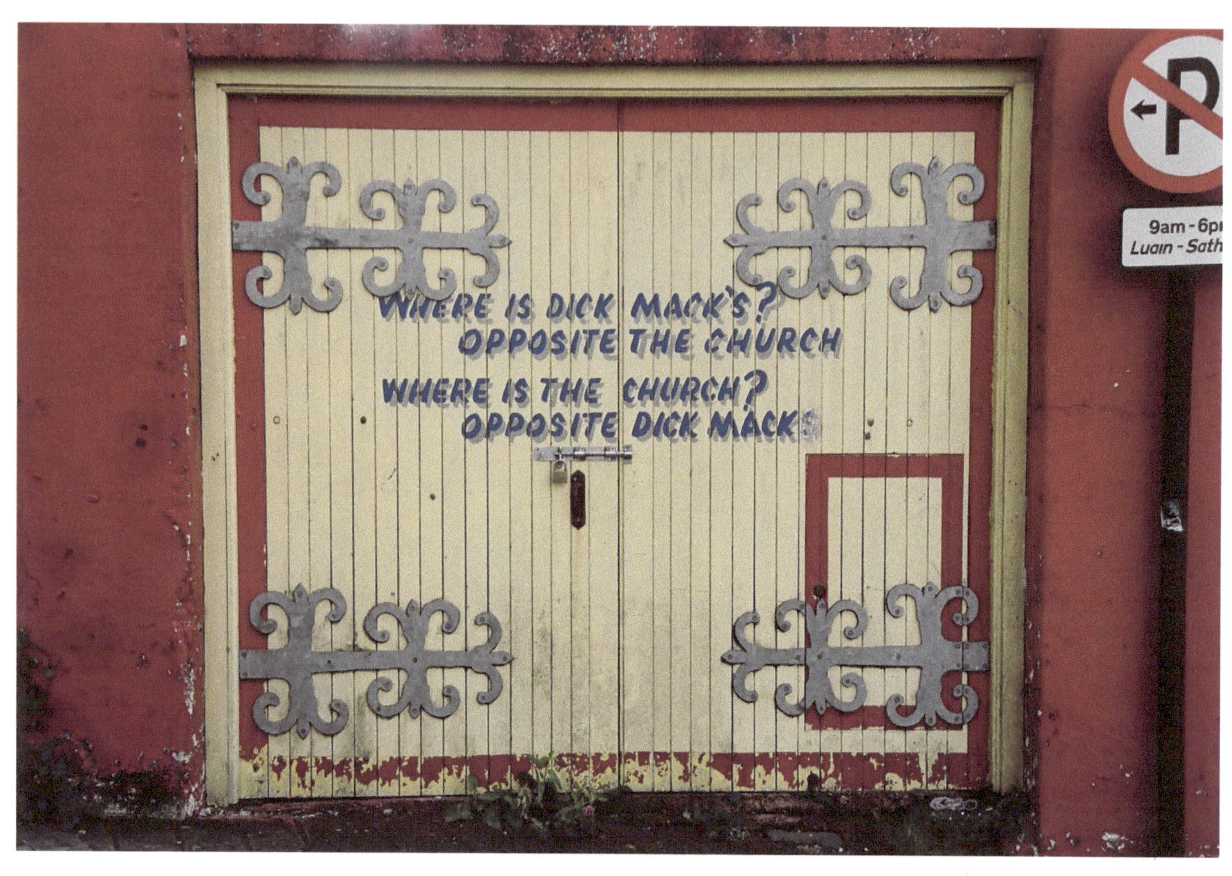


DingleTown, Ireland

God enters by a private door into every individual.

--Ralph Waldo Emerson, 1803-1882

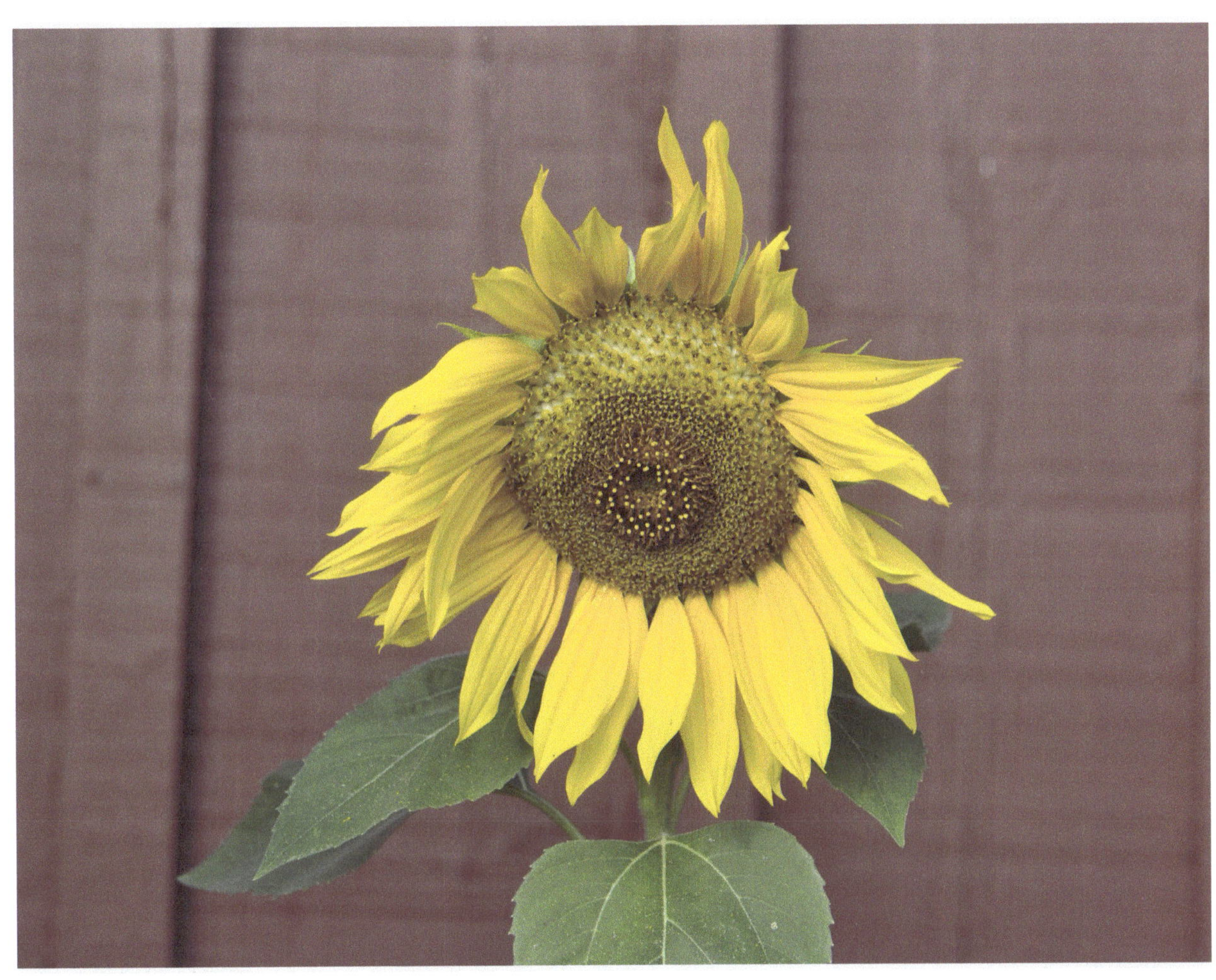

Eastham, Massachusetts

Nor is it an objection to say that we must understand a prayer if it is to have its true effect.
That simply is not the case. Who understands the wisdom of a flower?
Yet we can take pleasure in it.
– Rudolph Steiner, 1861-1925

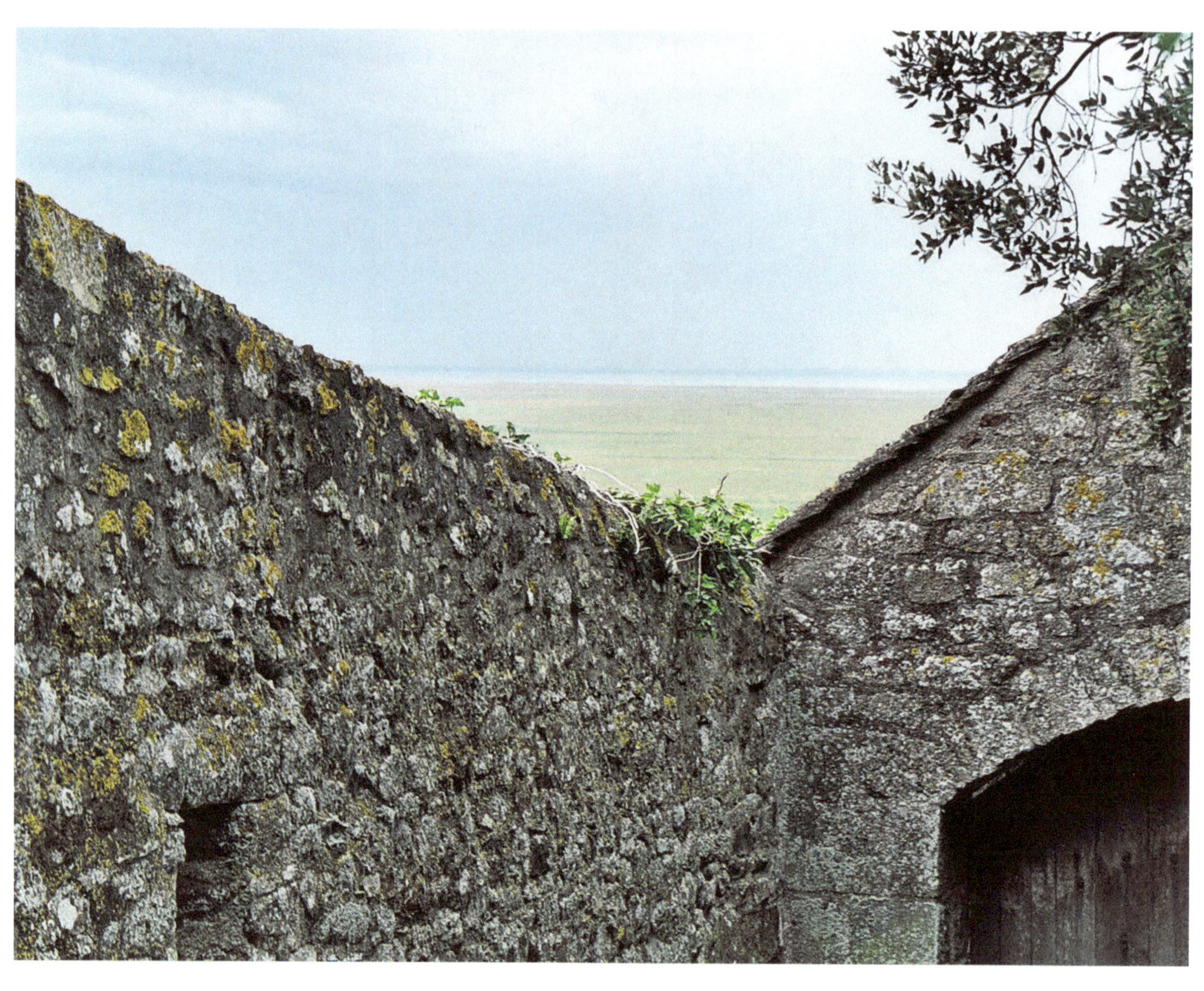

Mont Saint-Michel, France

Faith is the response of our spirits to beckonings of the eternal.

--George A. Buttrick, 1892-1980

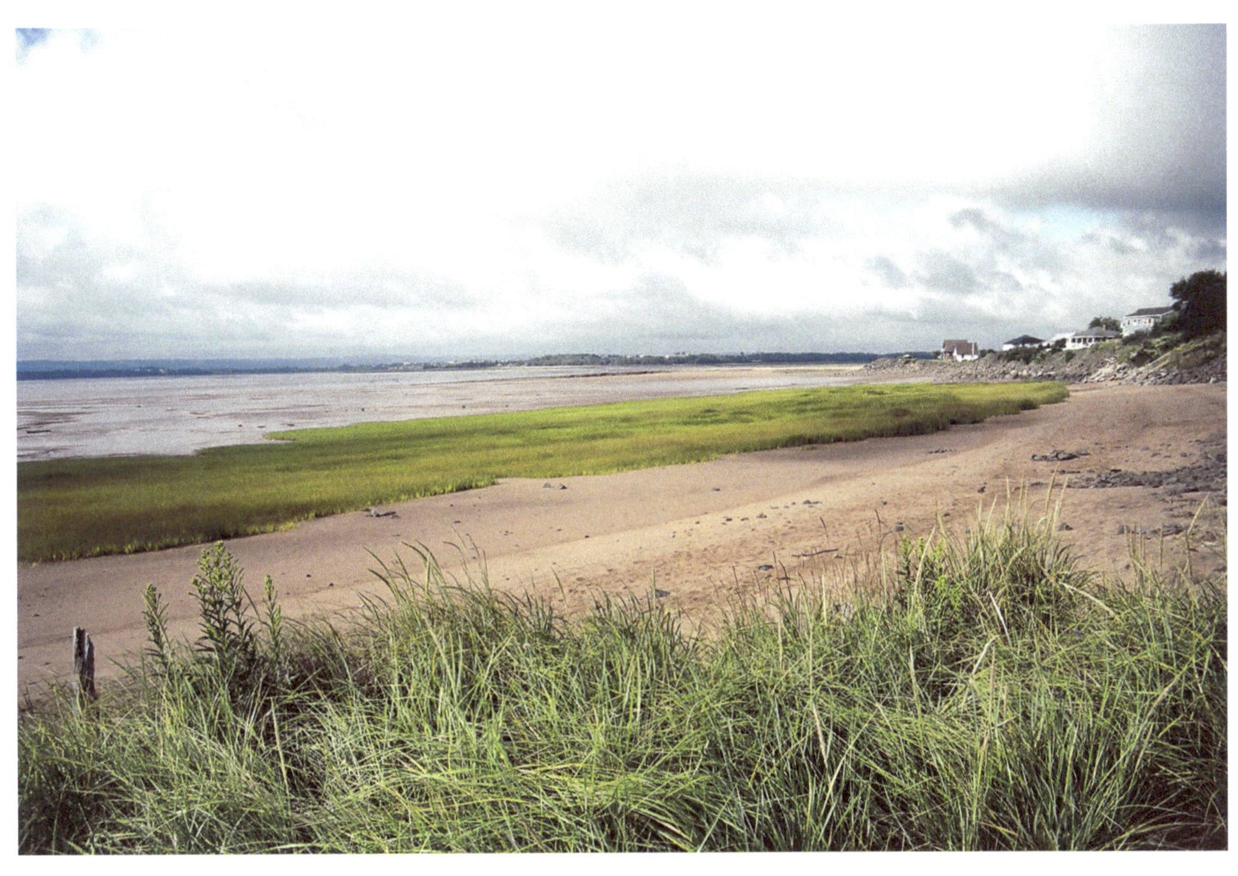

Bay of Fundy, Nova Scotia

The nature of God is a circle of which the centre is everywhere
and the circumference is nowhere.

--Anonymous

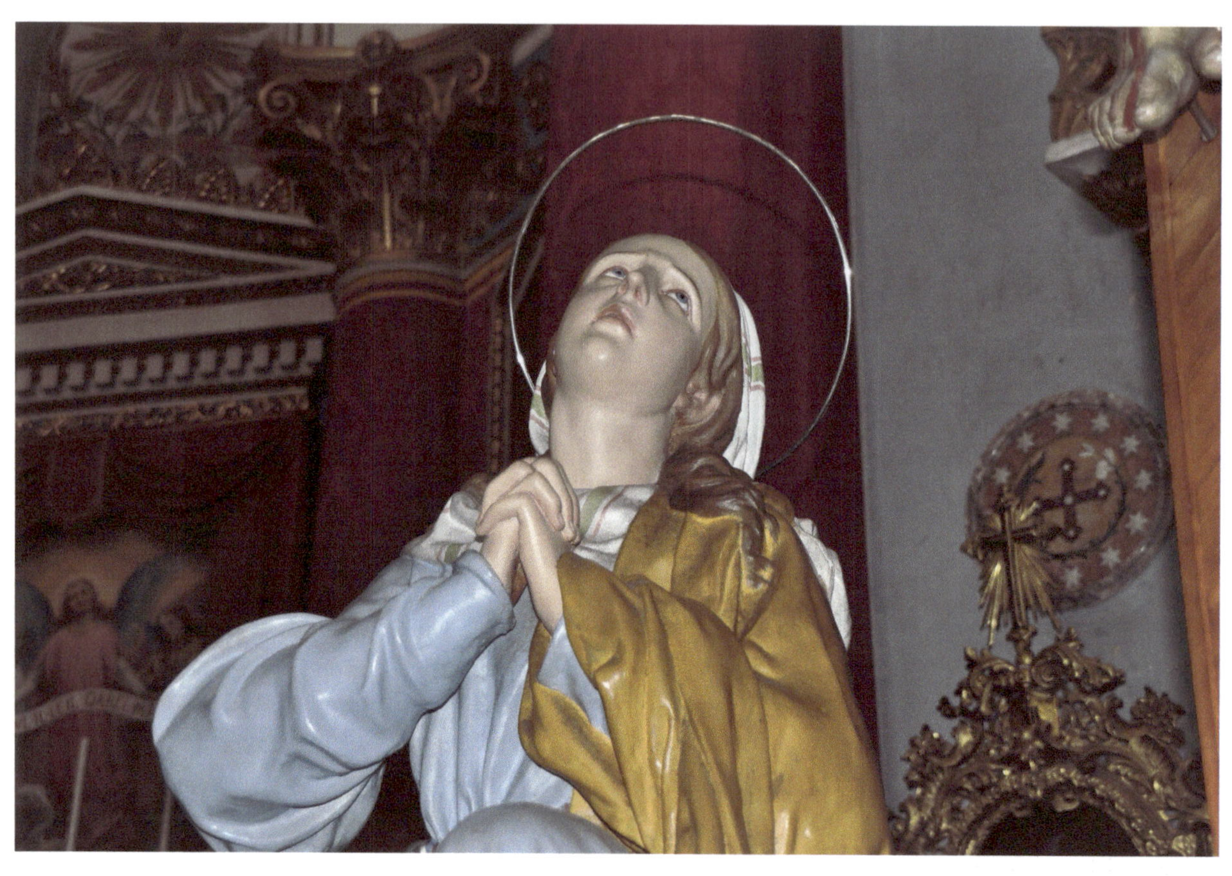

Mosta, Malta

Until the day when God shall deign to reveal the future to man,
all human wisdom is summed up in these two words, -- "Wait and hope."
--Alexandre Dumas, 1802-1870

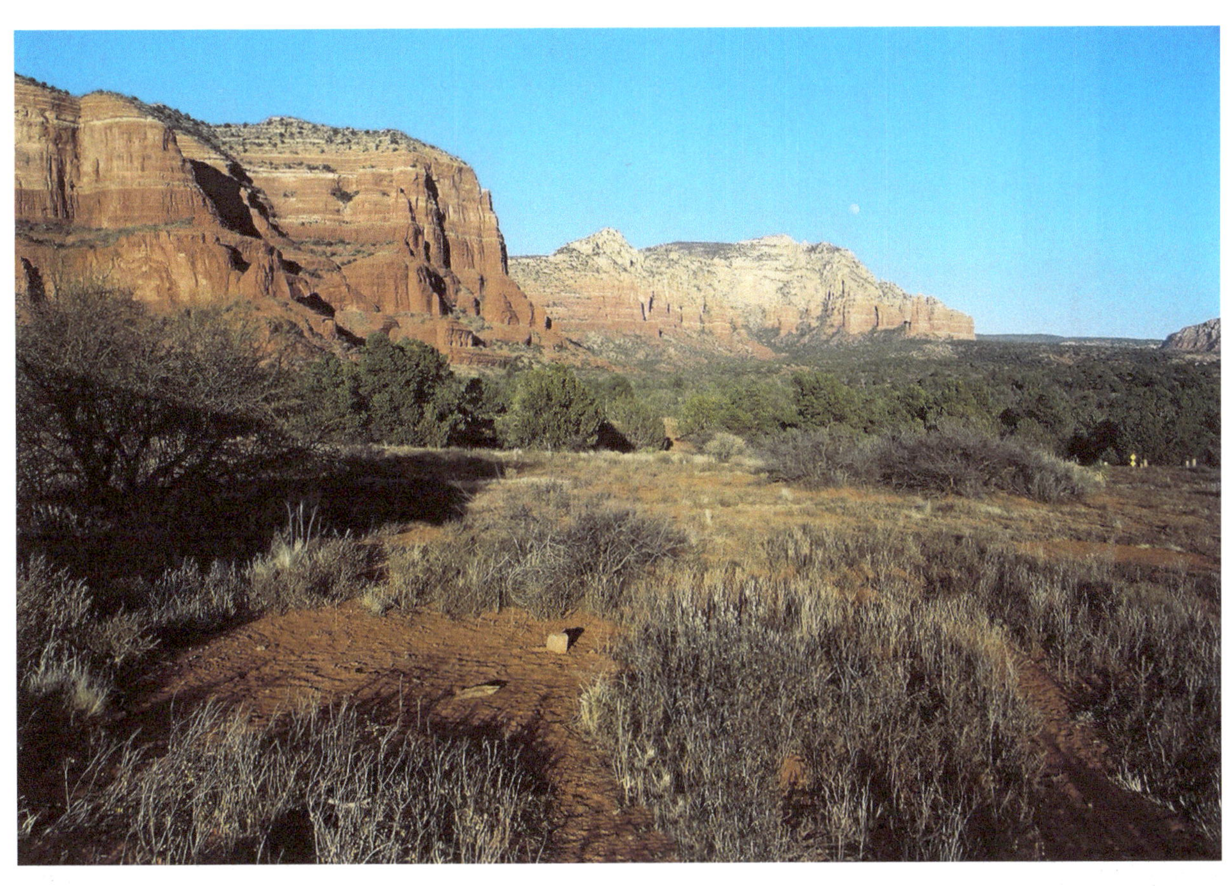

Sedona, Arizona

To pray is to pay attention to something or someone other than oneself.
Whenever a man so concentrates his attention, on a landscape, a poem,
a geometrical problem, an idol, or the true God--
that he completely forgets his own ego and desires, he is praying.
– W.H. Auden, 1907-1973

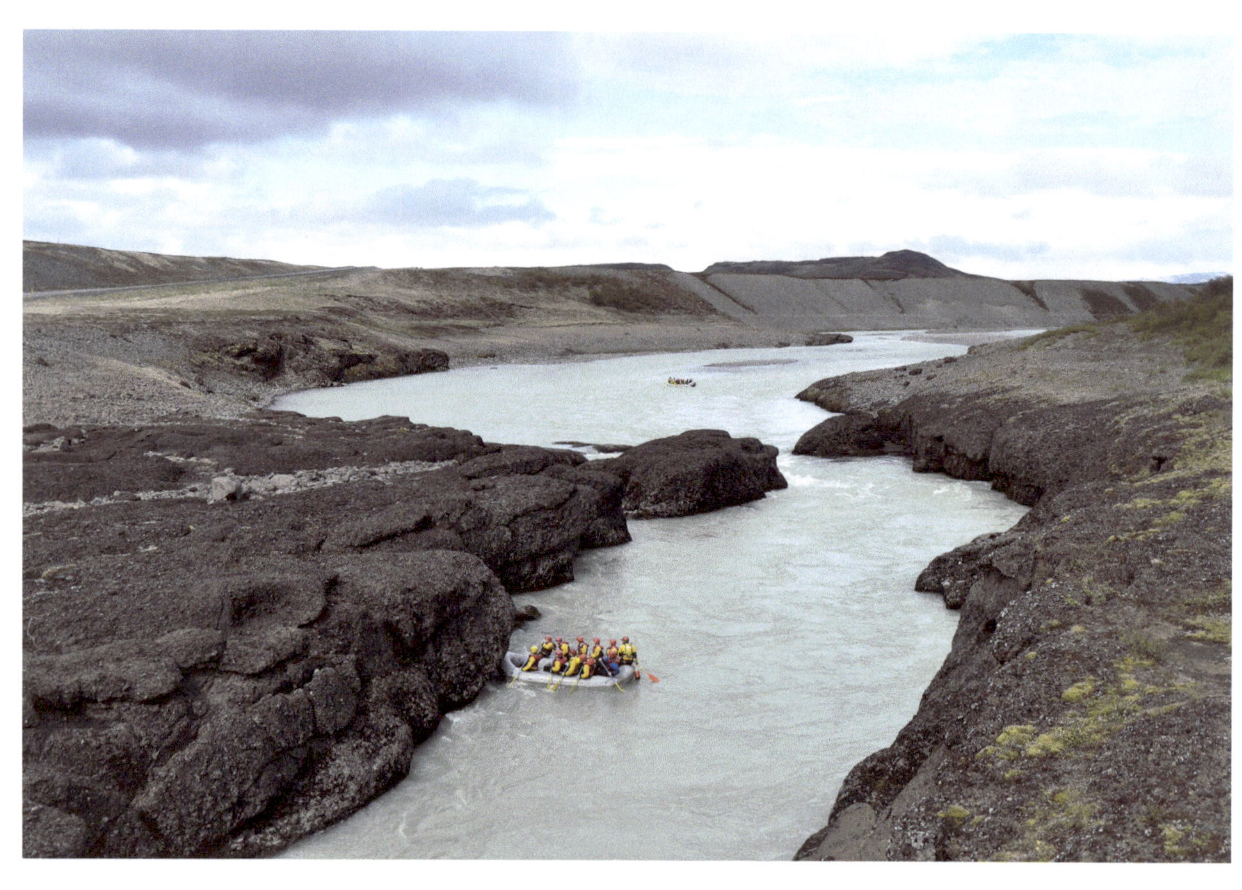

Hvitá River, Iceland

Hope is definitely not the same thing as optimism.
It is not the conviction that something will turn out well
but the certainty that something makes sense,
regardless of how it turns out.
--Vaclav Havel, 1936-

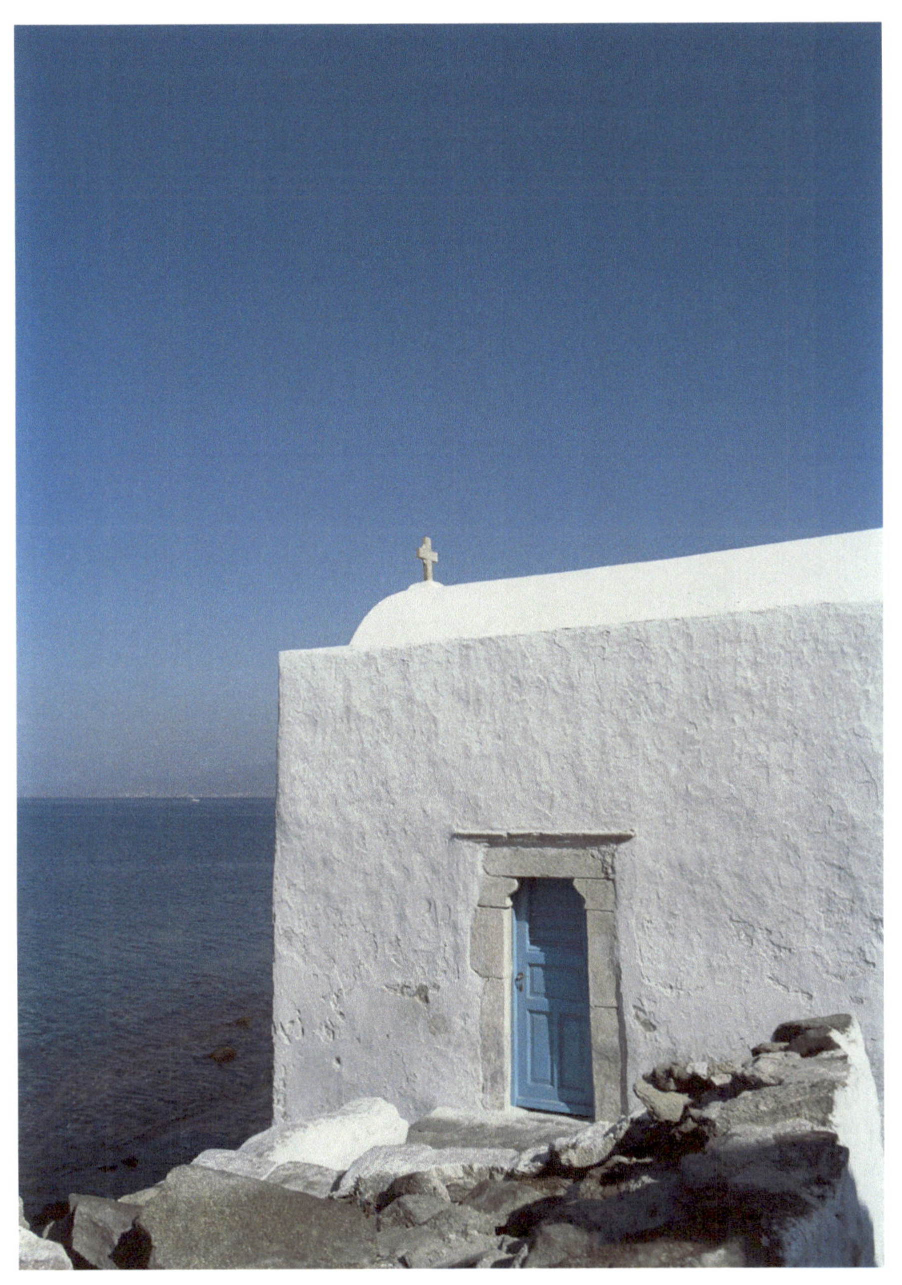

Mykonos, Greece

Ask and it shall be given you; seek and ye shall find;
knock, and it shall be opened unto you.
--New Testament, Matthew vii

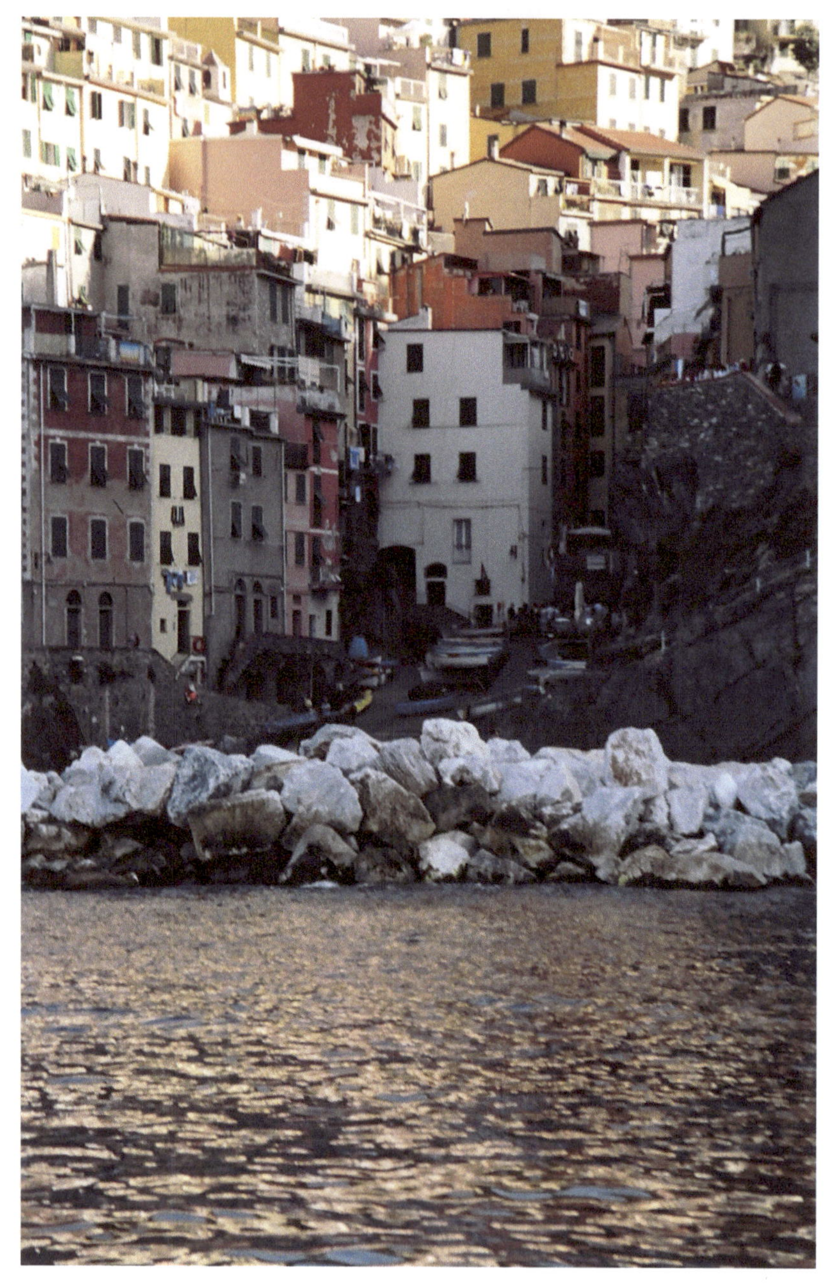

Riomaggiore, Italy

I live and love in God's peculiar light.

--Michelangelo, 1475-1564

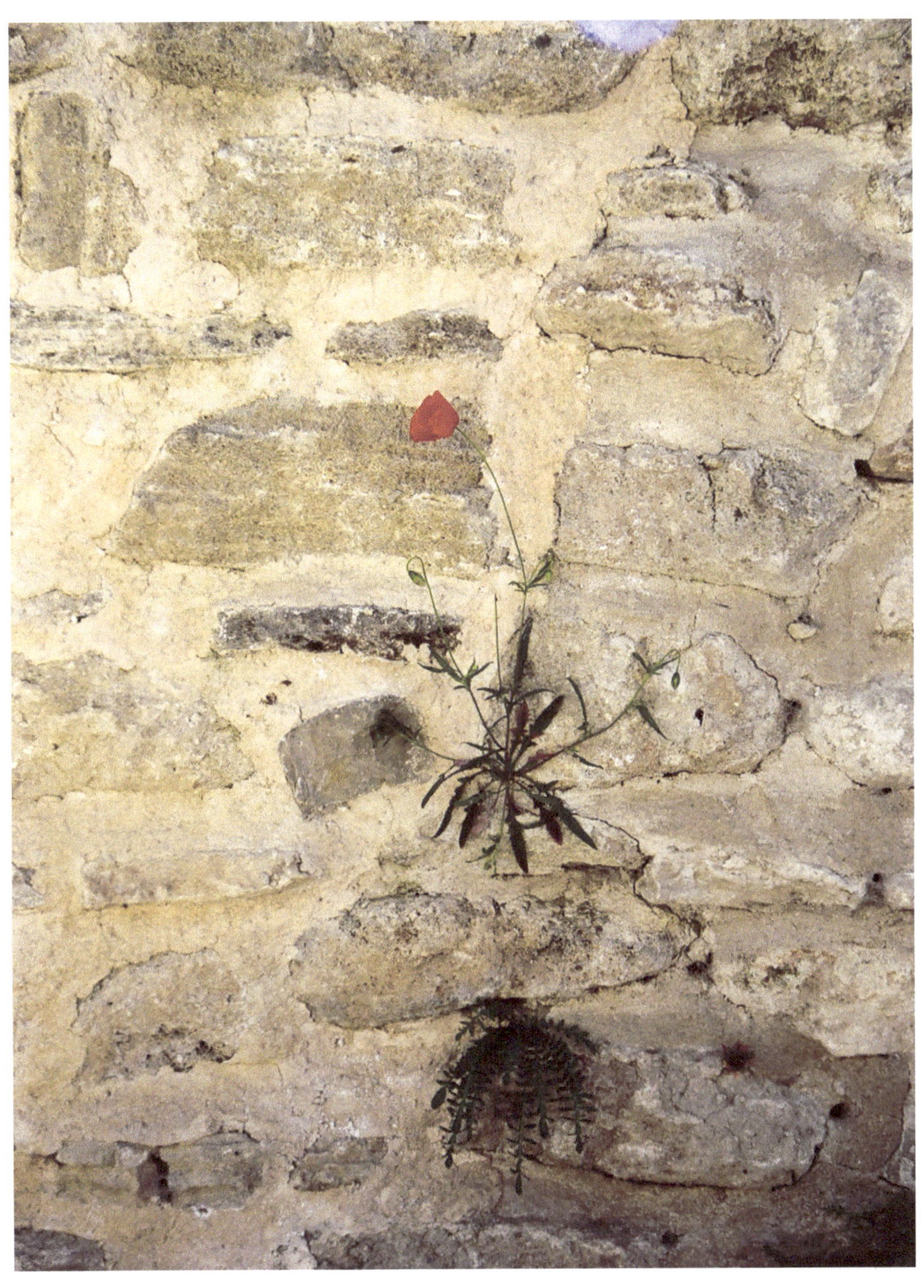

Ronda, Spain

I have seen flowers come in stoney places
and kind things done by men with ugly faces
and the gold cup won by the worst horse at the races.
So I trust too.
– John Masefield, 1878-1967

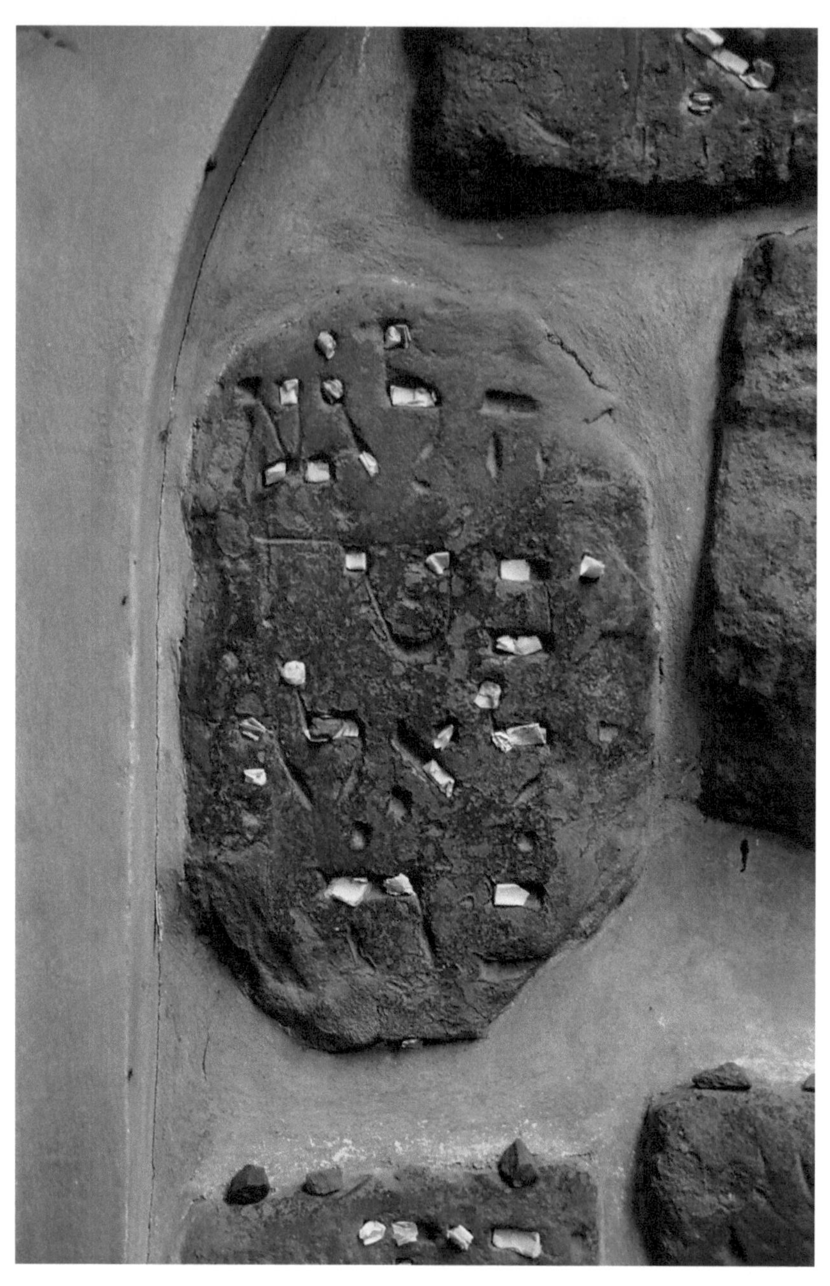

Prague, Czech Republic

If we could all hear one another's prayers,
God might be relieved of some of his burden.
Ashleigh Brilliant, 1933-

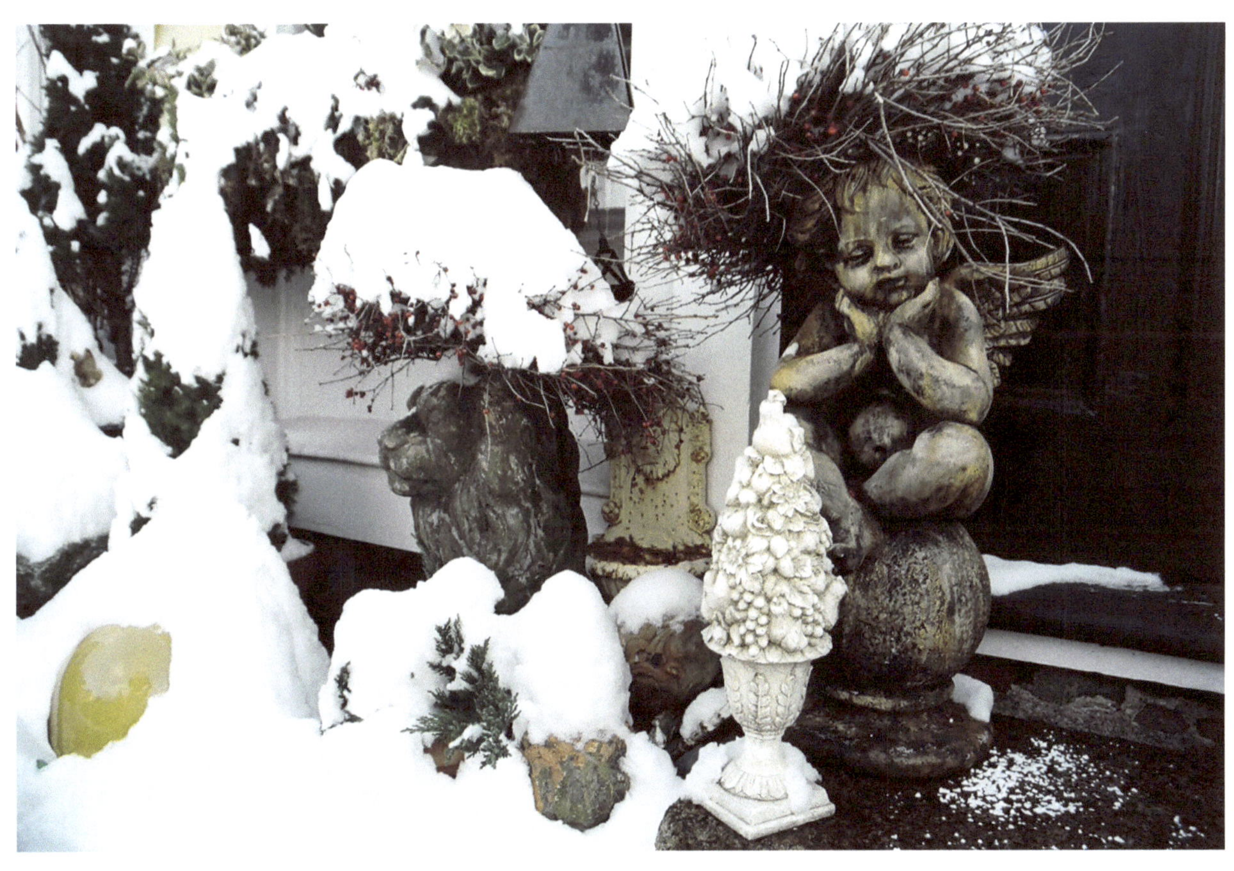

Marblehead, Massachusetts

Angels deliver fate to our doorstep --

and anywhere else it is needed.

--Jessi Lane Adams

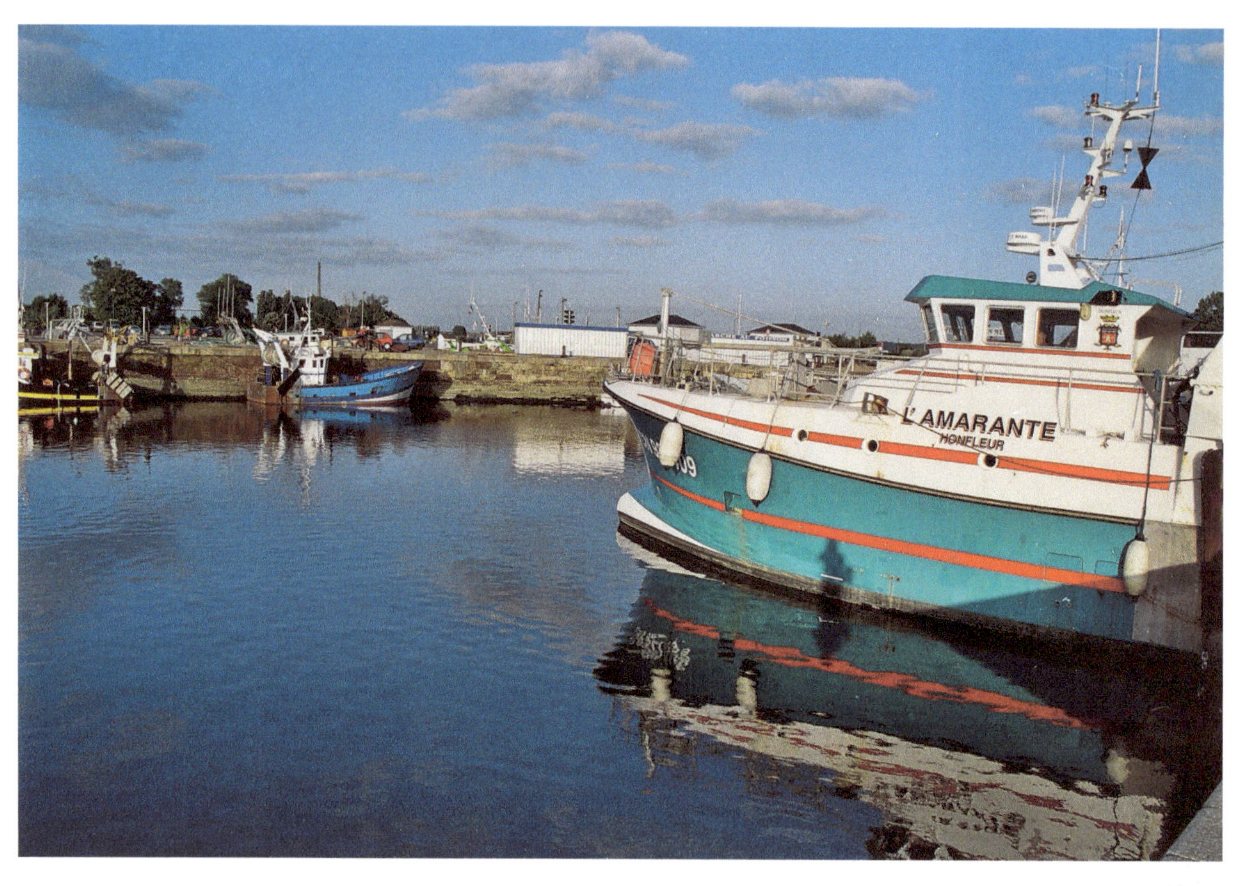


Honfleur, France

Faith is the soul riding at anchor.

--Josh Billings, 1818-1885

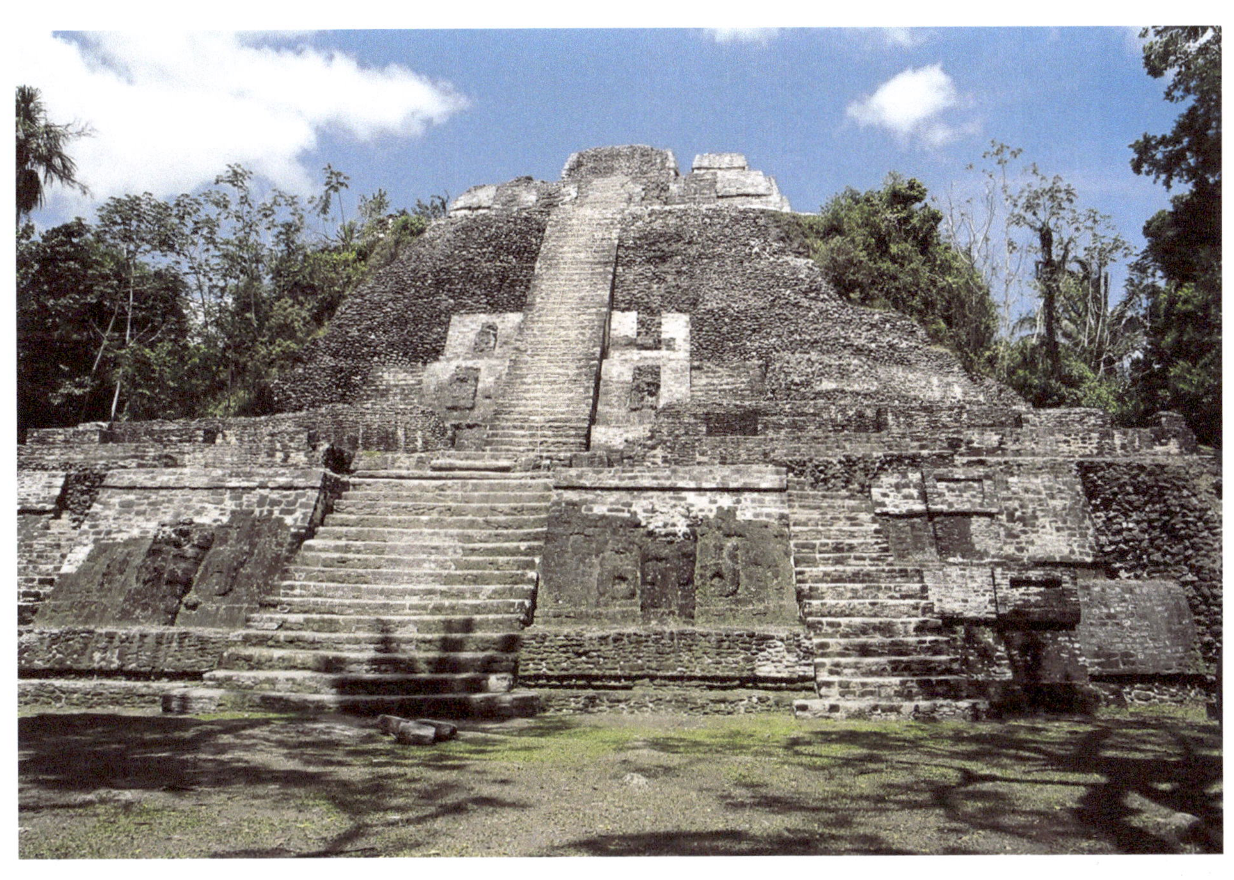

Lamanai, Belize

As I grow older, part of my emotional survival plan must be to actively seek inspiration instead of passively waiting for it to find me.

--Bebe Moore Campbell, 1950-2006

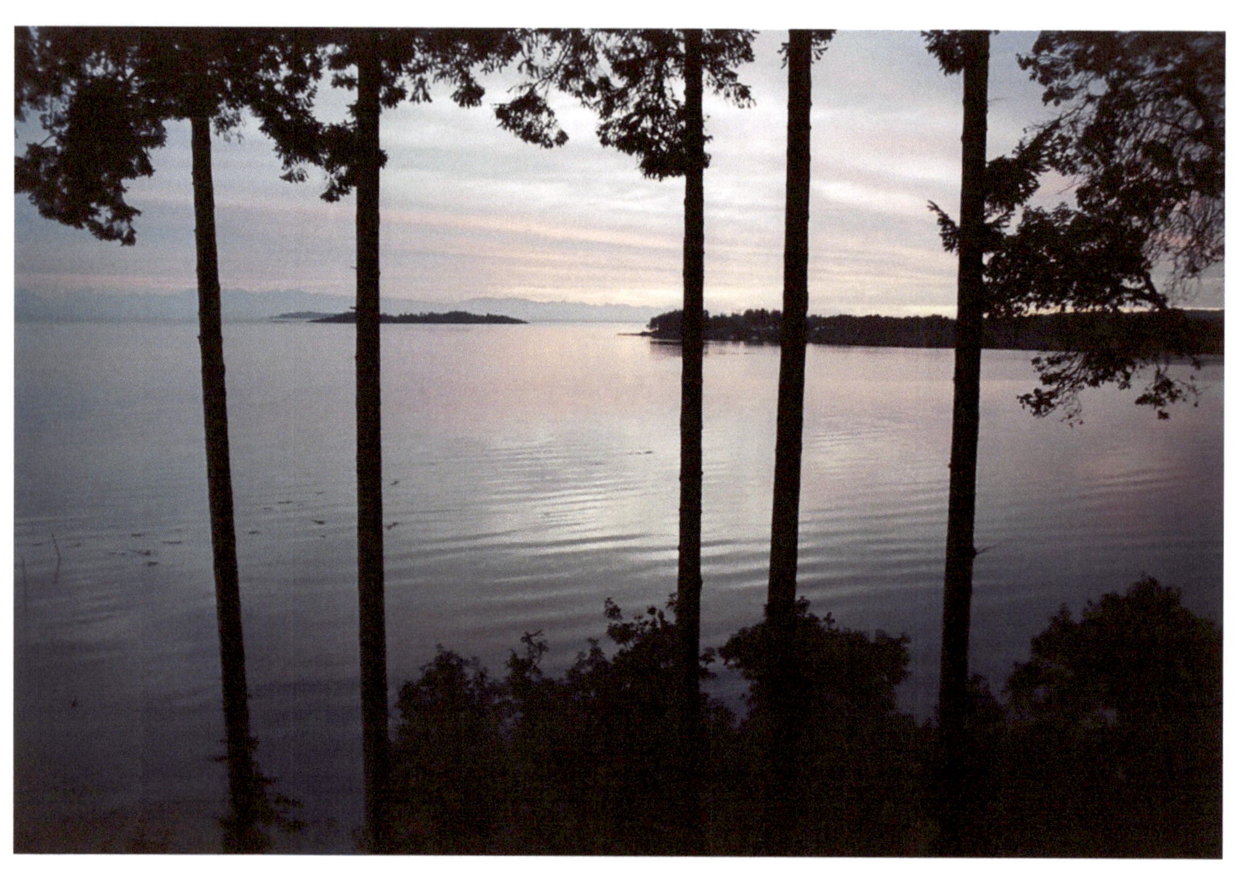

Craig Bay, British Columbia

All that I have seen teaches me to trust the creator for all that I have not seen.

--Ralph Waldo Emerson, 1803-1882

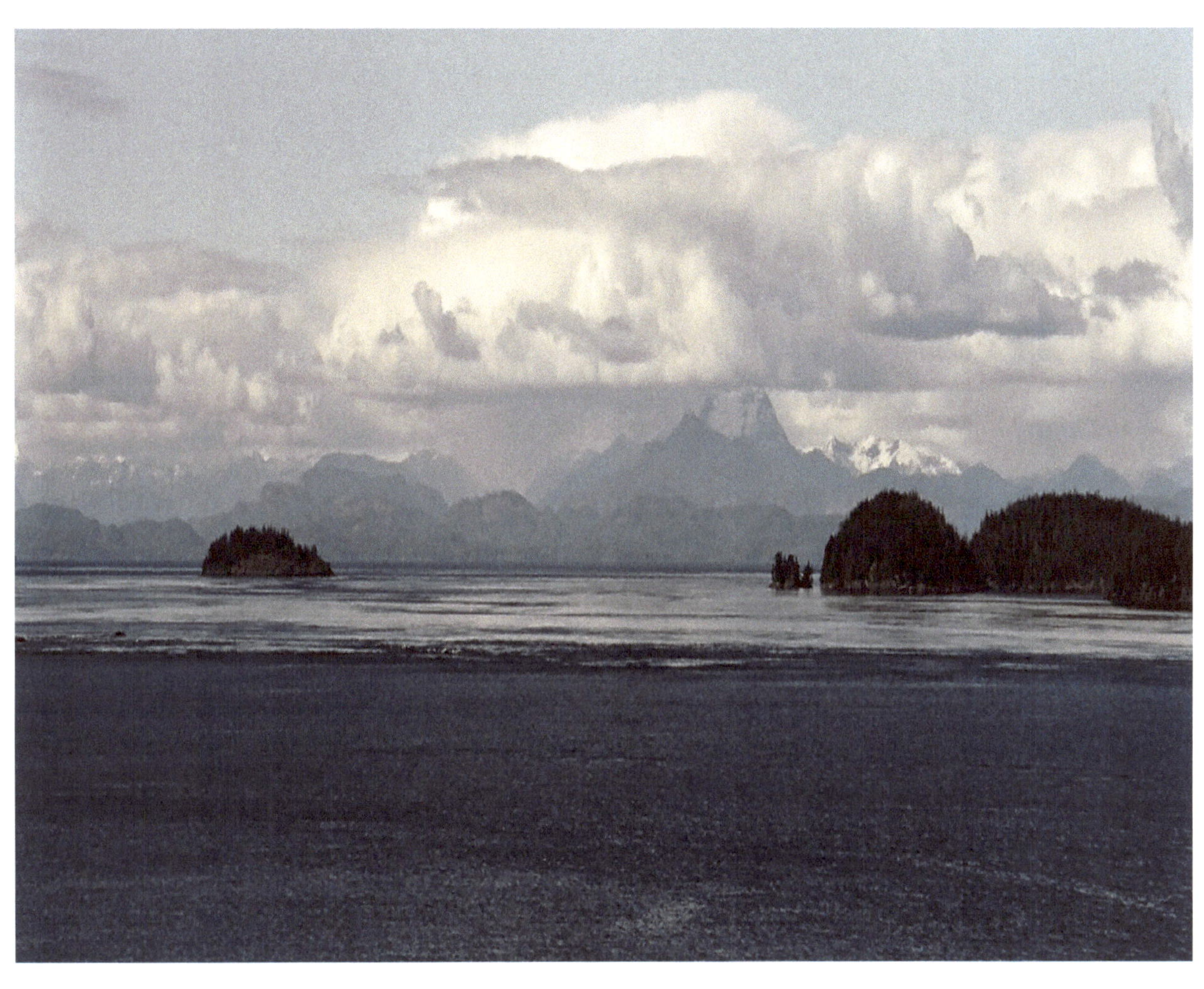

Gulf of Alaska

To one who has faith, no explanation is necessary.
To one without faith, no explanation is possible.
--Saint Thomas of Aquinas, 1225-1274

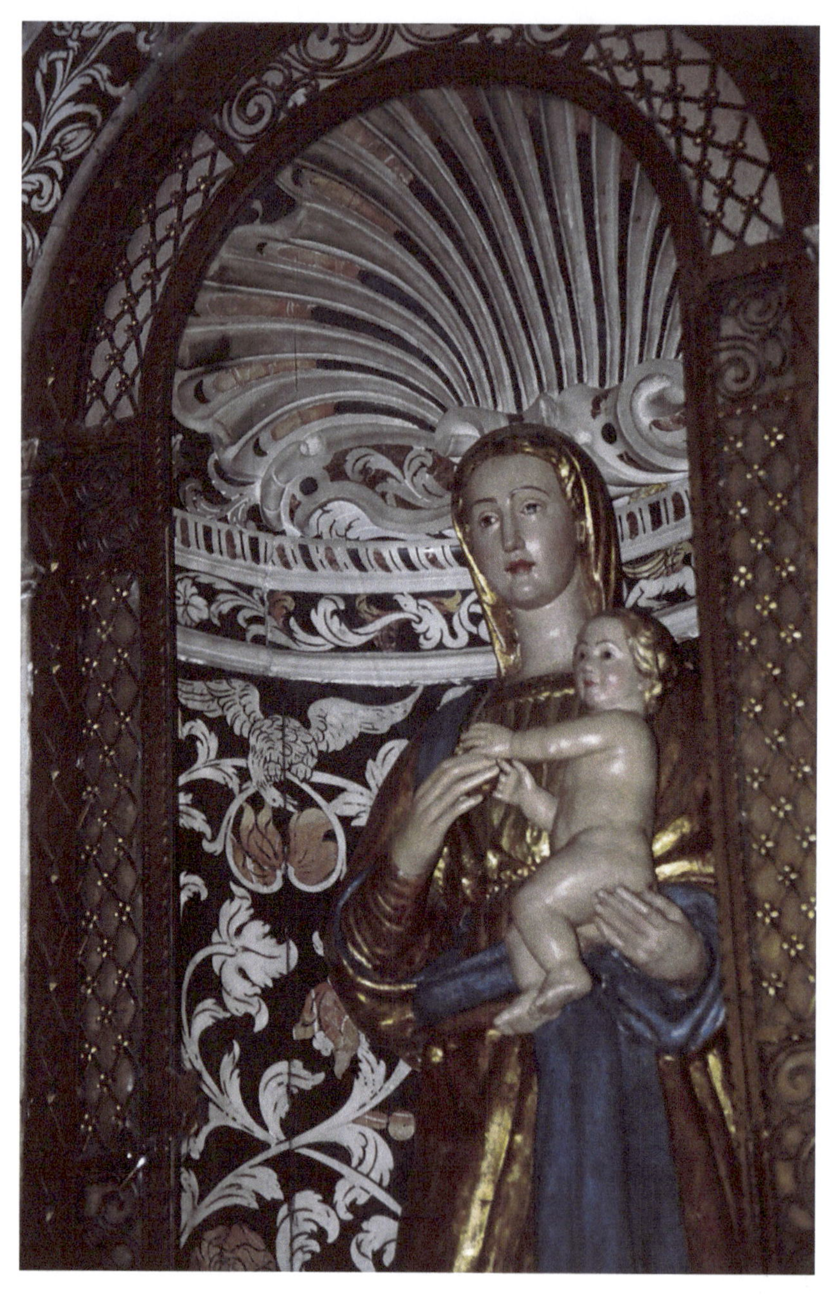

Noto, Sicily

A prayer in its simplest definition is a wish turned Godward.

--Phillip Brooks, 1835-1893

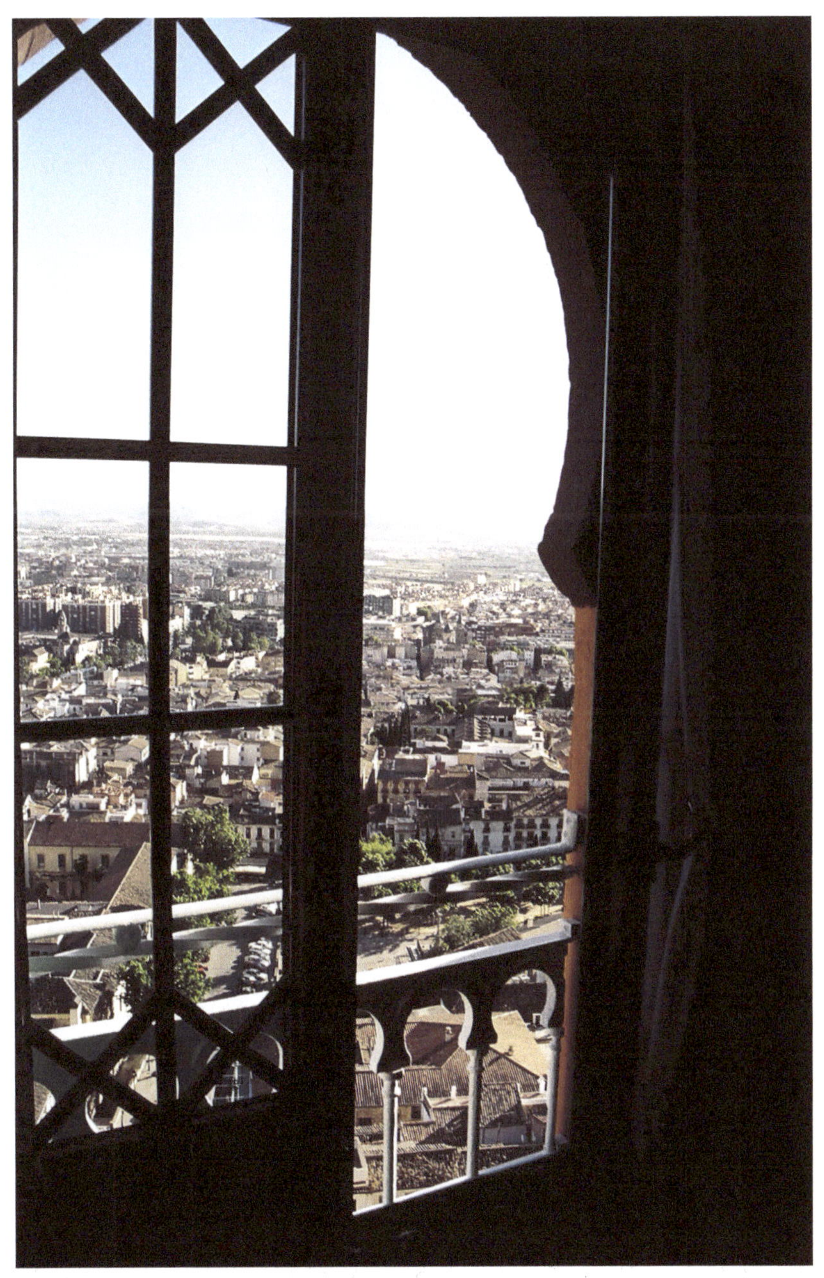

Granada, Spain

I was always looking outside myself for strength and confidence, but it comes from within. It is there all the time.

--Anna Freud, 1895-1982

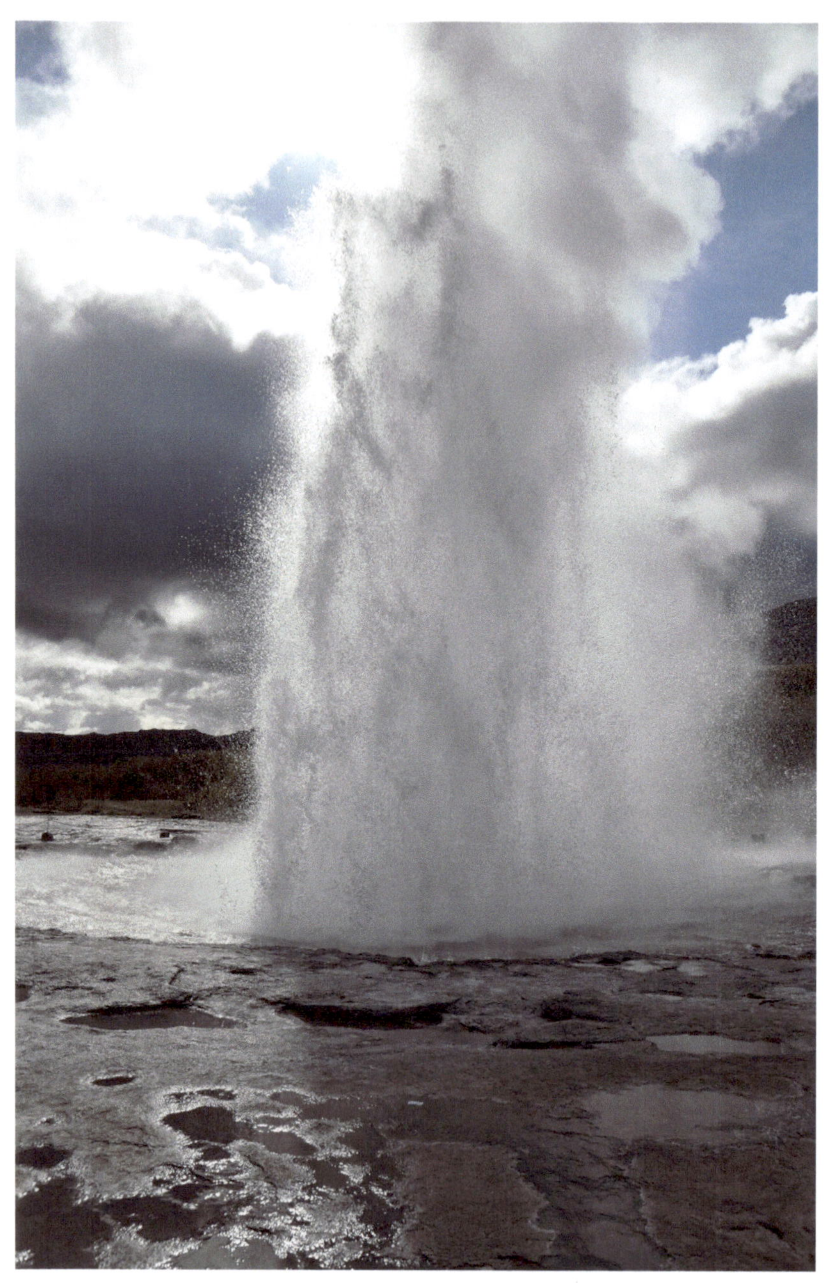

Geysir, Iceland

...I believe that God is born anew each morning,...creating the world at this very moment. He did not create it at a distant moment in time, then forget about it.

--Leon Joseph Cardinal Suenens, 1904-1996

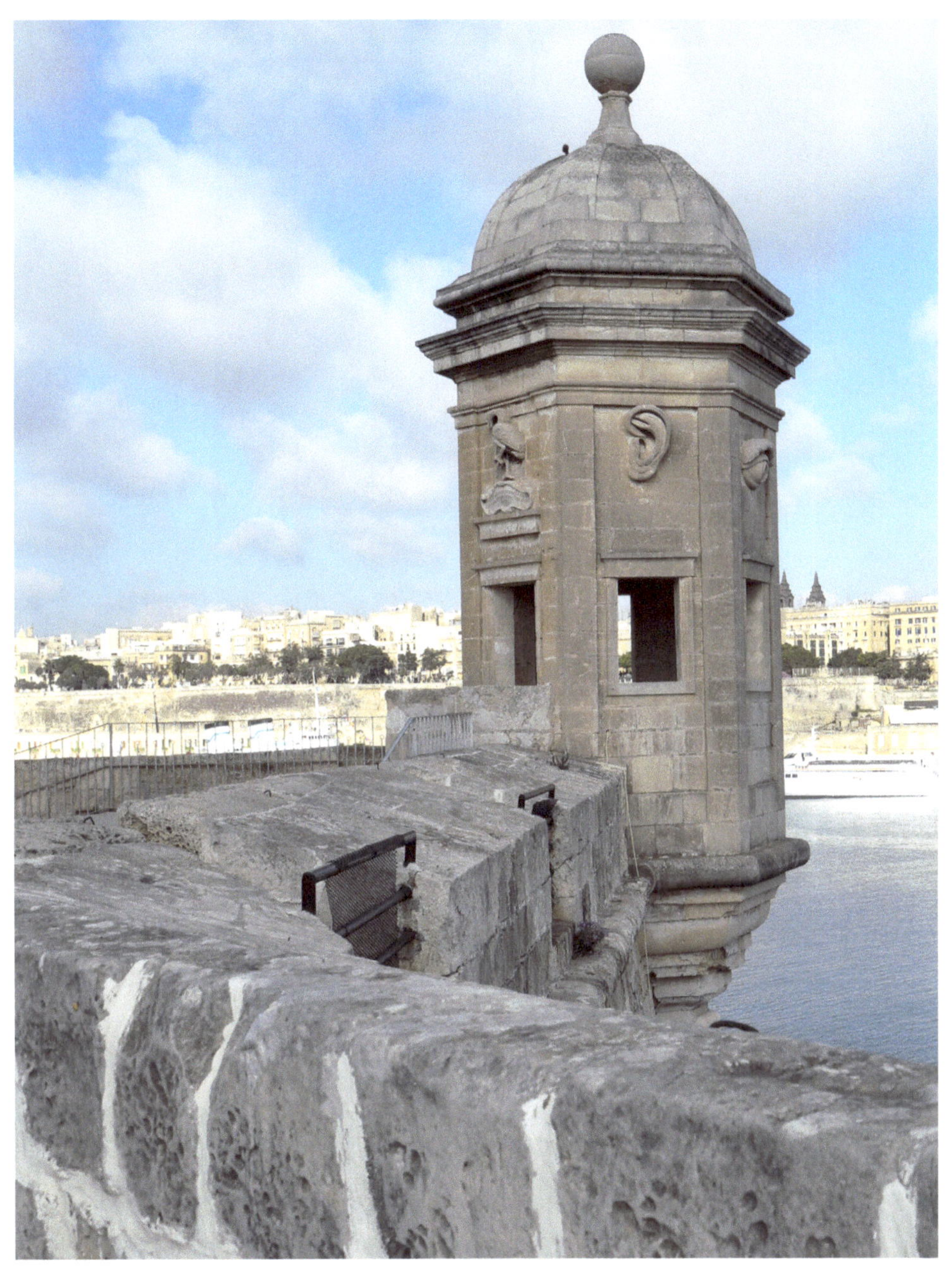

Grand Harbor, Malta

You are used to listening to the buzz of the world,
but now is the time to develop the inner ear that listens to the inner world.
It is time to have a foot in each world and it can be done.

--Saint Bartholomew

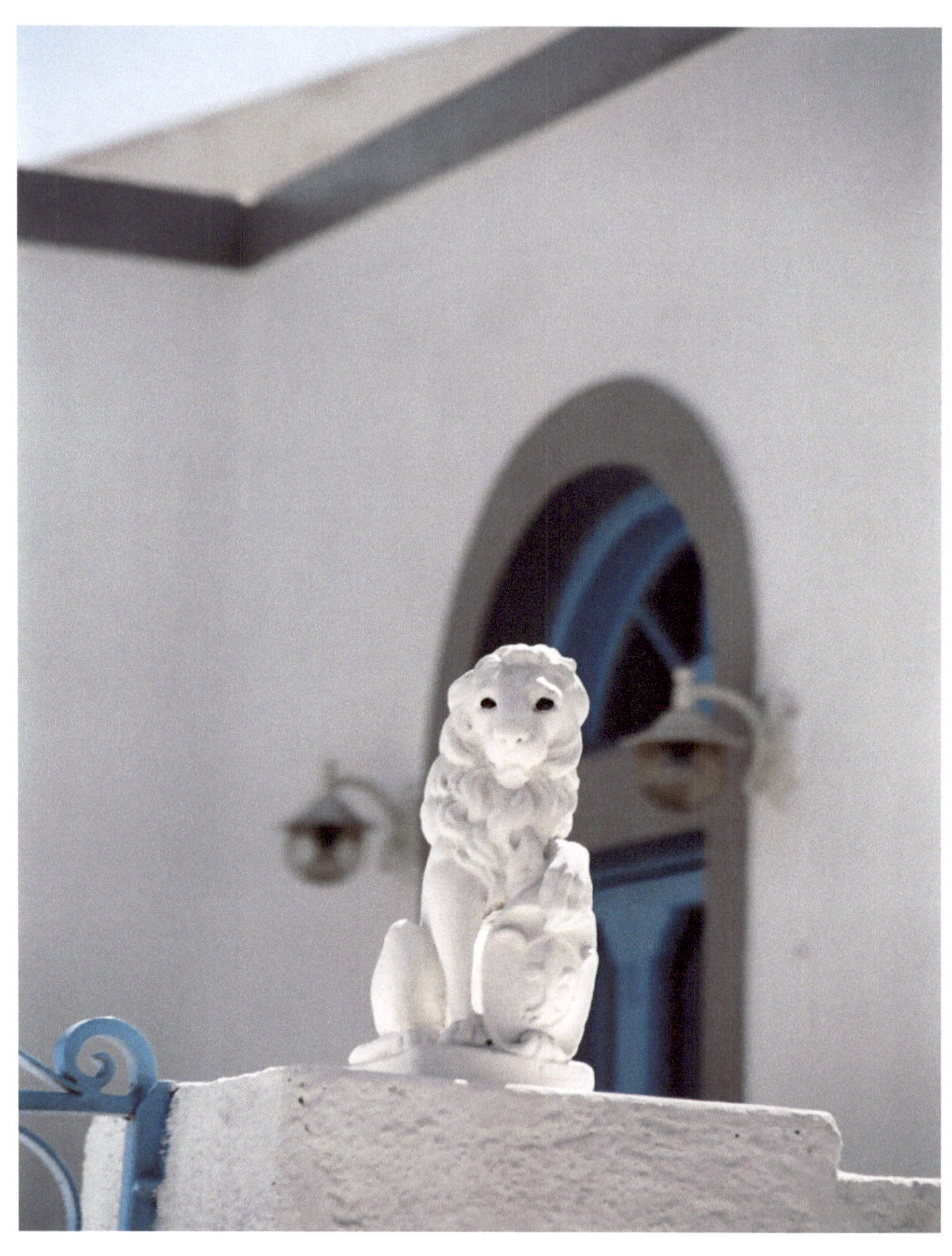

Santorini, Greece

Courage is fear that has said its prayers.

--Dorothy Bernard, 1890-1955

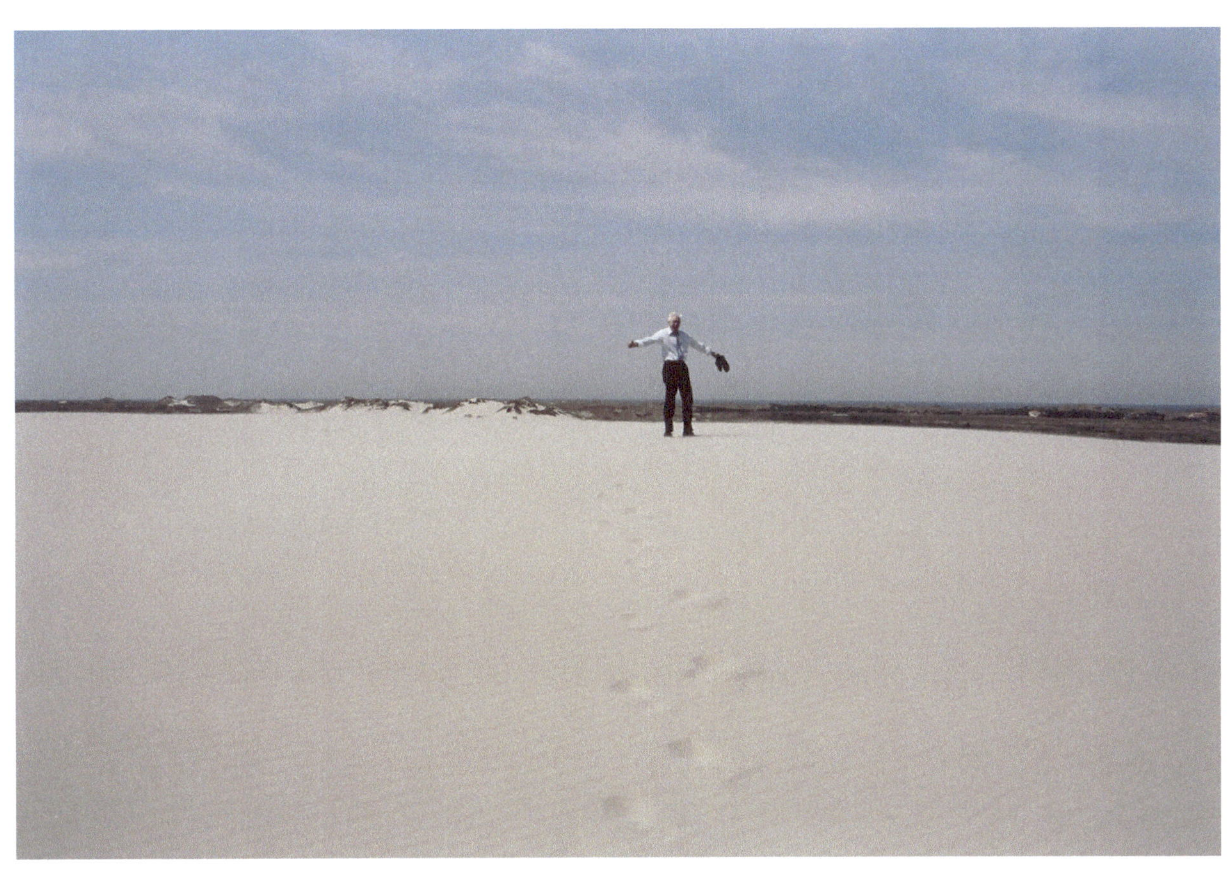

Skagen, Denmark

When you see only one set of footprints,

it was then that I carried you.

--Mary Stevenson Zangare, 1922-1999

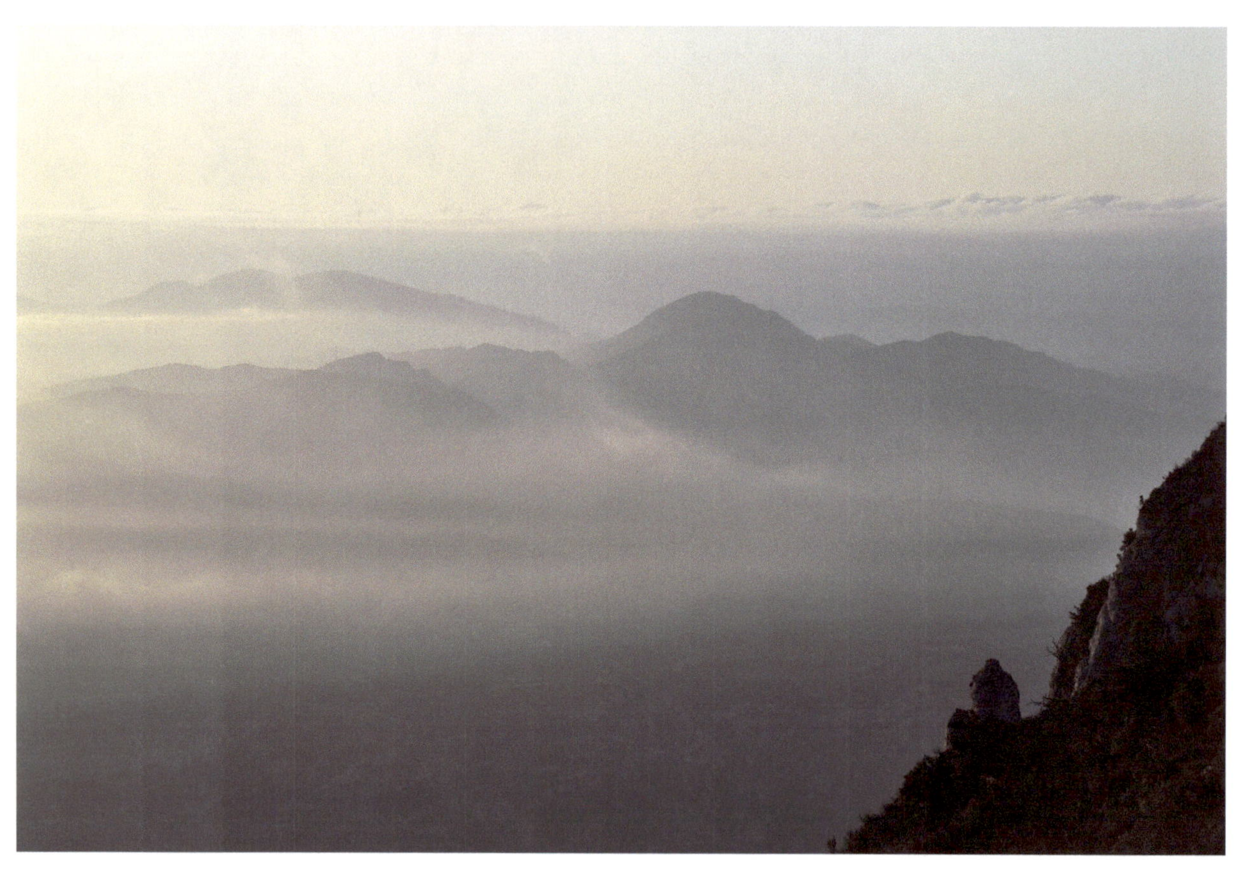

Montserrat, Spain

Faith is the daring of the soul to go farther than it can see.

--William Newton Clark, 1841-1912

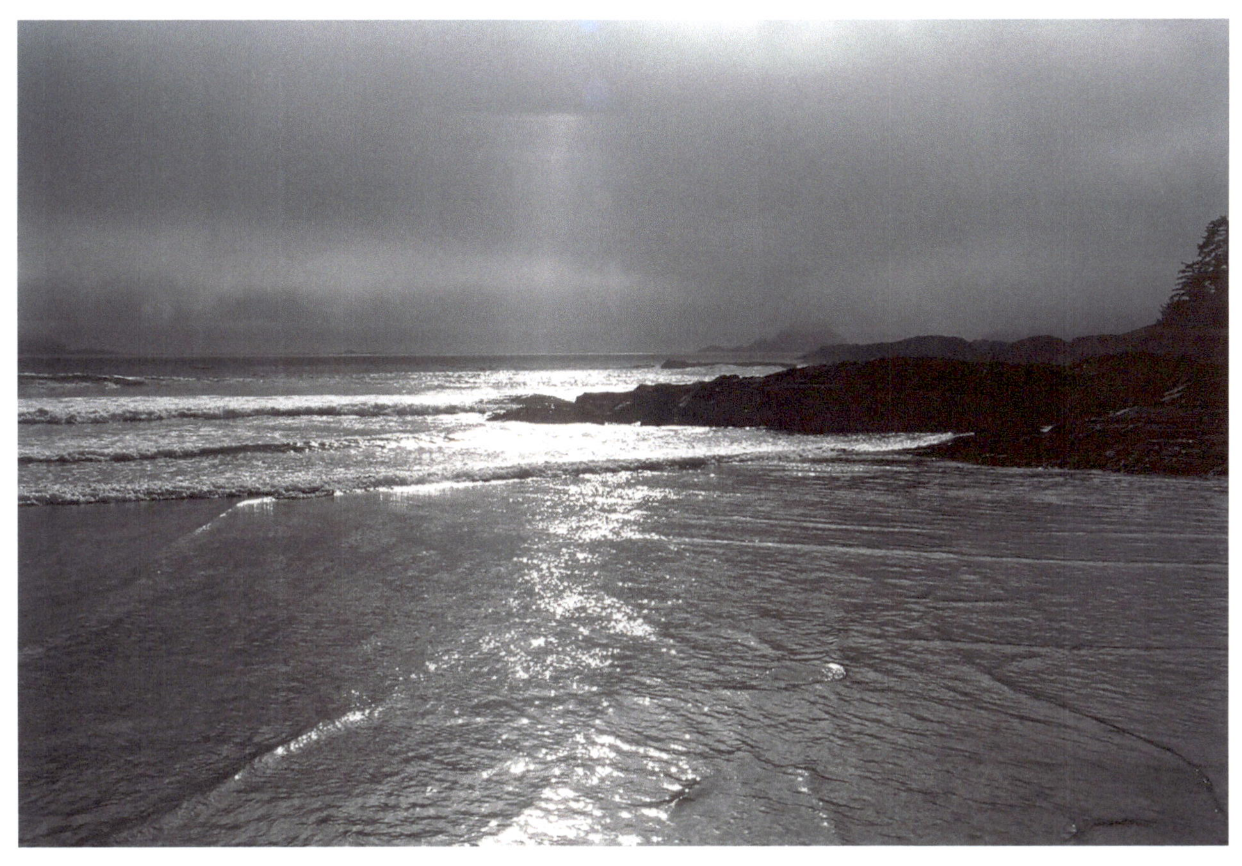

Chesterman Beach, British Columbia

Hope begins in the dark, the stubborn hope that if you just show up
and try to do the right thing, the dawn will come.
You wait and watch and work. You don't give up.
– Anne Lamott, 1954-

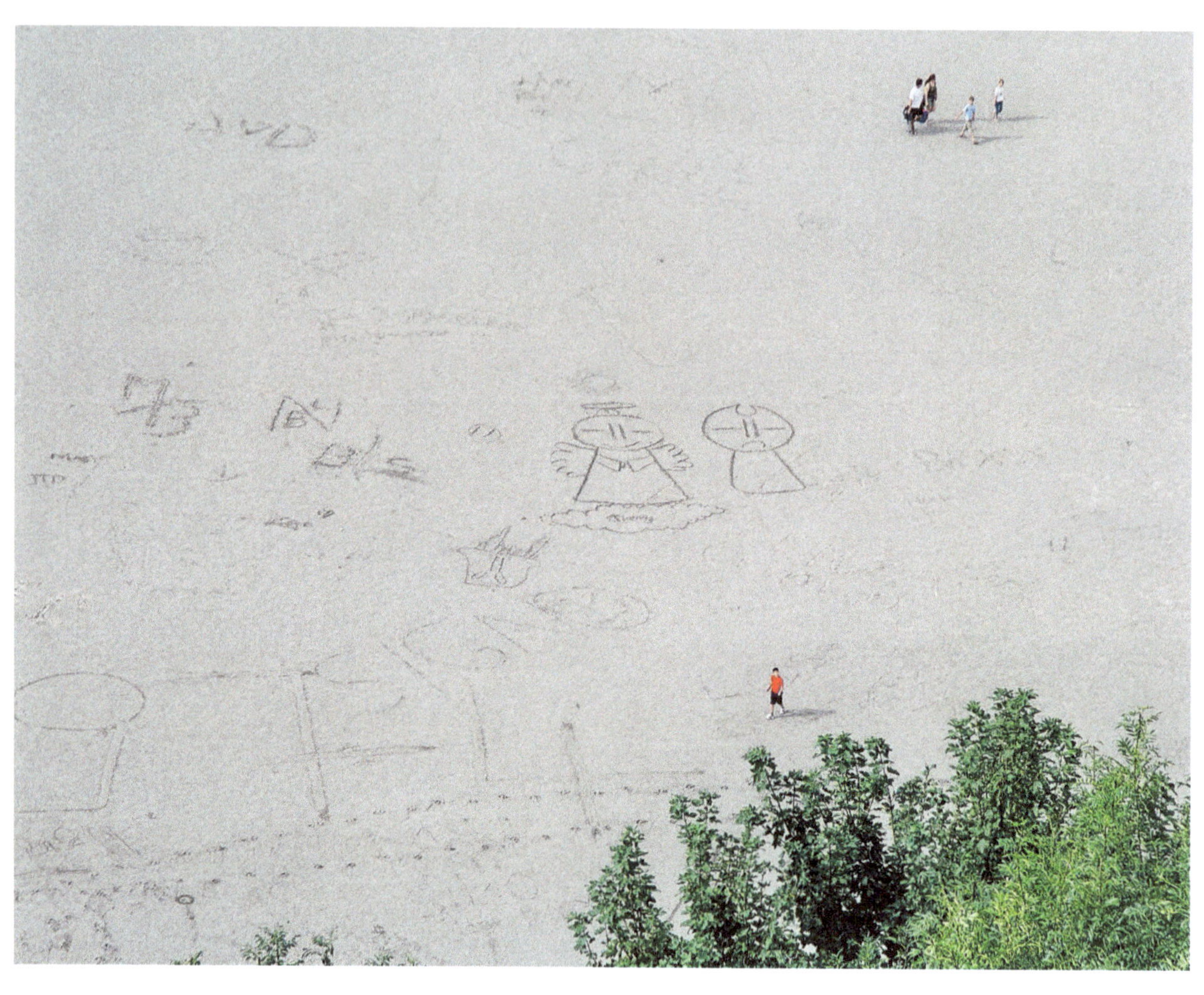

Mont Saint-Michel, France

"What do you think of God," the teacher asked.
After a pause, the young pupil replied, "He's not a think, he's a feel."
--Paul Frost

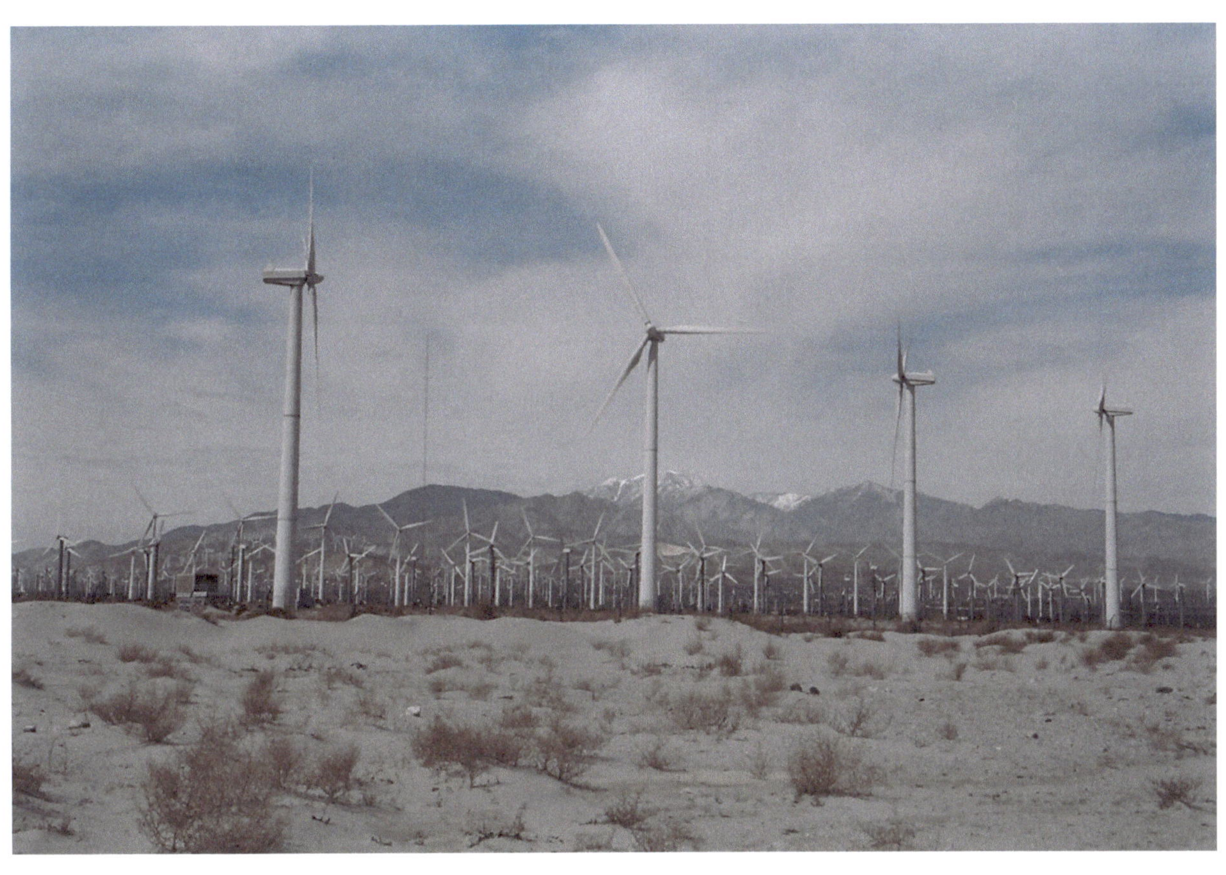

Palm Springs, California

Someday, after we have mastered the winds, the waves, the tide and gravity,
we shall harness for God the energies of love,
Then, for the second time in the history of the world,
man wll have discovered fire.
– Pierre Telhard de Chardin, 1881-1955

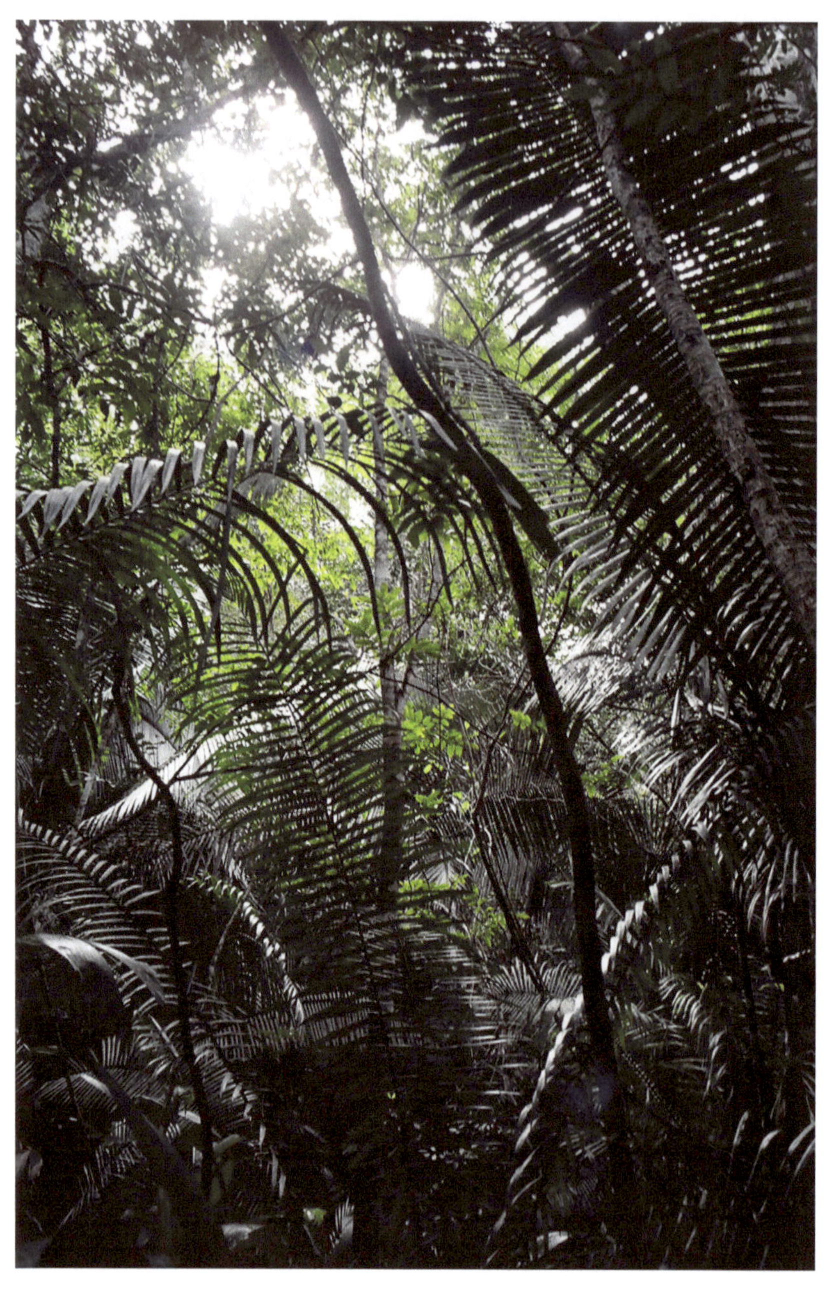

Chaa Creek, Belize

Hunting God is a great adventure.

--Marie de Flores

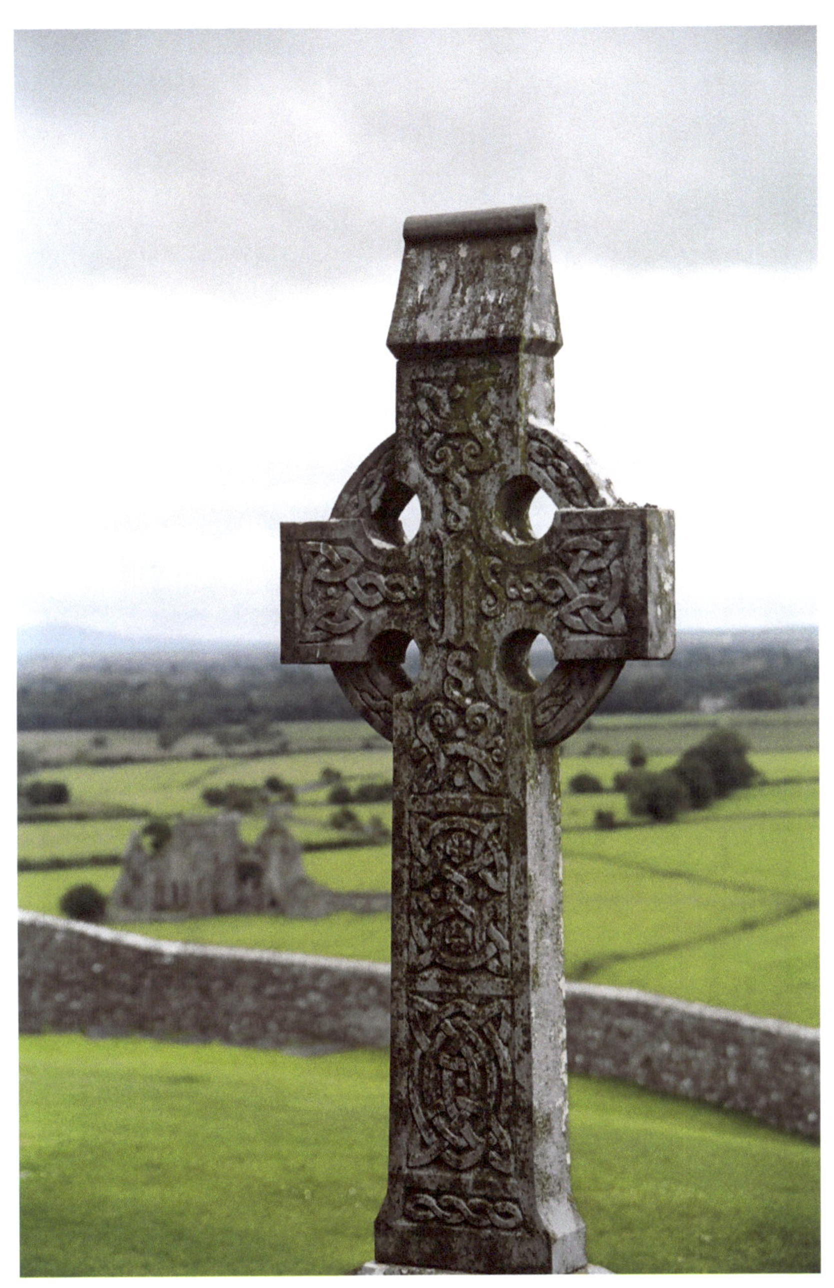

Cashel, Ireland

The great act of faith is when man decides he is not God.

--Oliver Wendell Holmes, 1841-1935

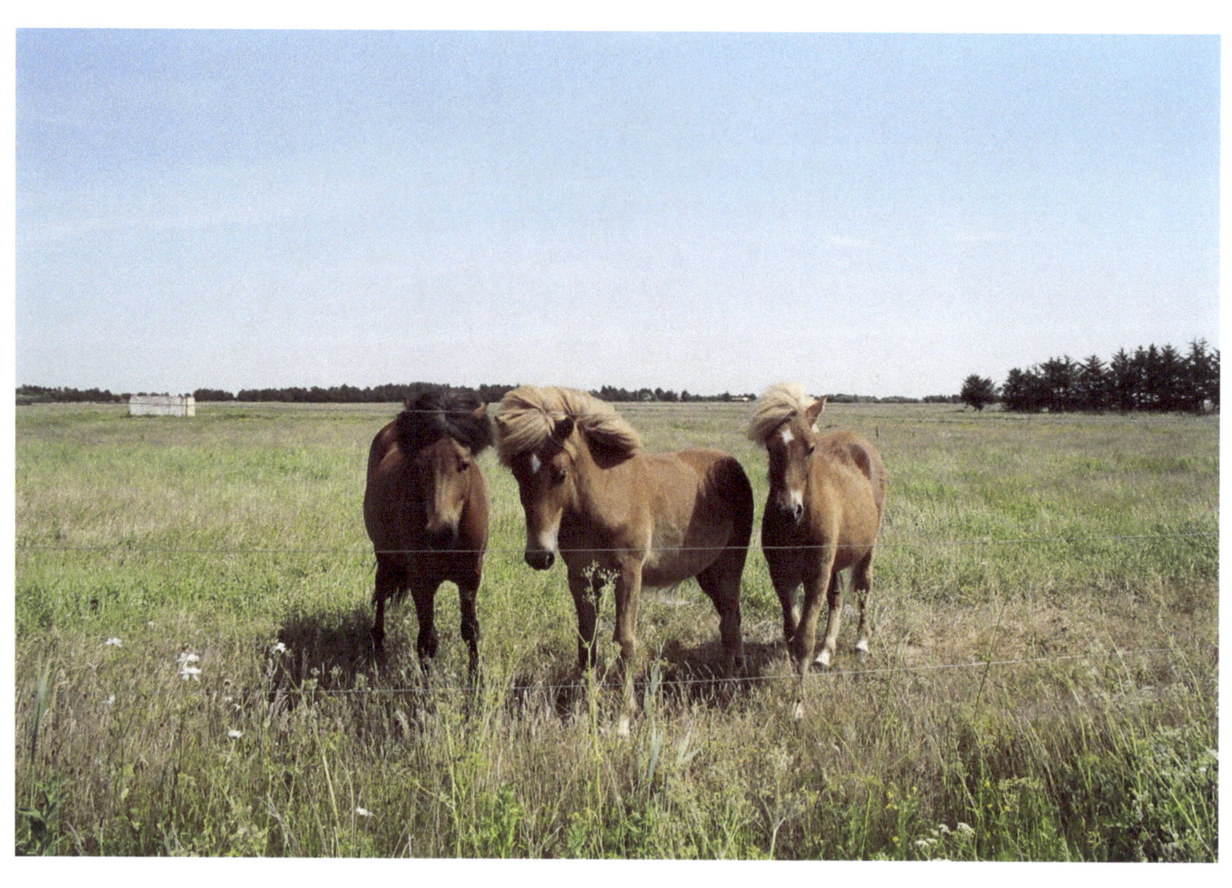

North Jutland, Denmark

Will is to grace as the horse is to the rider.

--Saint Augustine of Hippo, 354-430 A.D.

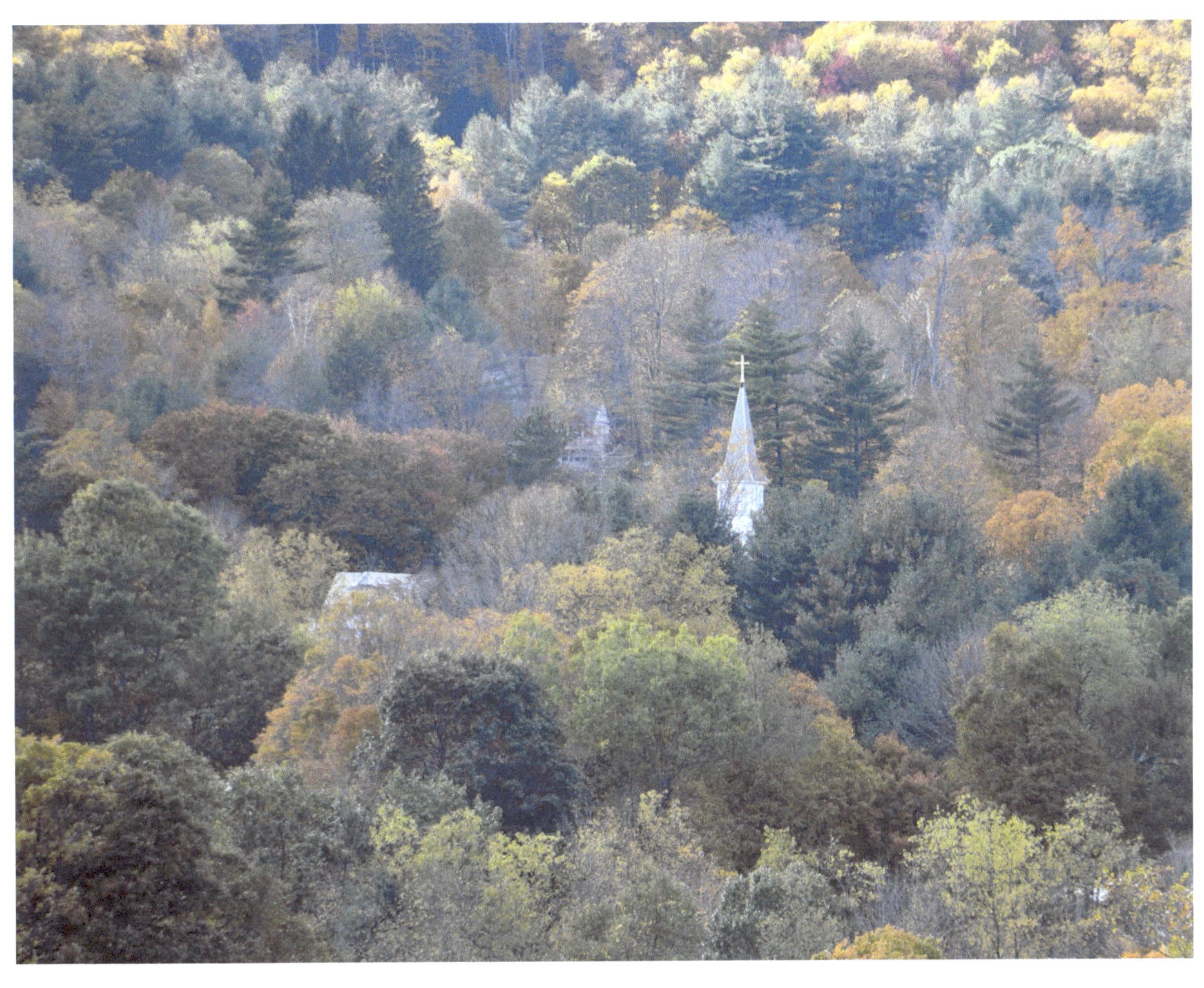

Shelburne Falls, Massachusetts

Life is a wilderness of twists and turns, where faith is your only compass.

–Paul Santaguida

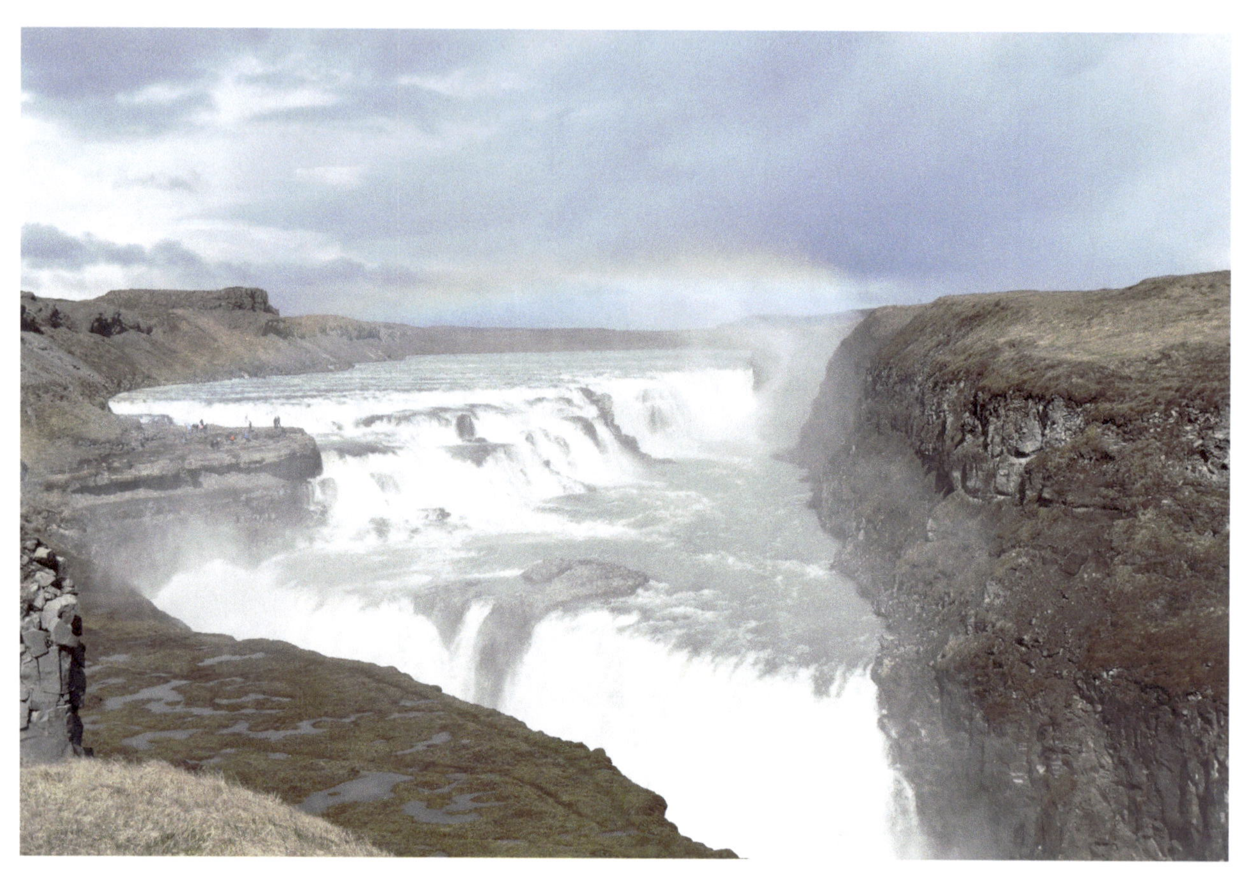

Gullfoss, Iceland

I believe in God, only I spell it Nature.

--Frank Lloyd Wright, 1867-1959

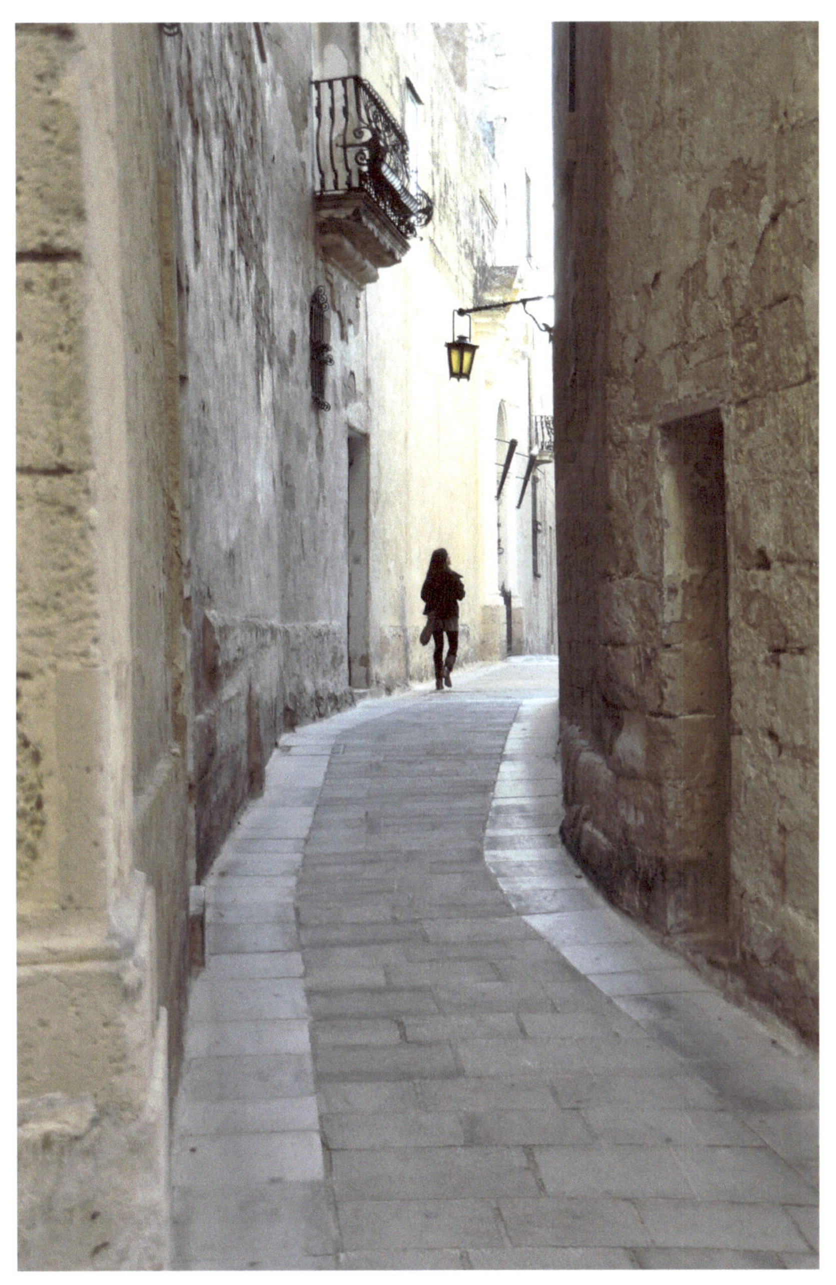

M'dina, Malta

Never be afraid to trust an unknown future to a known god.

--Corrie ten Boom, 1892-1983

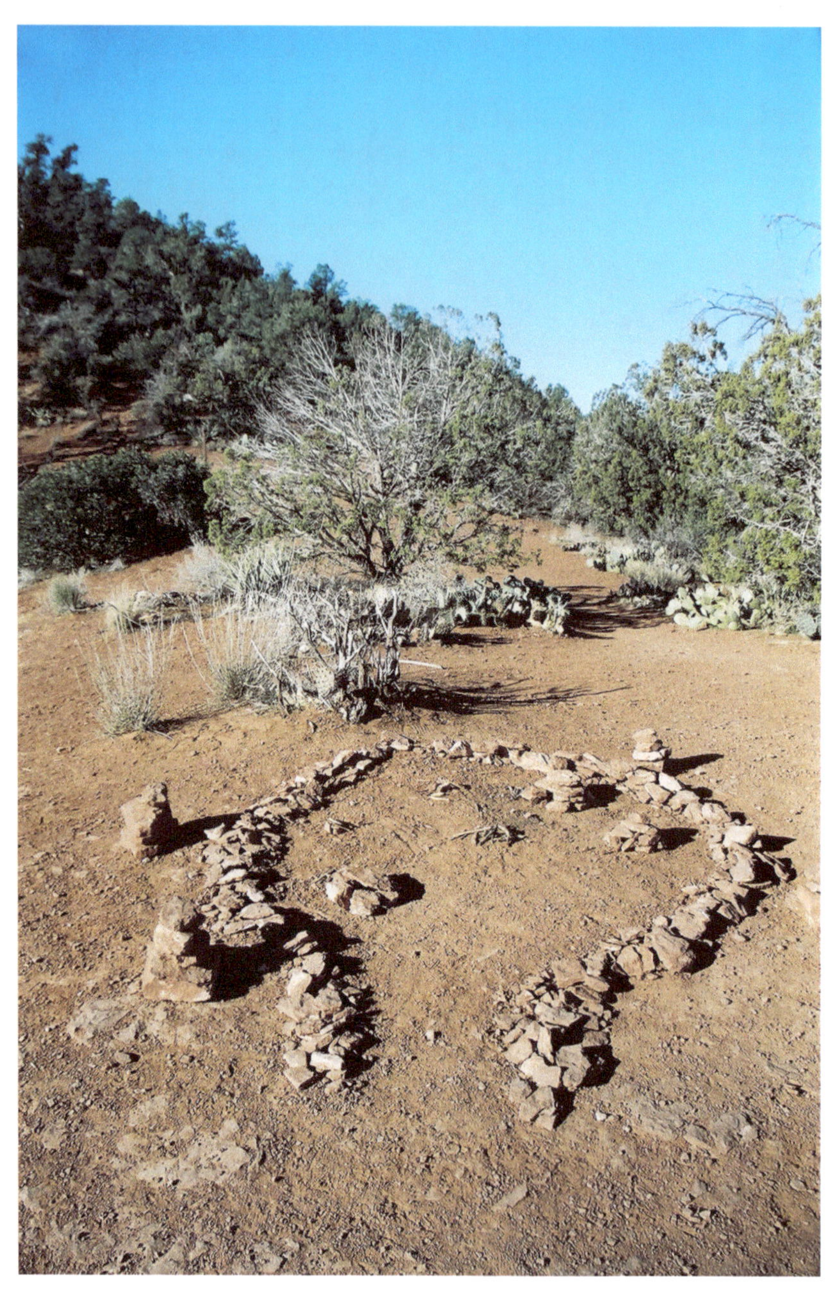

Sedona, Arizona

Ritual is the way you carry the presence of the sacred.
Ritual is the spark that must not go out.
--Christina Baldwin

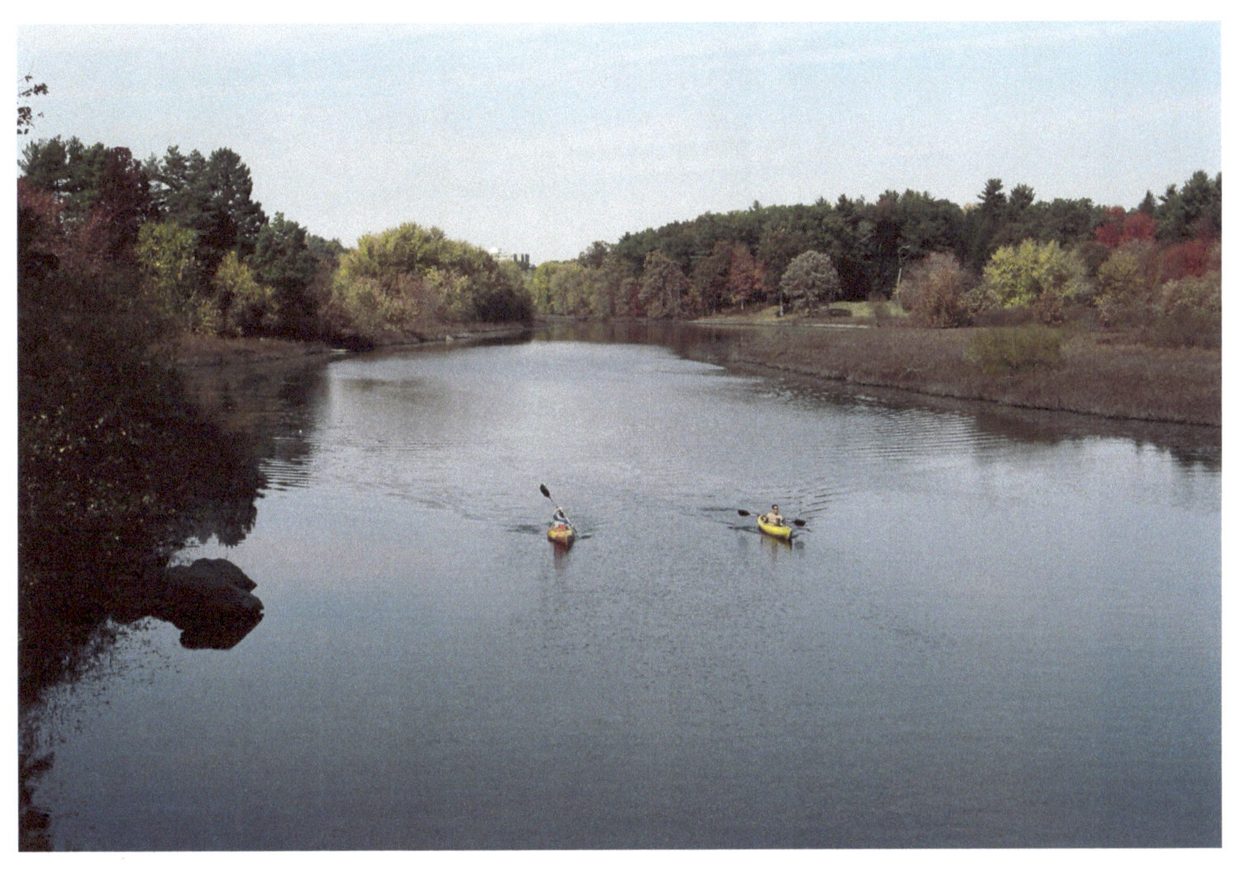

Sudbury, Massachusetts

I am suddenly filled with that sense of peace and meaning which is, I suppose,
what the pious have in mind when they talk about
the practice of the presence of God.
--Valerie Taylor

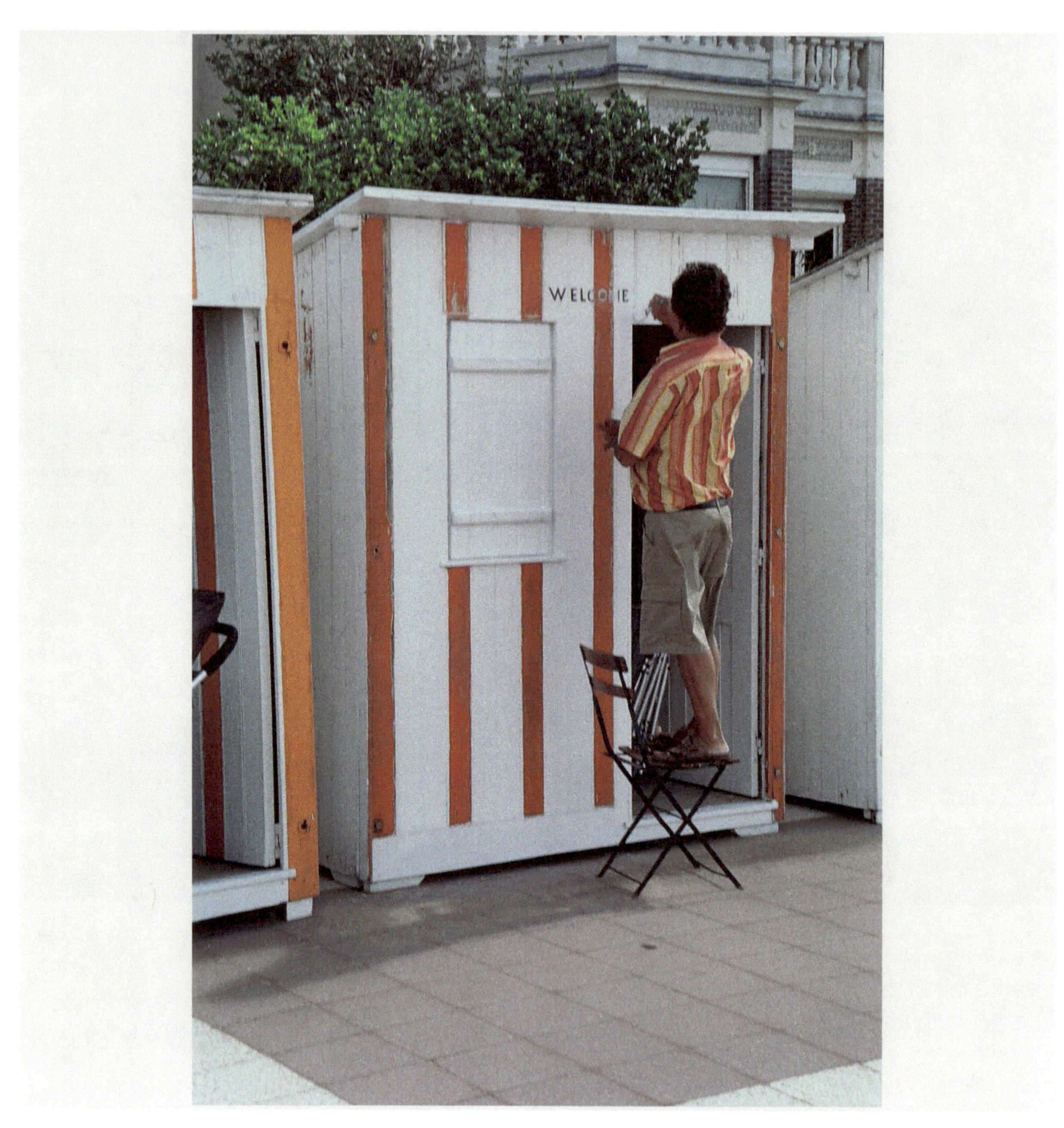

Houlgate, France

When I pray, coincidences happen, and when I don't, they don't.

--William Temple, 1881-1944

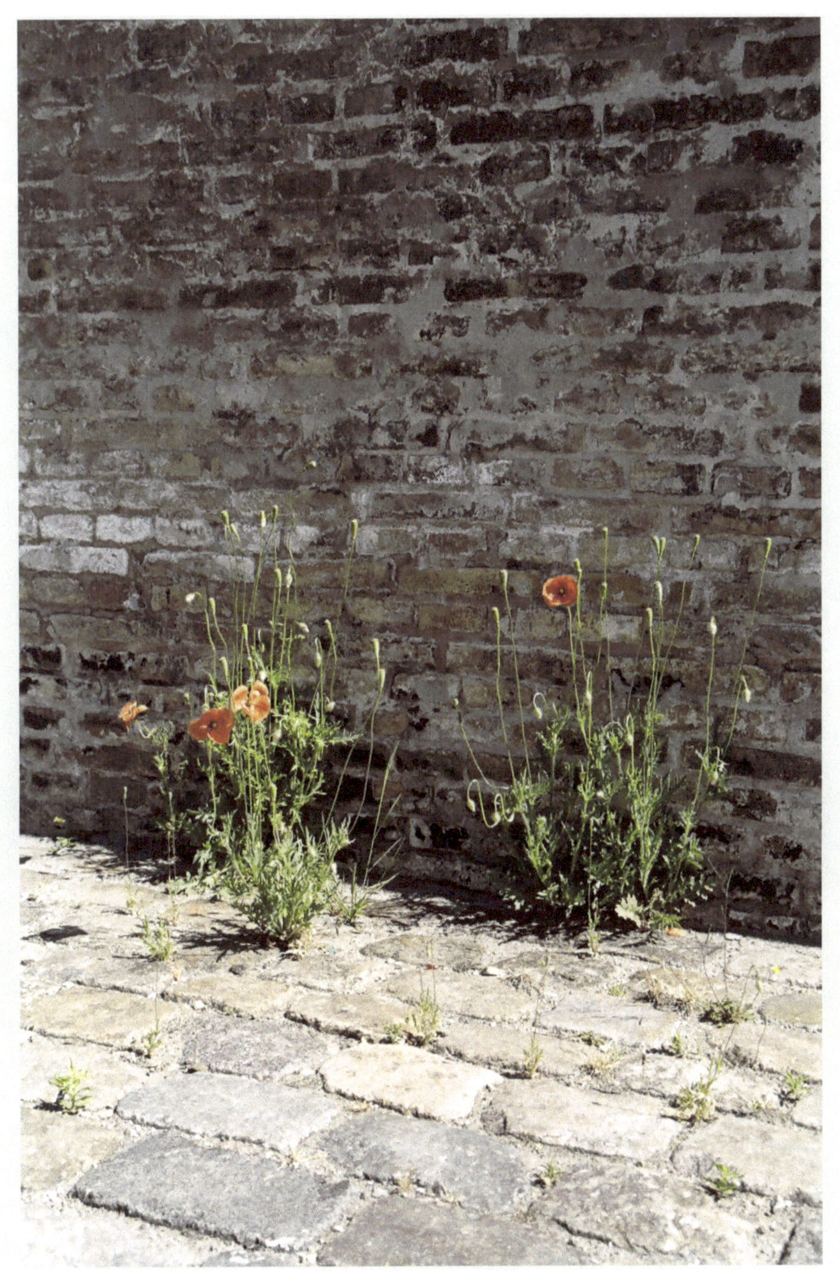

Copenhagen, Denmak

Belief consists in accepting affirmations of the soul.

--Ralph Waldo Emerson, 1803-1882

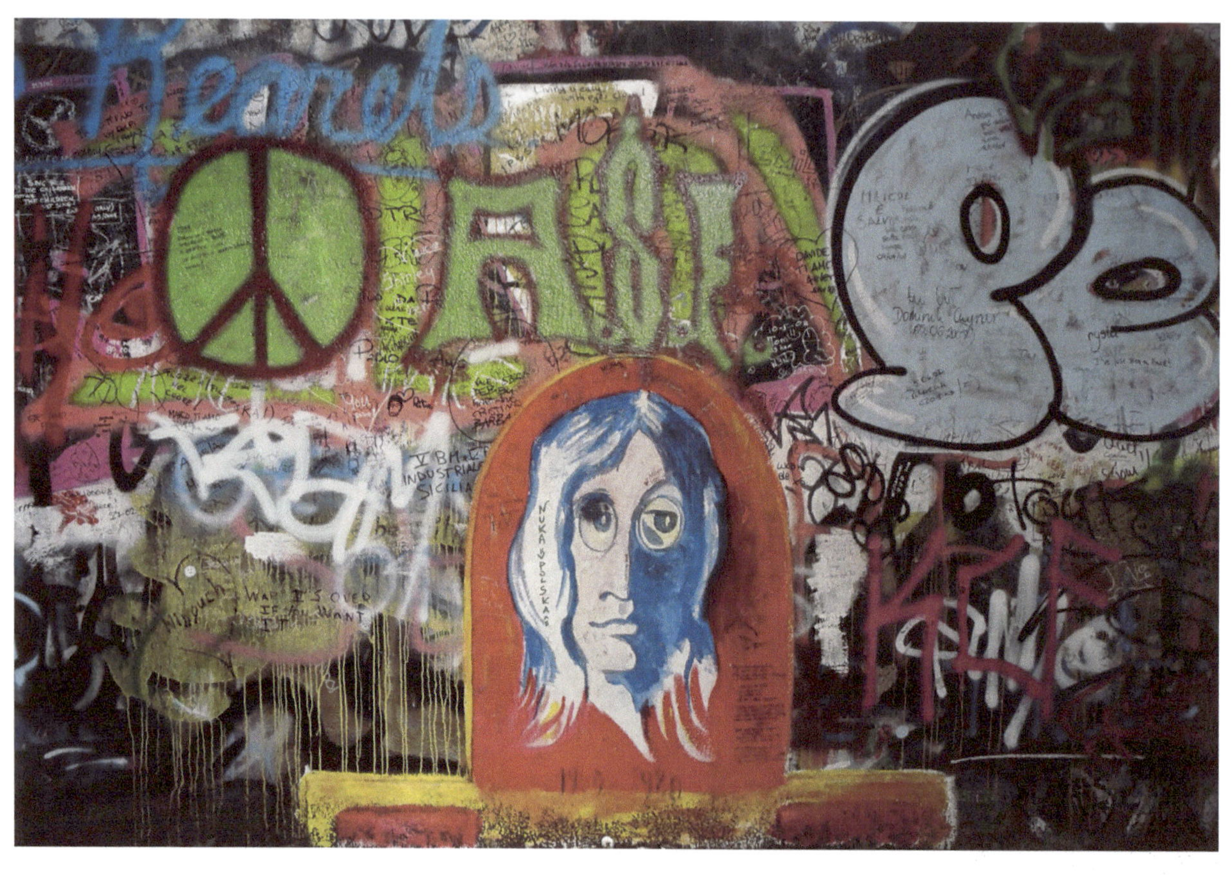

Prague, Czech Republic

We can say "Peace on Earth,"
we can sing about it, preach about it, or pray about it,
but if we have not internalized the mythology to make it happen inside us,
then it will not be.
– Betty Shabazz, 1936-1997

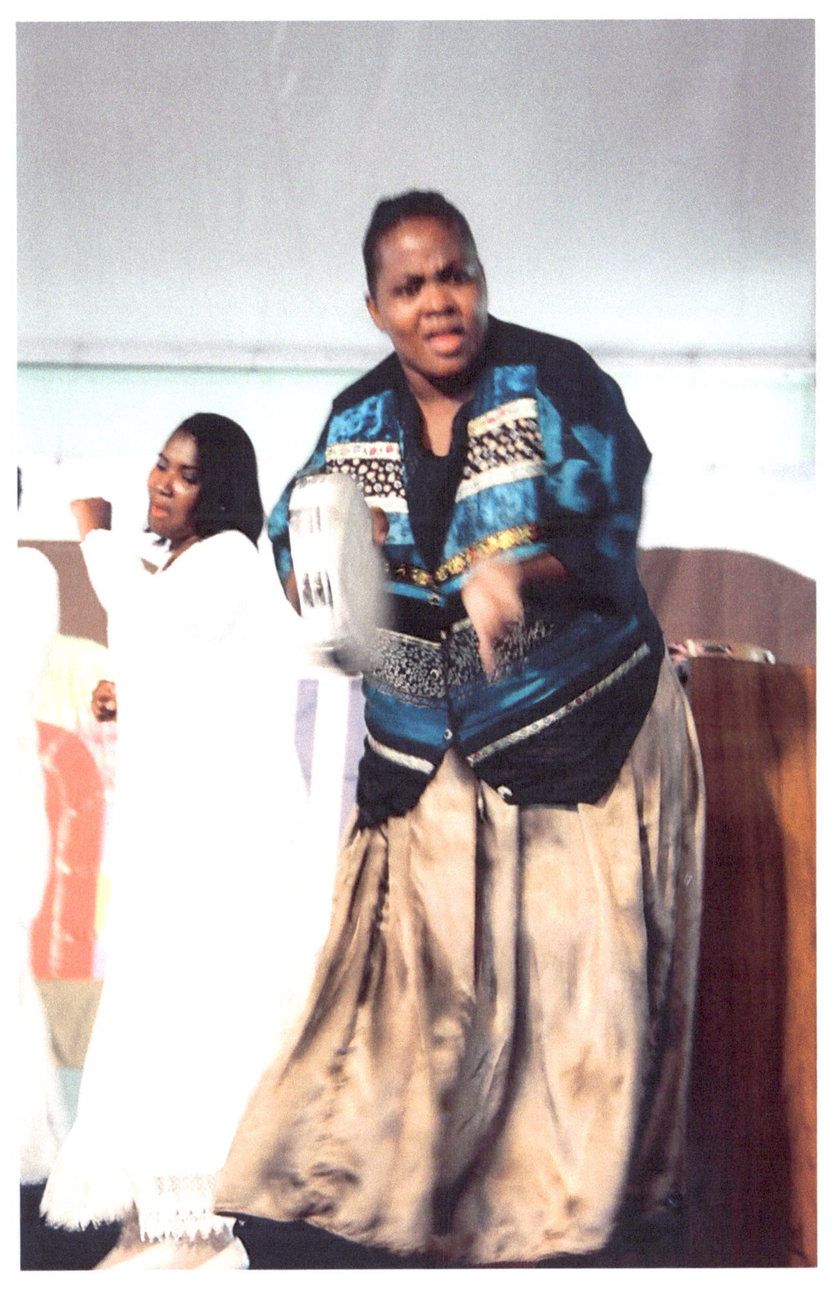

New Orleans, Louisiana

Joy is prayer, joy is strength,
joy is a net of love by which you can catch souls.
--Mother Teresa, 1910-1997

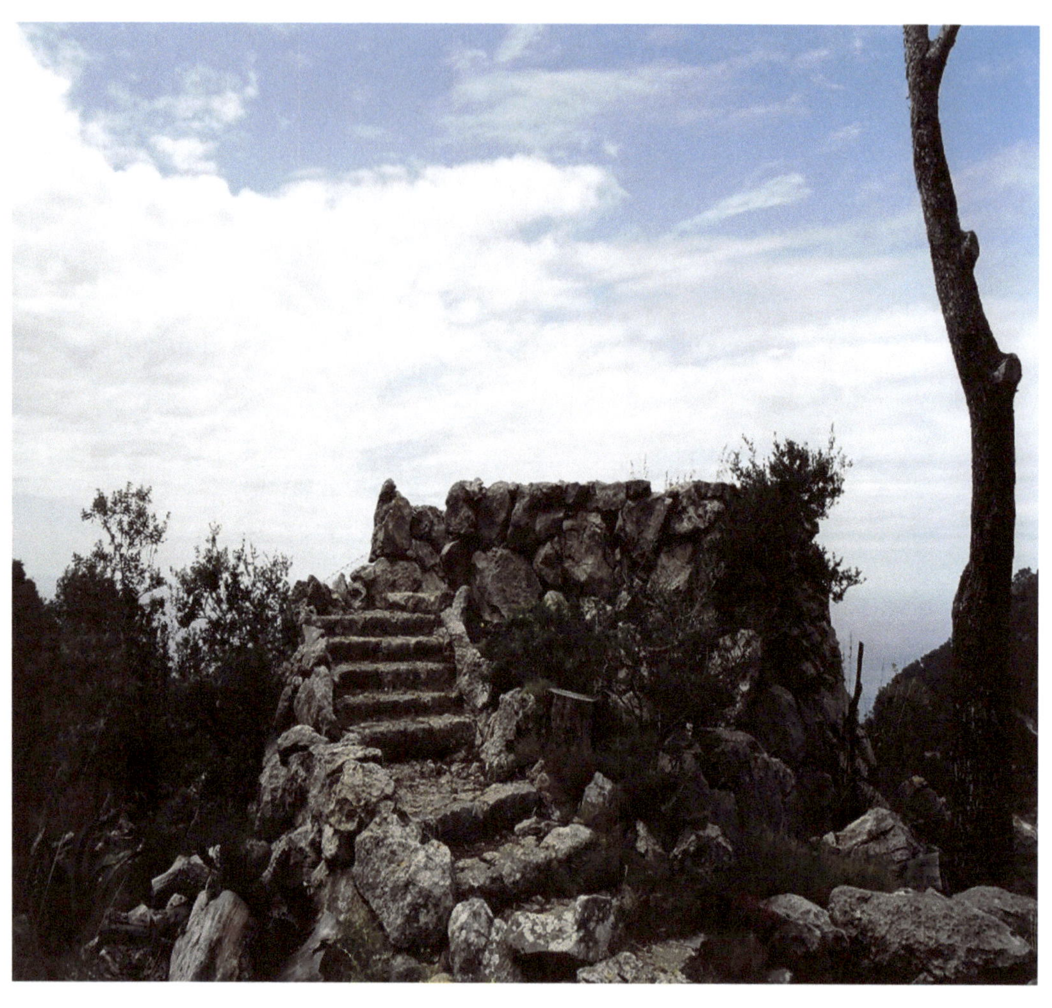

Majorca, Spain

God can be realized through all paths...The important thing is to reach the roof. You can reach it by stone stairs or by wooden stairs or by bamboo steps or by a rope.

--Ramakrishna, 1836-1886

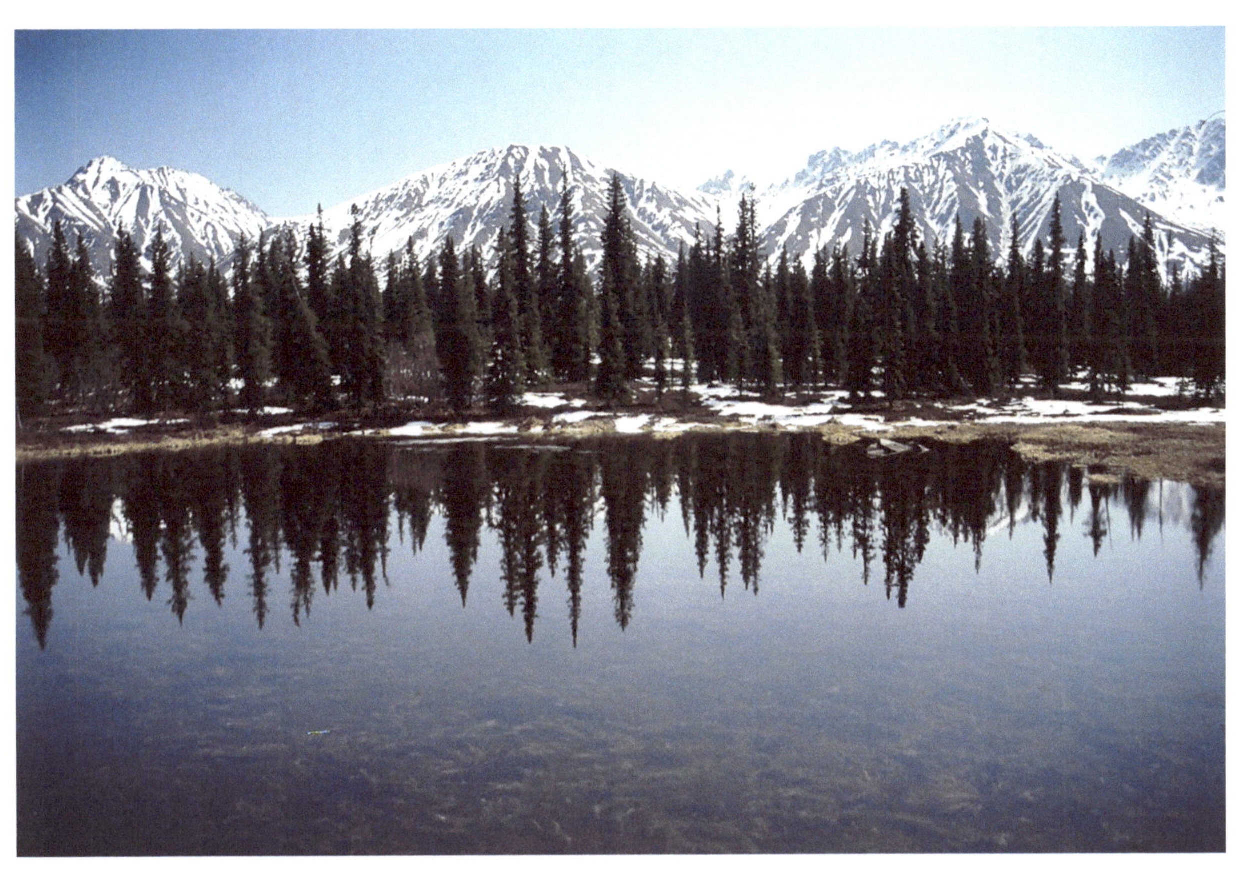

Denali National Park, Alaska

Prayer is exhaling the spirit of man and inhaling the spirit of God.

--Edwin Keith

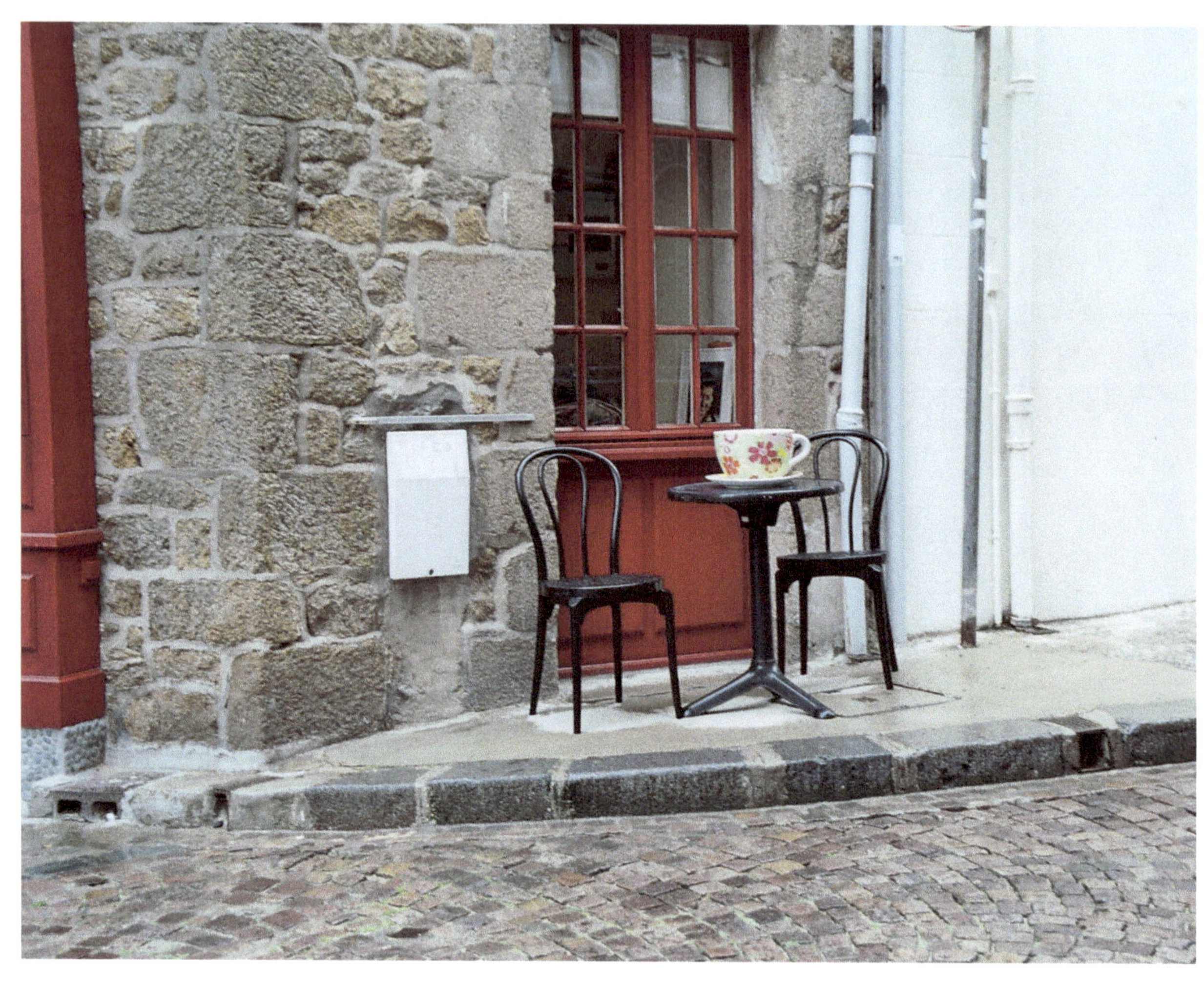

Saint-Malo, France

Spend time every day listening to what your muse it trying to tell you.

--Saint Bartholomew

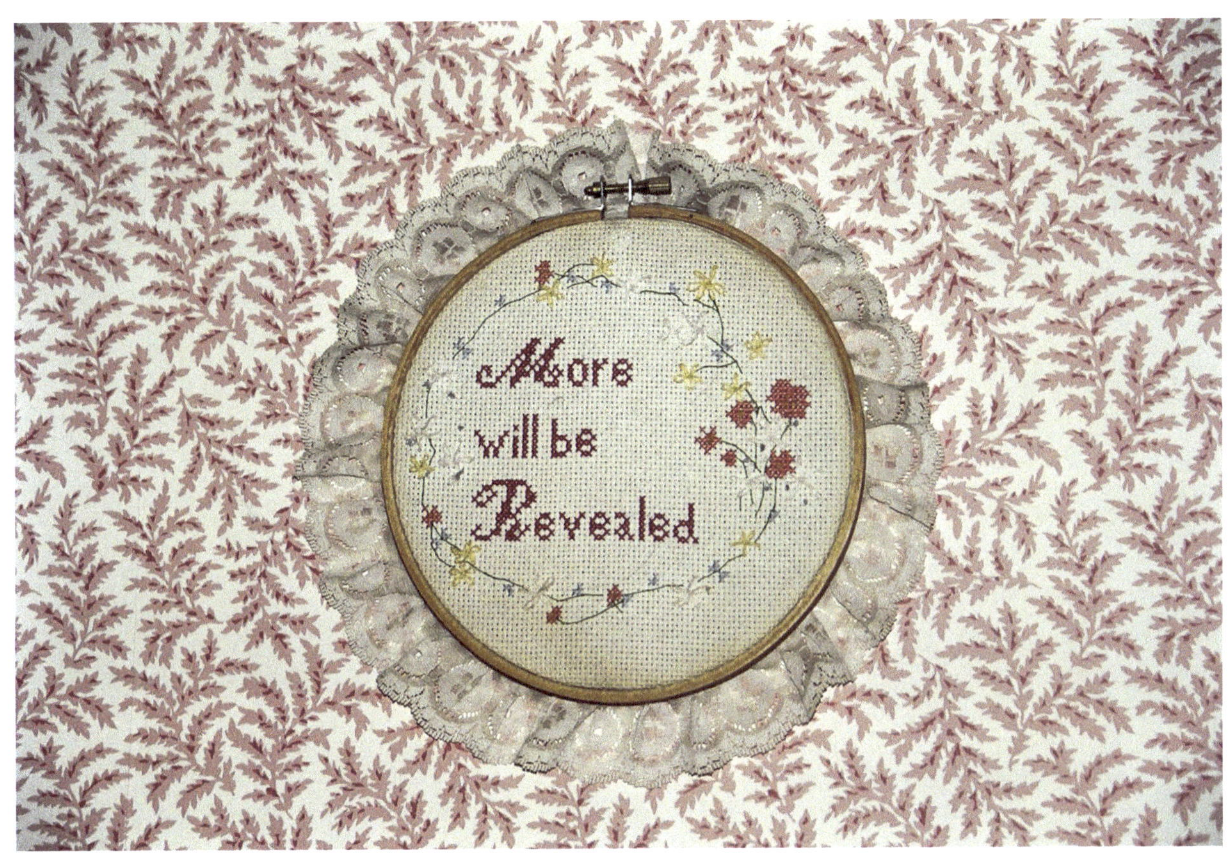


East Dorset, Vermont

God is in the world, or nowhere, creating continually in us and around us.
Insofar as man partakes of this creative process does he partake of the divine,
of God, and that participation is his immortality.
– Alfred North Whitehead, 1861-1947

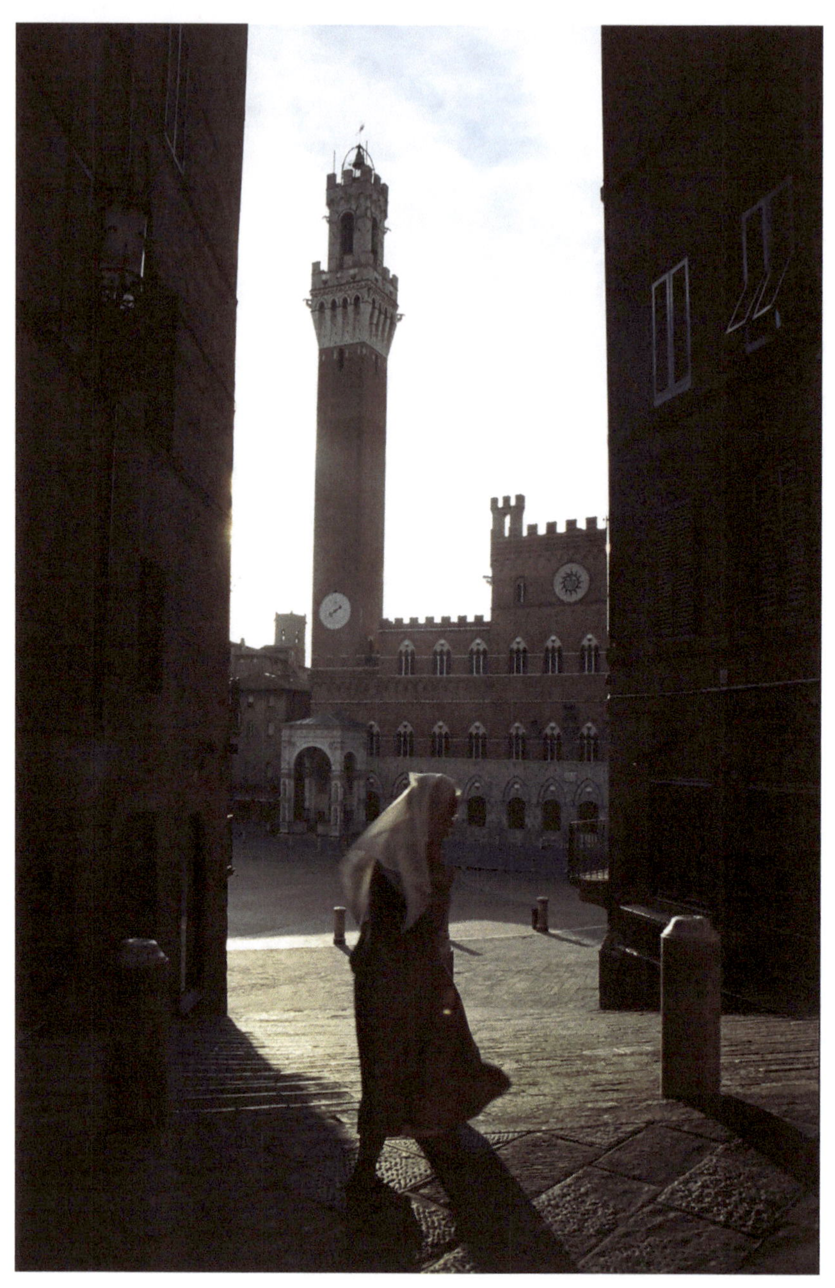

Siena, Italy

Two men please God--who serves him with all his heart because he knows him;
who seeks him with all his heart because he knows him not.

--Nikita Ivanovich Panin, 1718-1783

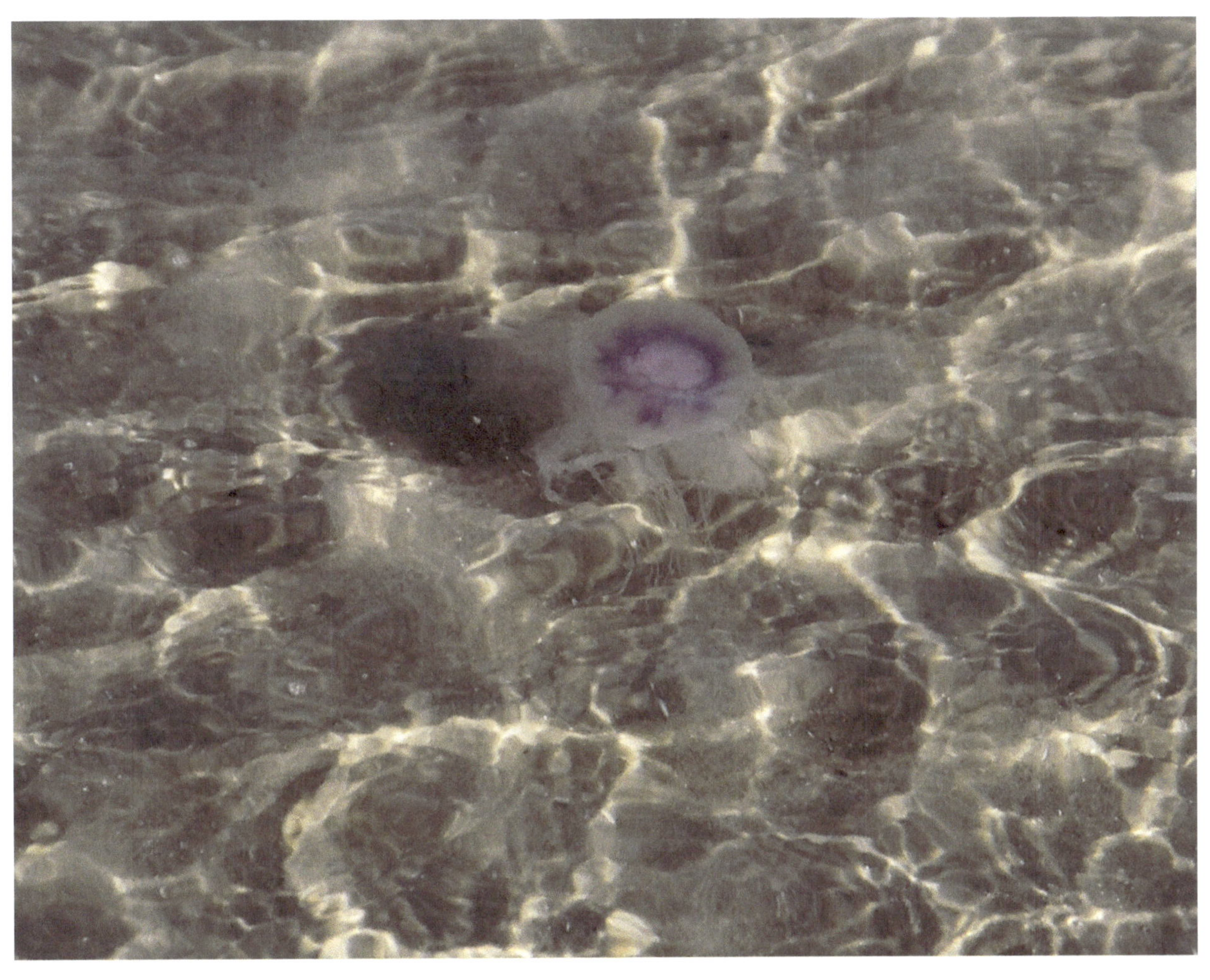

Skagen, Denmark

As your faith is strengthened you will find that there is no longer the need
to have a sense of control, things will flow as they will,
and that you will flow with them, to your great delight and benefit.
– Emmanuel Teney

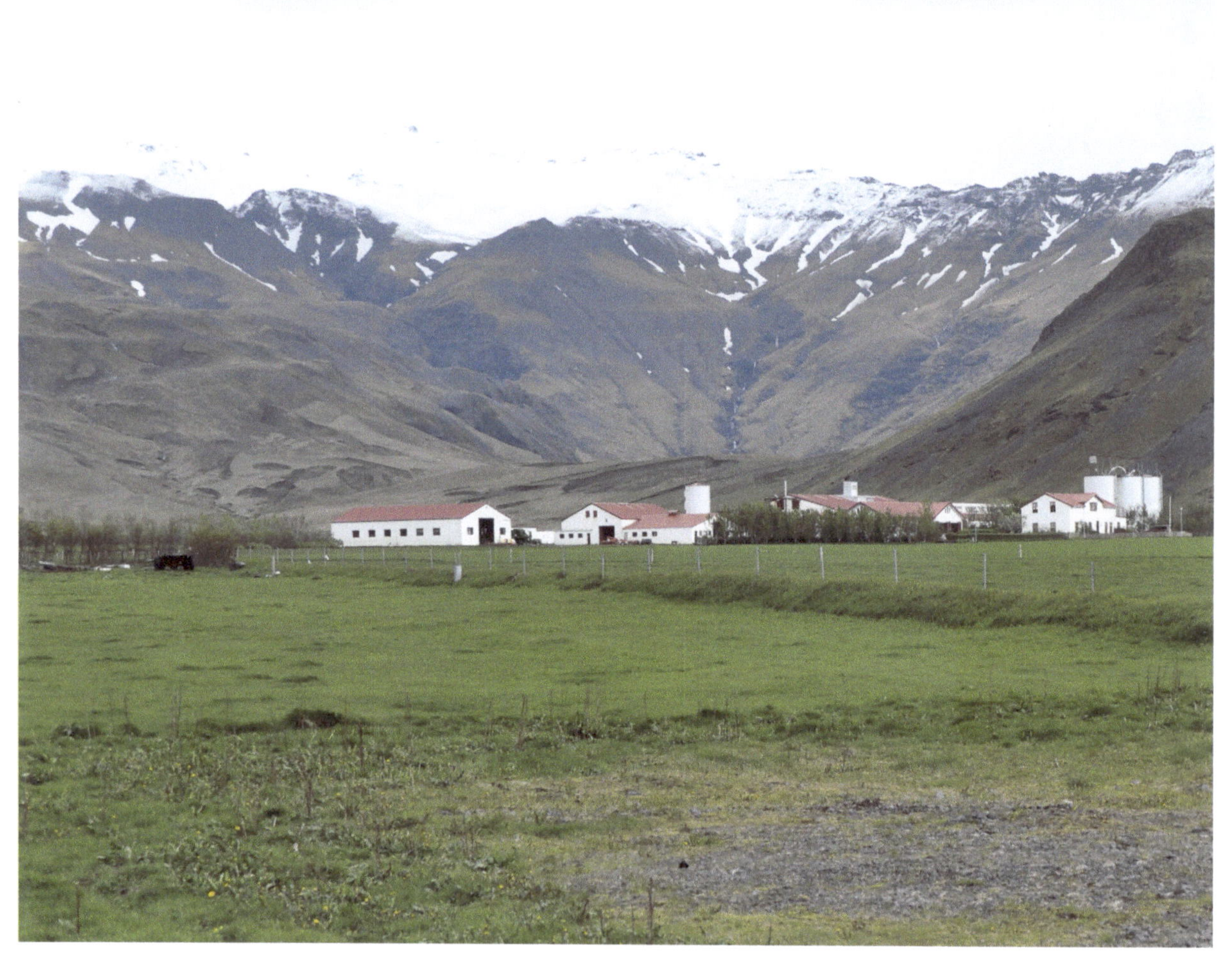

Skogar, Iceland

Prayer is a kind of calling home every day.
And there can come to you a serenity, a feeling of at-homeness in god's universe,
a peace that the world can neither give nor disturb, a fresh courage,
a new insight, a holy boldness that you'll never, never get any other way.
– Earl G. Hunt, Jr., 1918-2004

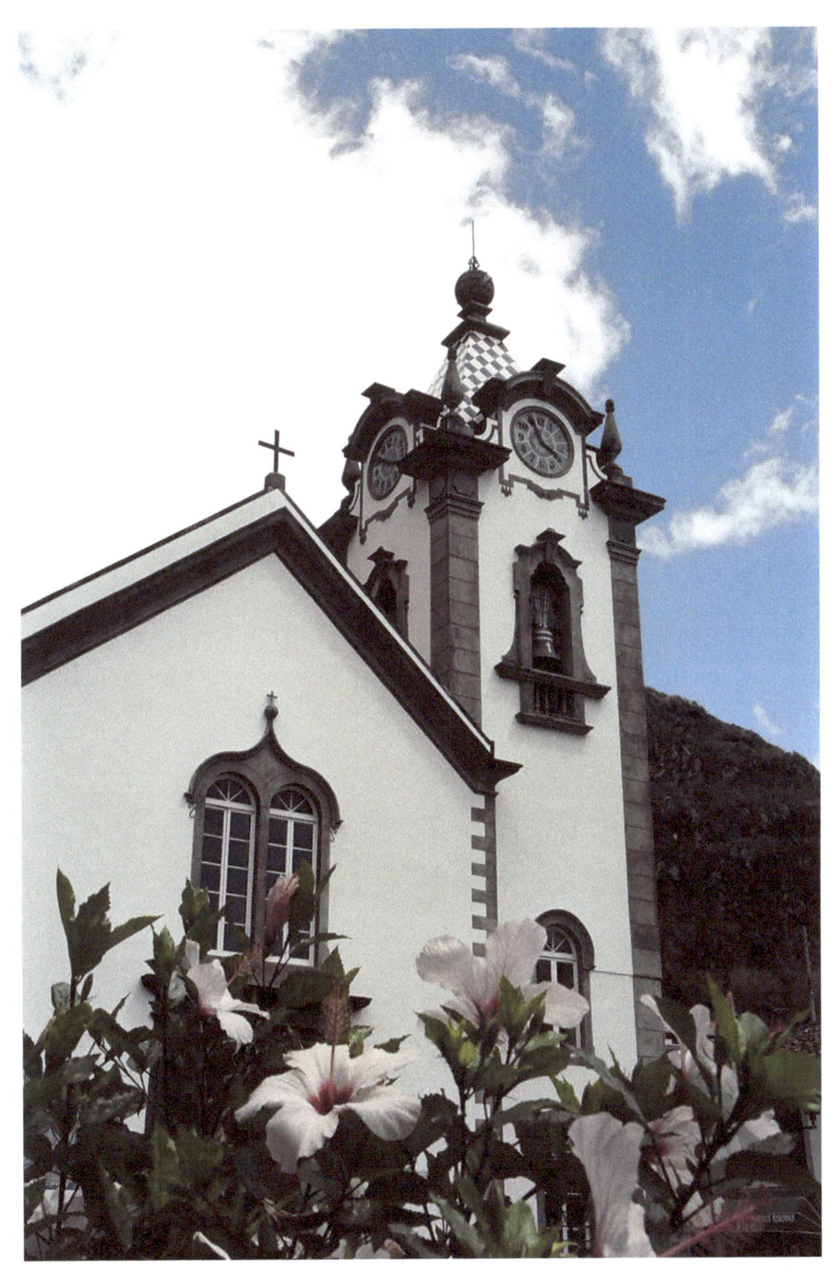

Madeira, Portugal

For prayer is nothing else than
being on terms of friendship with God.
--Saint Teresa of Avila, 1515-1582

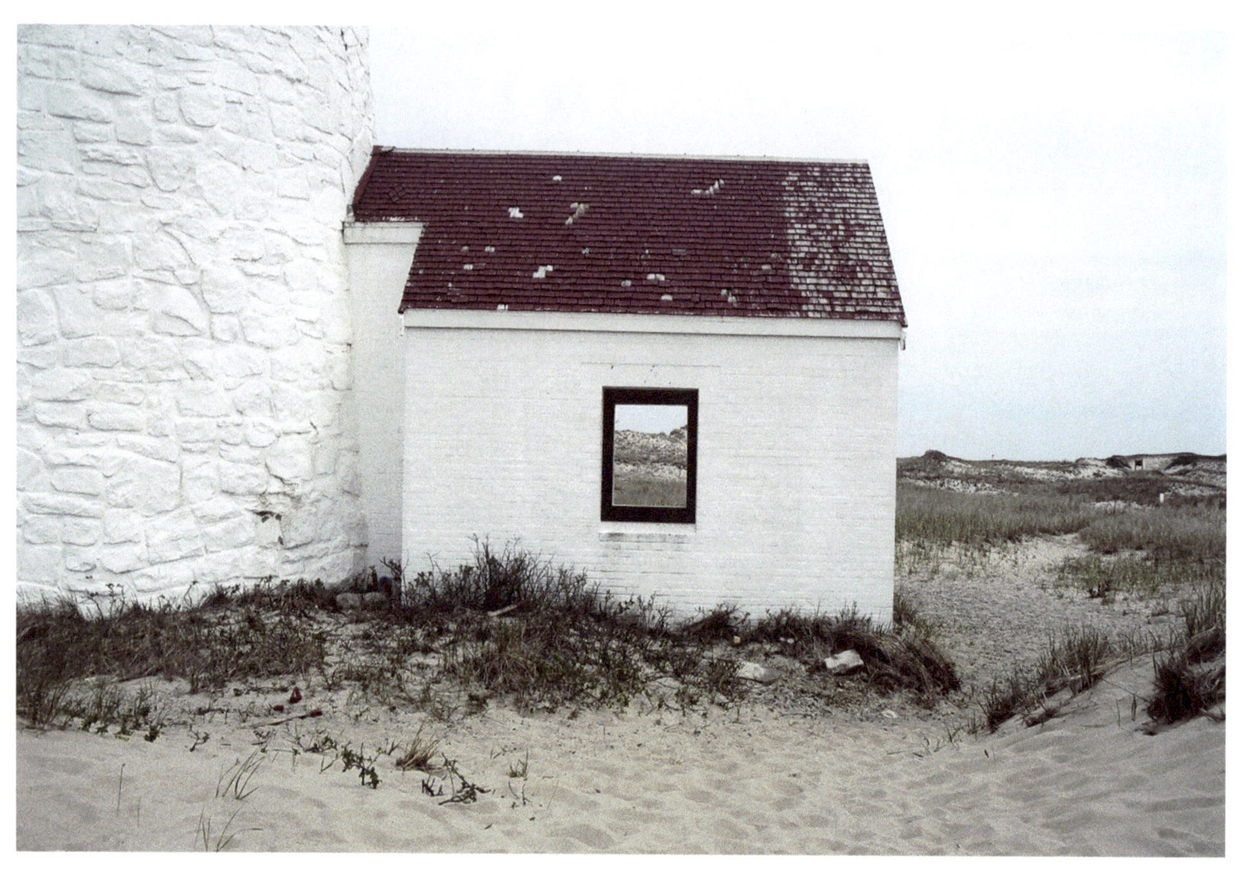

Nantucket, Massachusetts

God dwells wherever man lets Him in.

--Jewish proverb

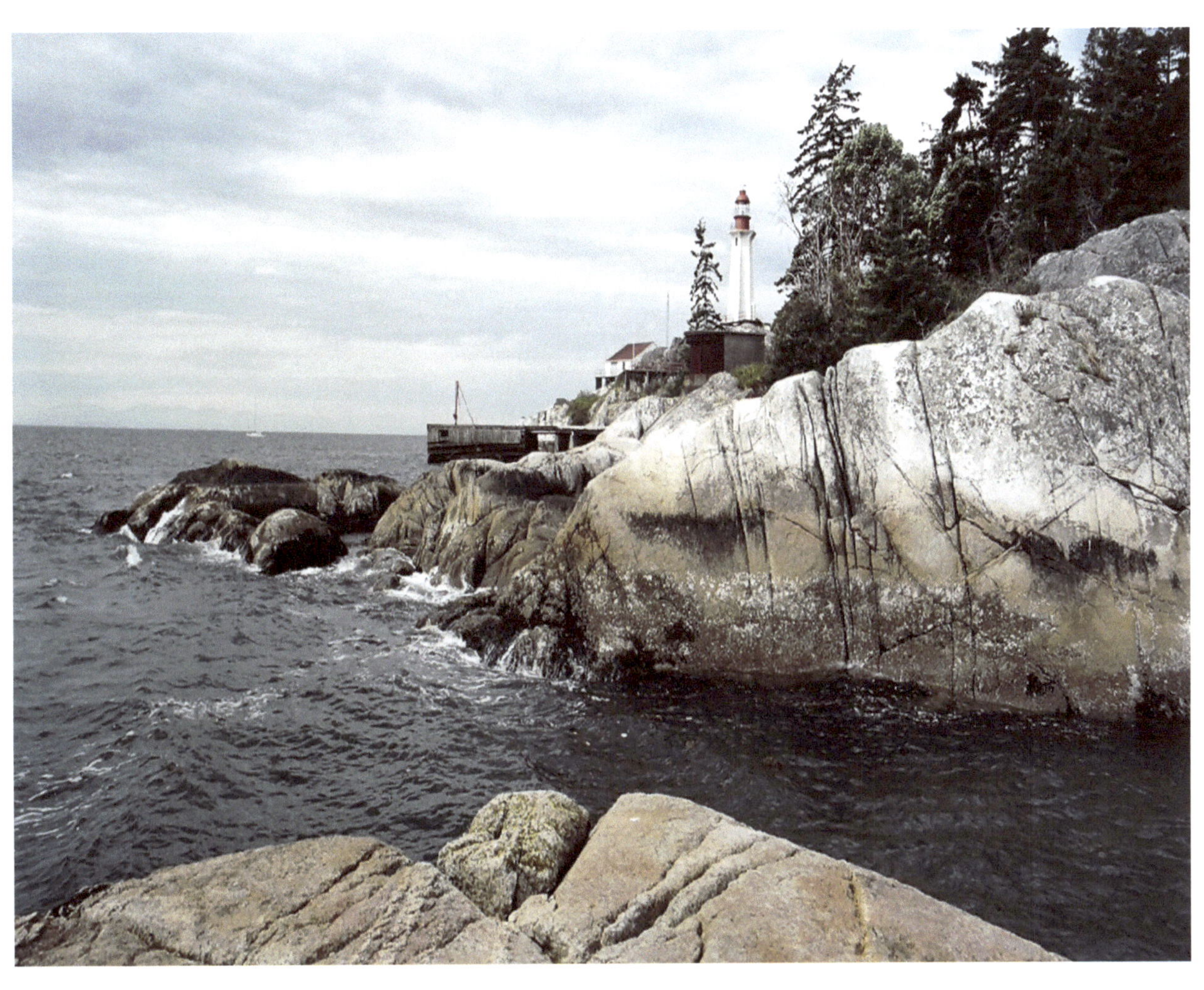

Howe Sound, British Columbia

Call on God,
but row away from the rocks.
--Indian proverb

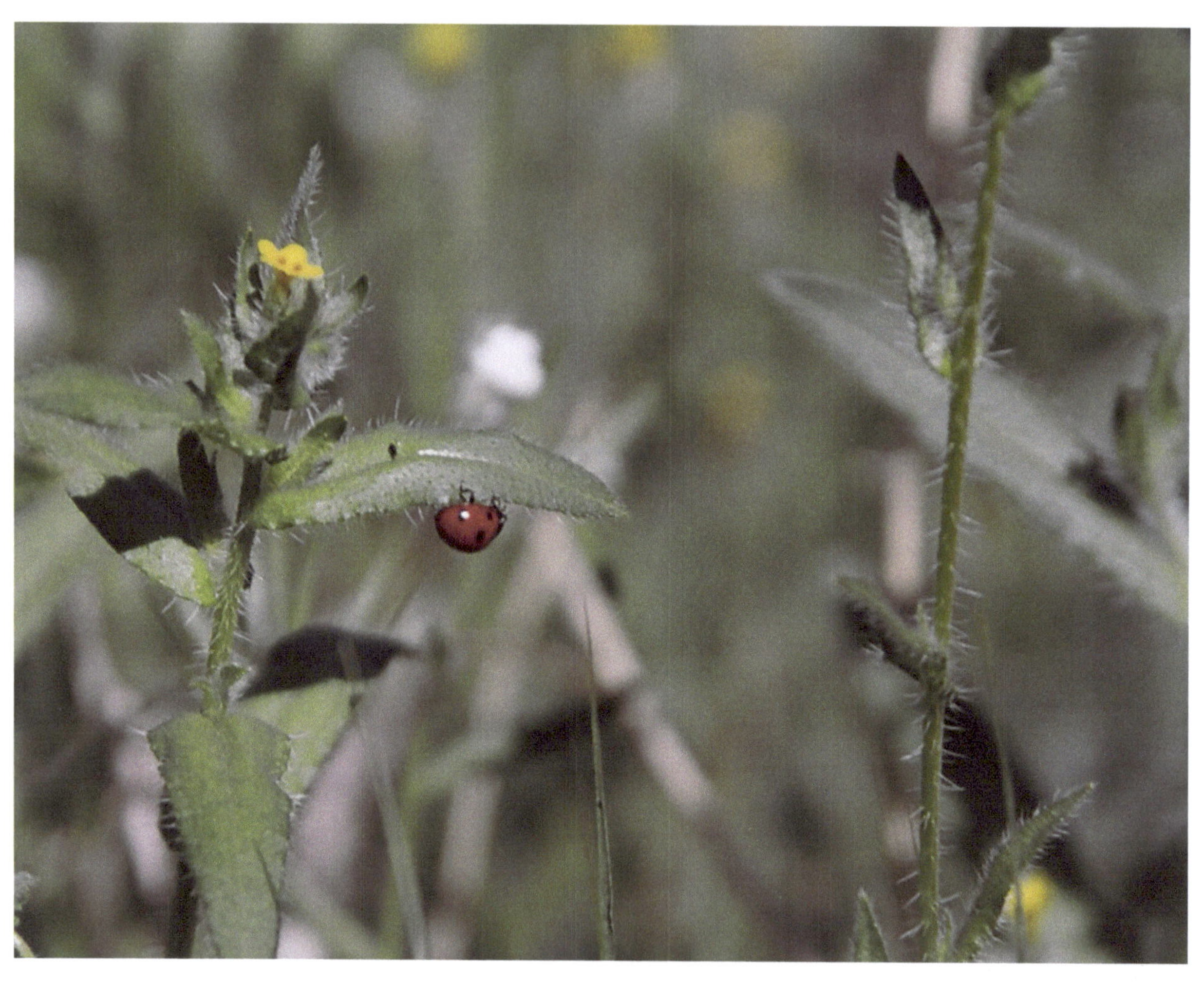

Tahquitz Canyon, California

It had only been my repeated experience that when you said to life calmly and firmly...
'I trust you; do what you must,'
life had an uncanny way of responding to your need.
--Olga Ilyin, 1894 - 1991

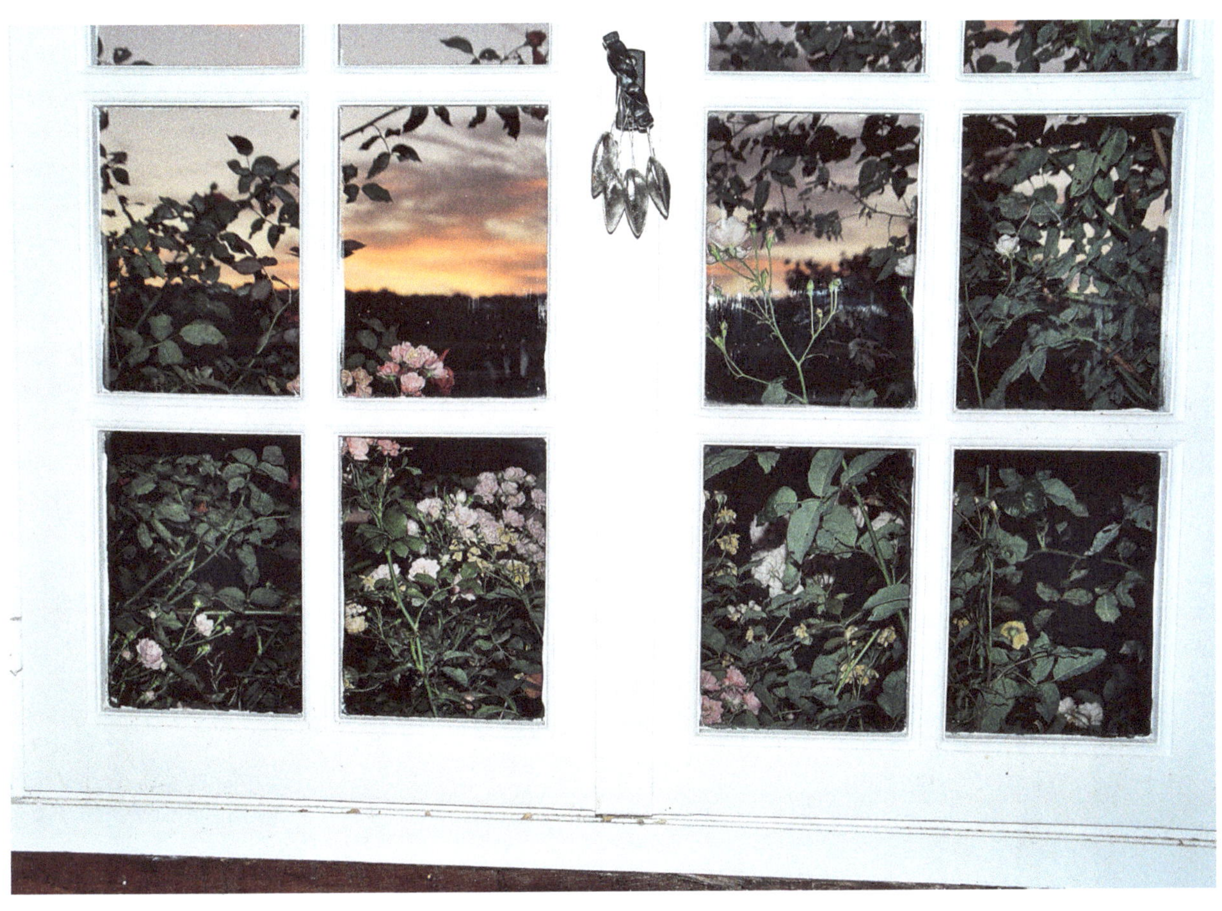

Normandy, France

Beauty puts a face on God.
When we gaze at nature, at a loved one, or at a work of art,
our soul immediately recognizes and is drawn to the face of God.
--Margaret Brownley

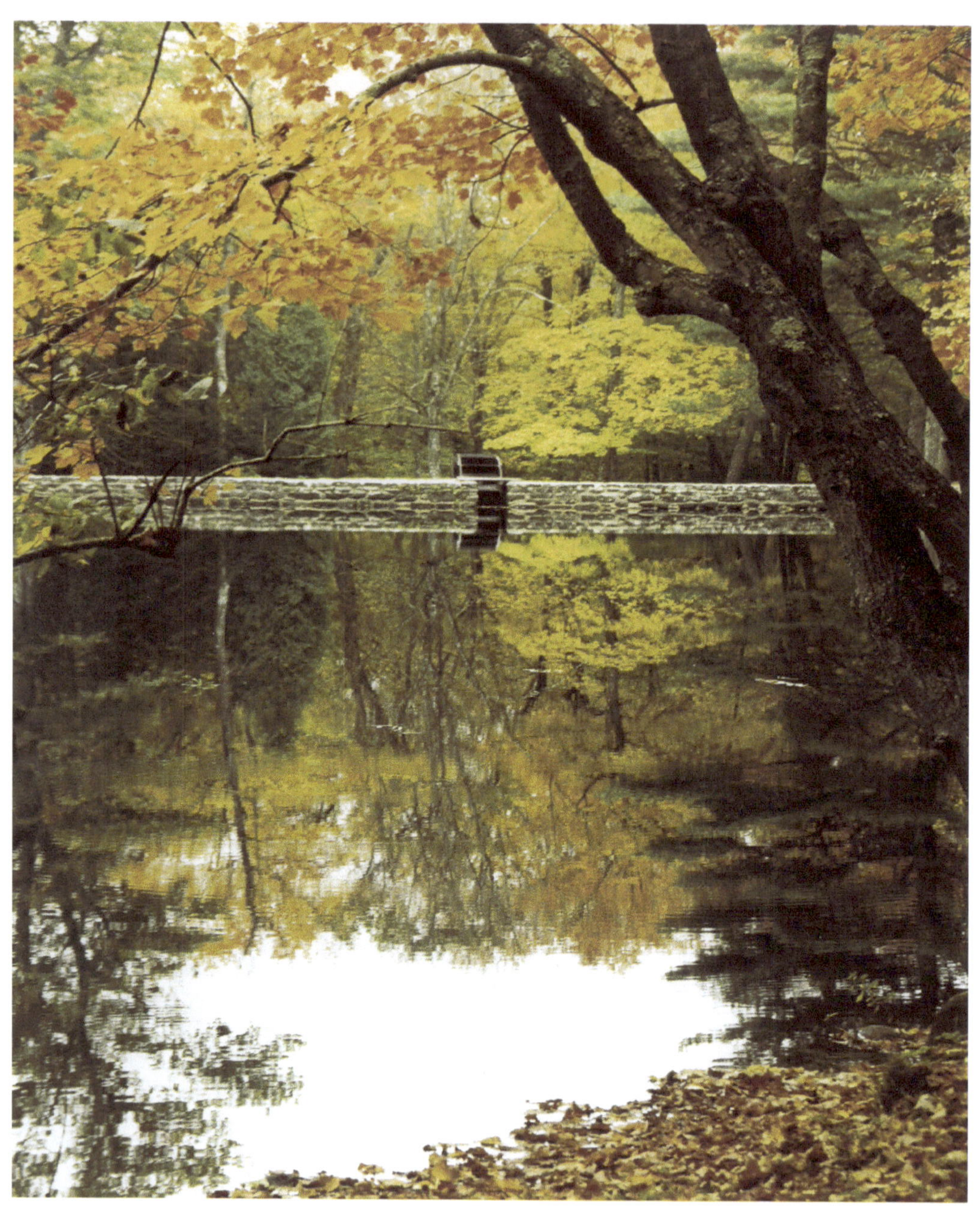

Chatfield Hollow State Park, Connecticut

There seems to be a kind of order in the universe, in the movement of the stars and the turning of the earth and the changing of seasons, and even in the cycle of human life.

--Katherine Anne Porter, 1890-1980

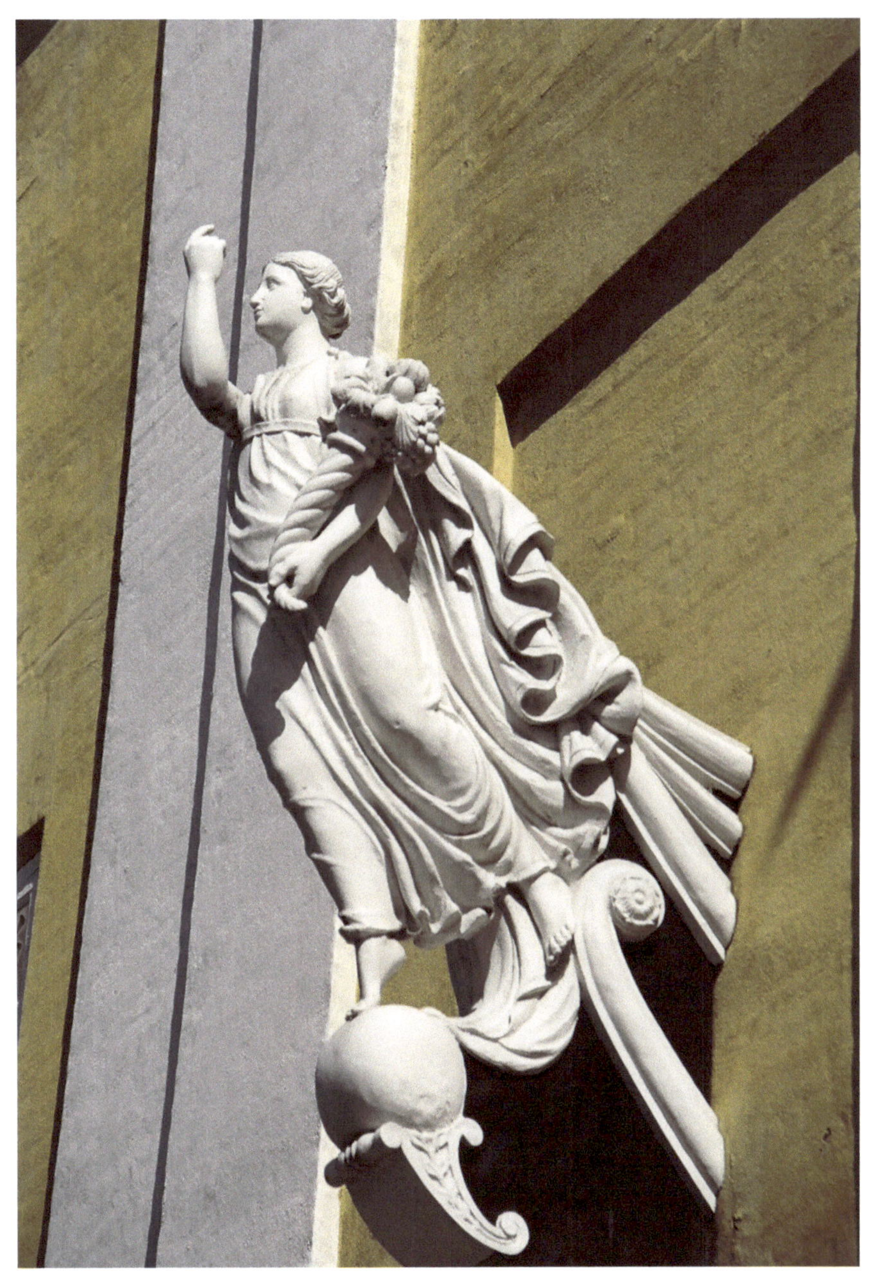

Copenhagen, Denmanrk

Intuition is a spiritual faculty and does not explain but simply points the way.

– Florence Scovel Shinn, 1871-1940

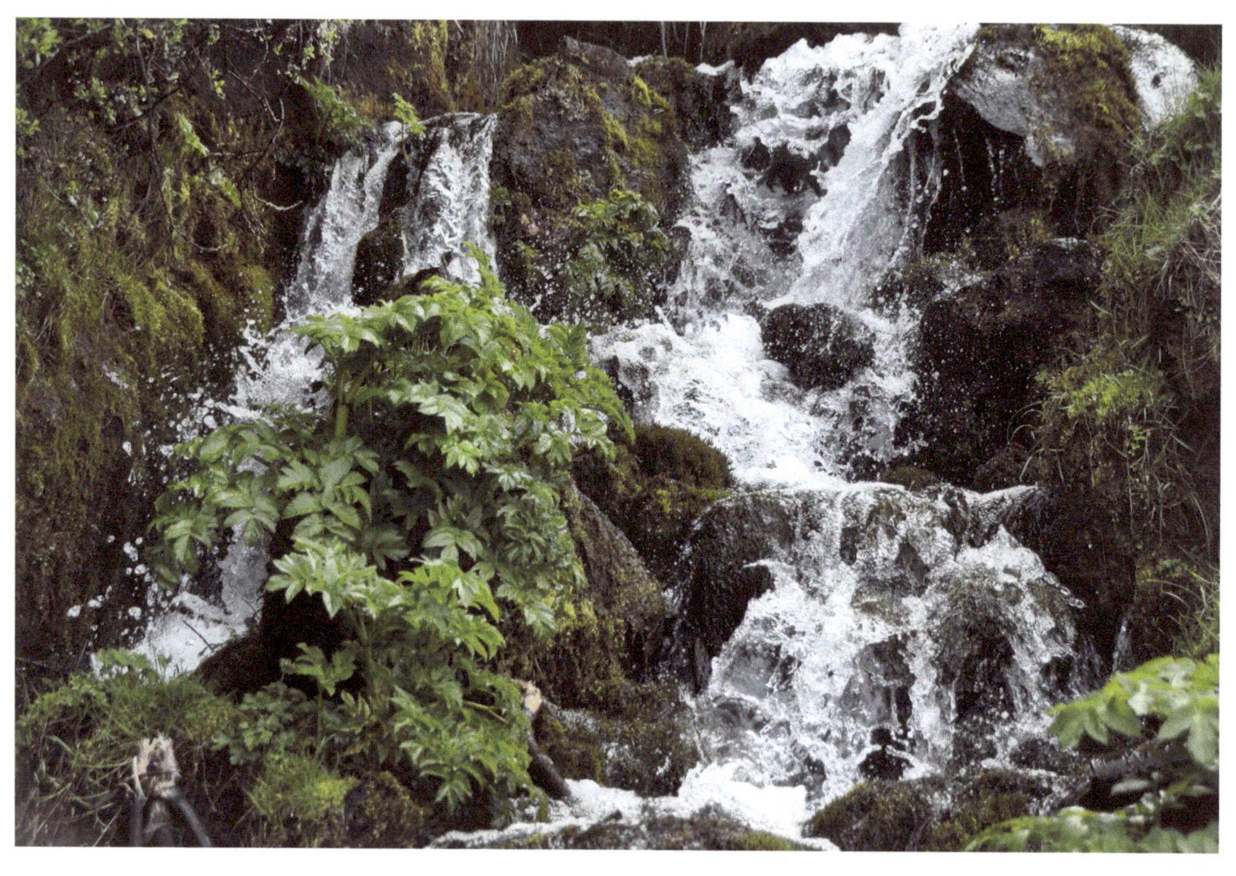

Seljalandsfoss, Iceland

Faith is a curious thing.
It must be renewed; it has its own spring.
--Gladys Taber, 1899-1980

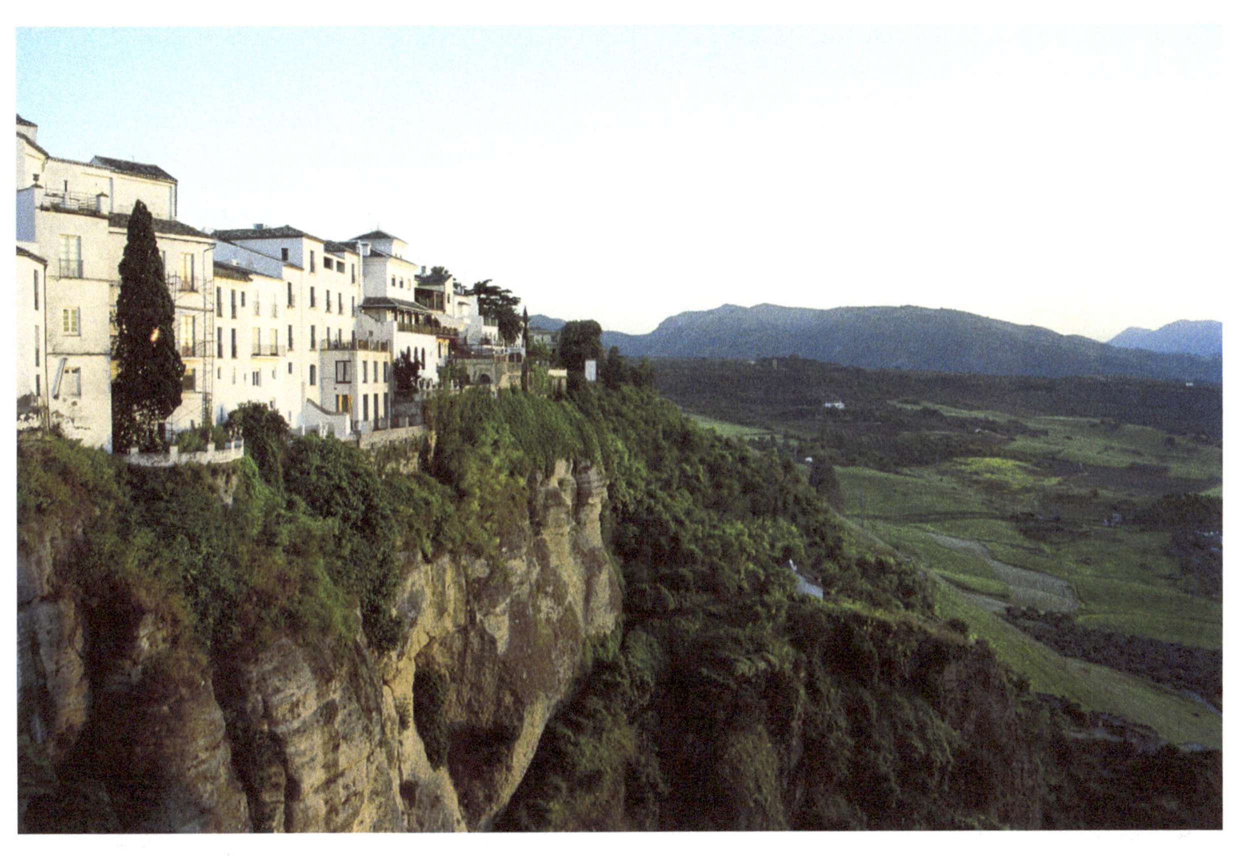

Ronda, Spain

So instead of getting to Heaven, at last--
I'm going, all along.
--Emily Dickinson, 1830-1886

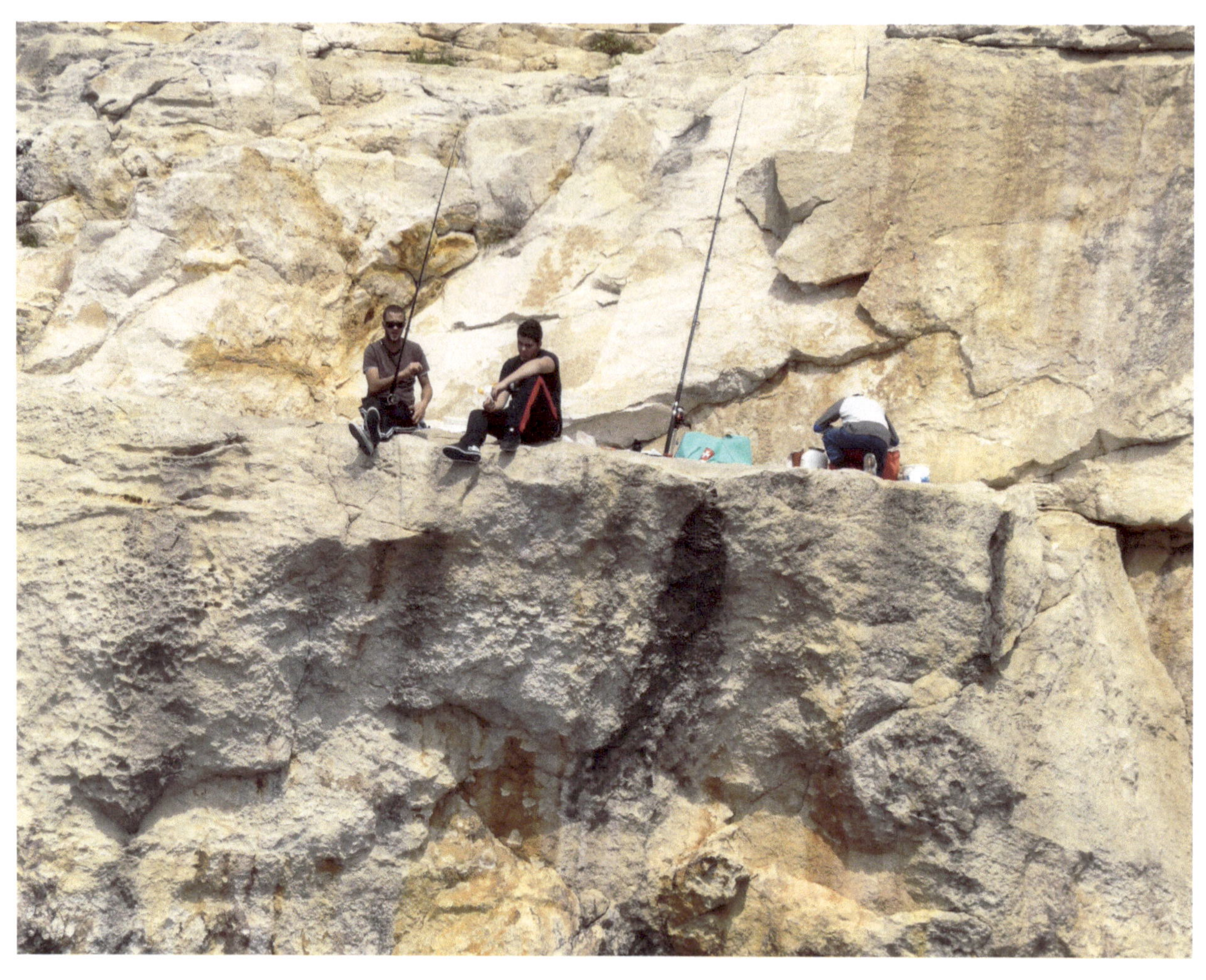

Blue Grotto, Malta

Sometimes the questions are complicated and the answers are simple.

--Dr. Seuss, 1904-1991

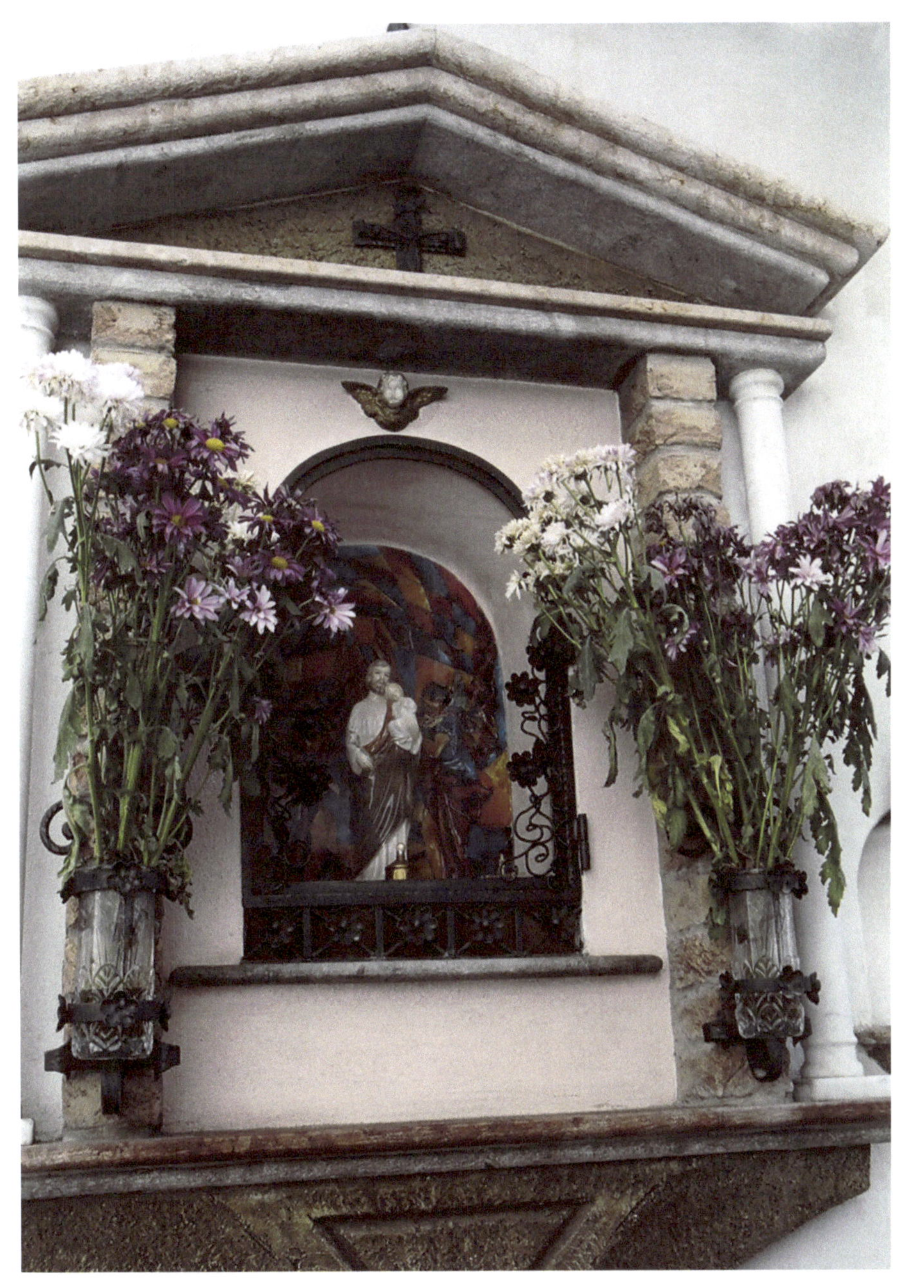

Cefalu, Sicily

We are not human beings having a spiritual experience,

we are spiritual beings having a human experience.

--Pierre Teilhard de Chardin, 1881-1955

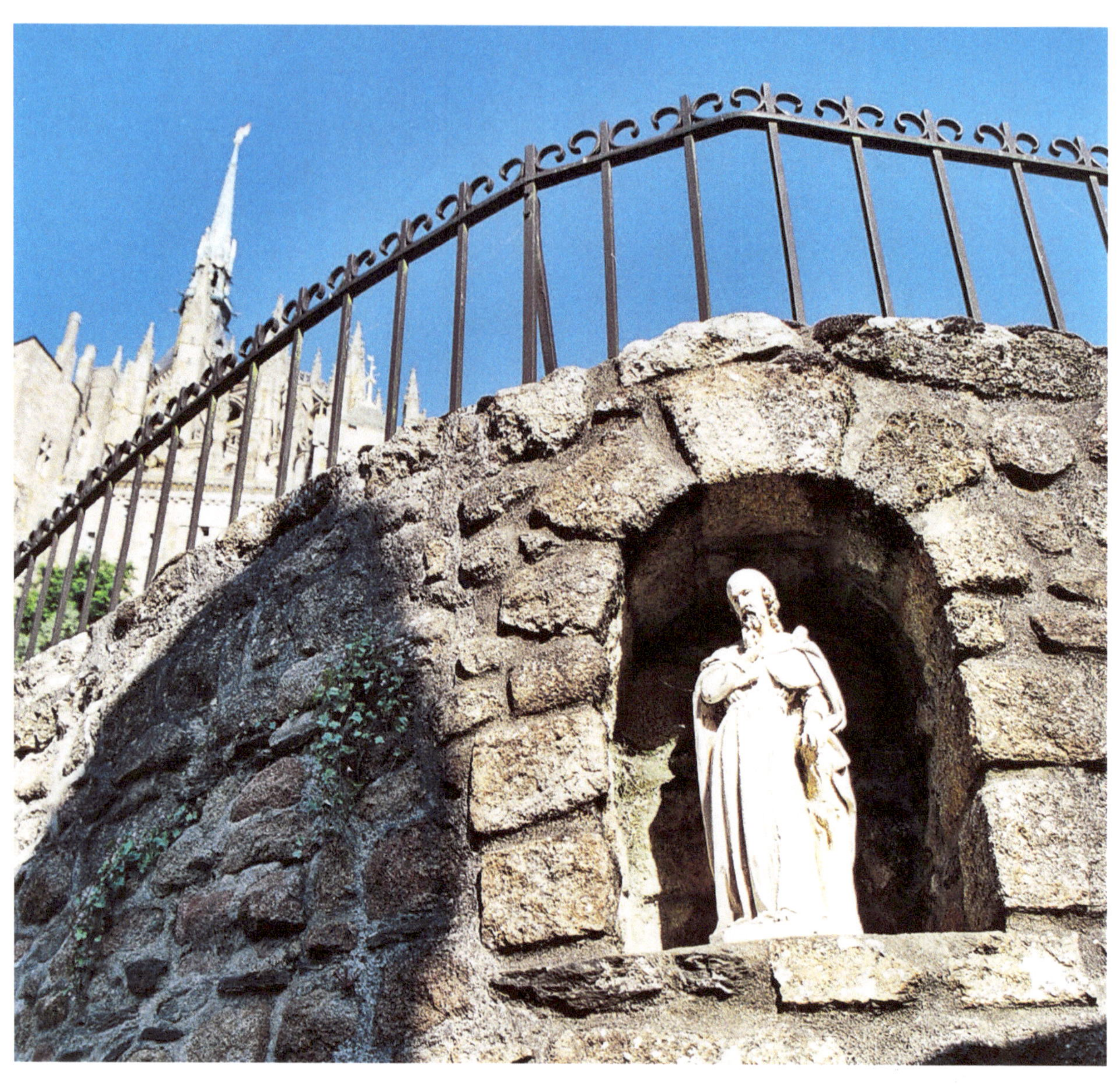

Mont Saint-Michel, France

Prayer serves as an edge and border to preserve the web of life from unraveling.

--Robert Hall

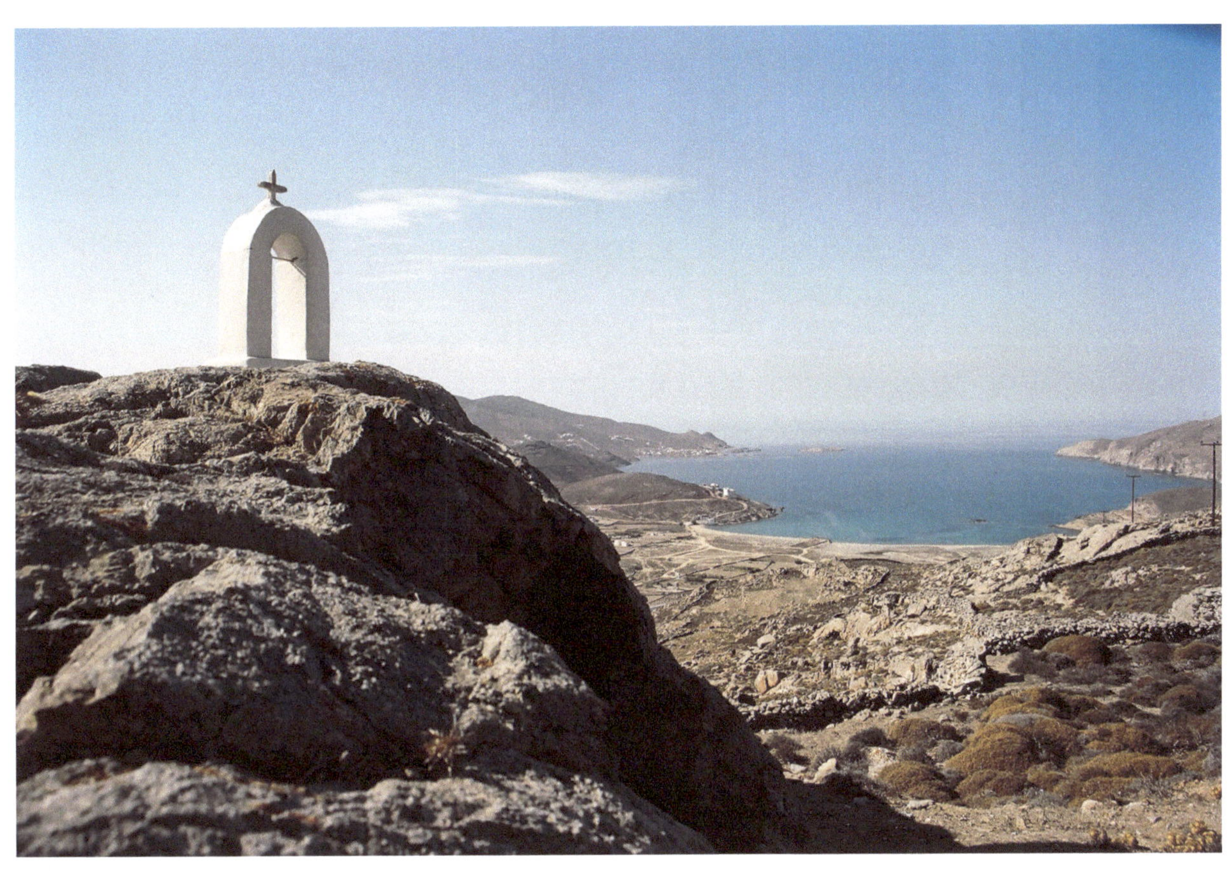

Mykonos, Greece

As long as rivers shall run down to the sea,
or shadows touch the mountain slopes, or stars graze in the vault of heaven,
so long shall your honor, your name, your praise endure.
– Virgil, 70-19 B.C.

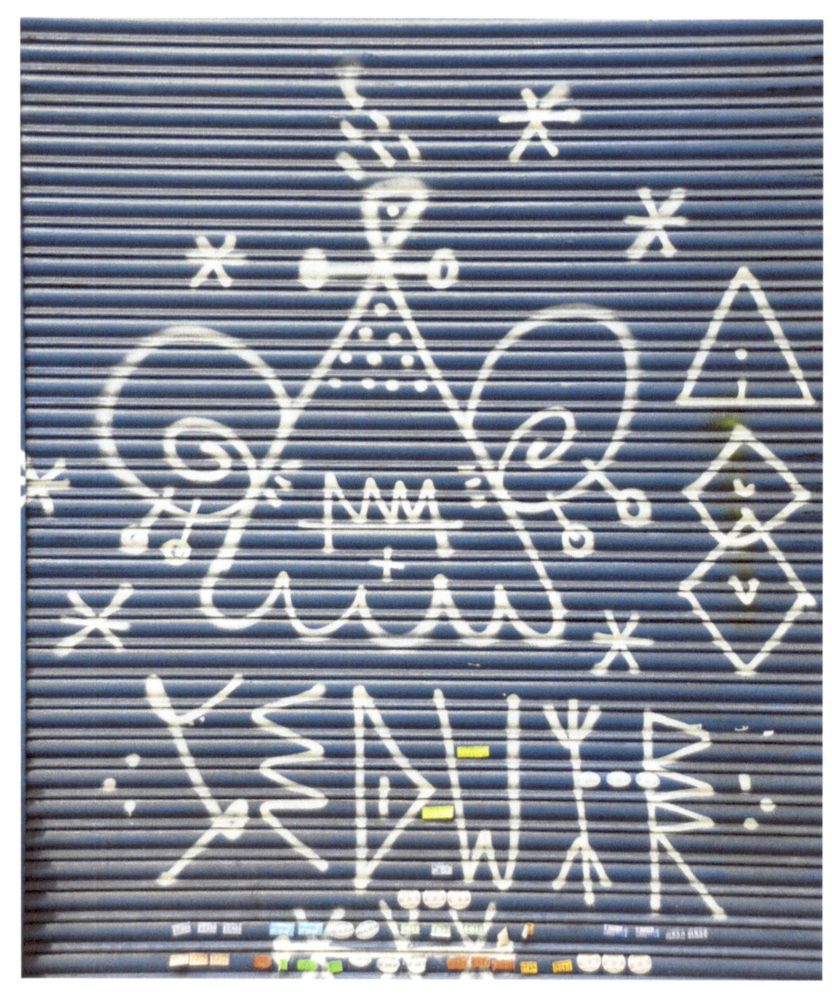

Barcelona, Spain

It is the creative potential itself in human beings that is the image of God.

--Mary Daly, 1928-

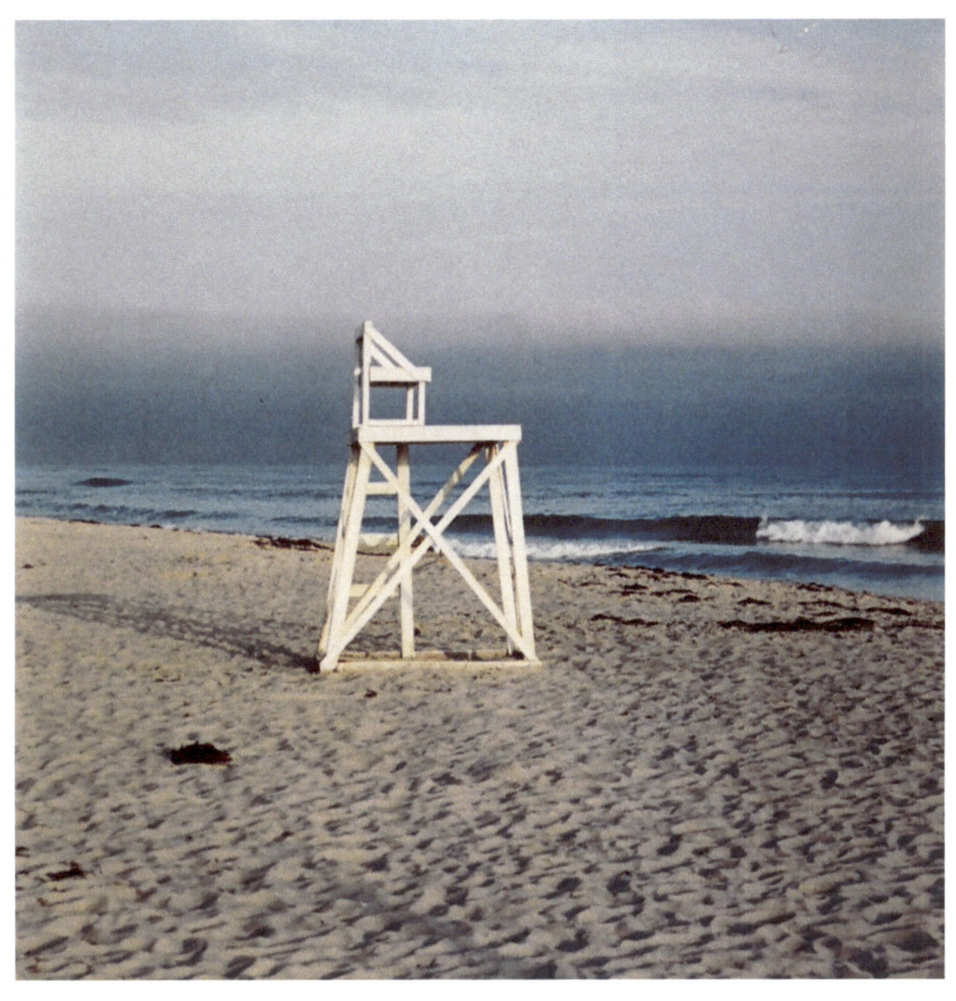

Nantucket, Massachusetts

Chance is perhaps the pseudonum of God
when he does not wish to sign his work.
--Anatole Frank, 1844-1924

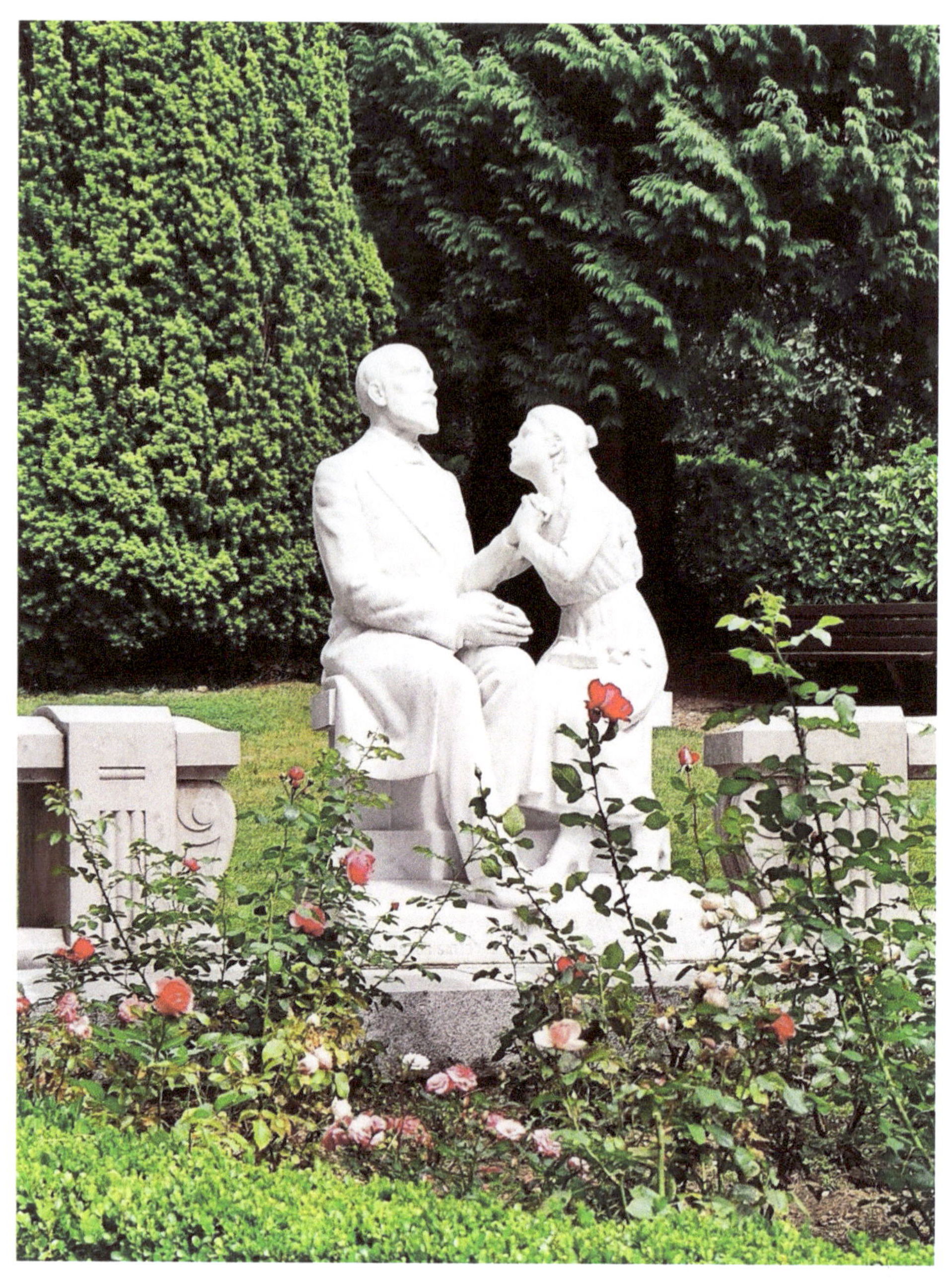

Liseaux, France

The value of consistent prayer is not that He will hear us,
but that we will hear Him.
--William McGill, 1922-1997

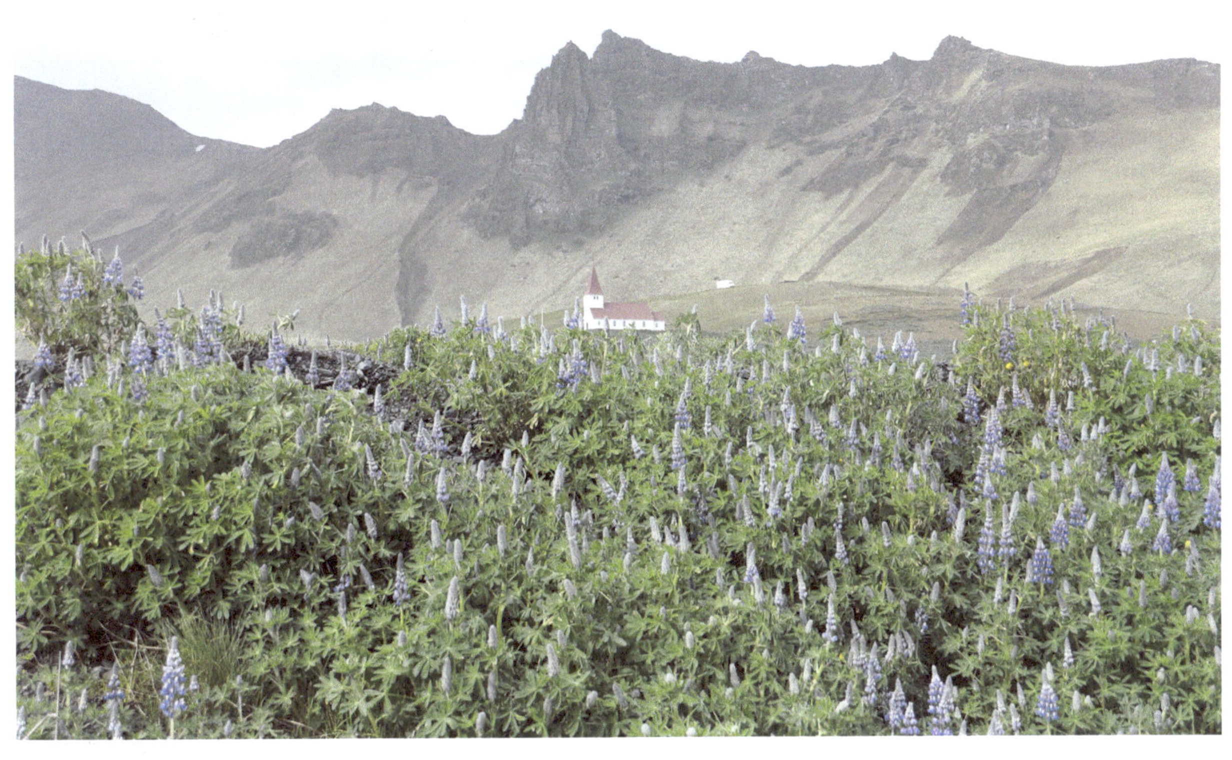

Vik, Iceland

I don't say what God is, but a name that somehow answers us
when we are driven to feel and think how little we have to do with what we are.
--Edwin Arlington Robinson, 1869-1935

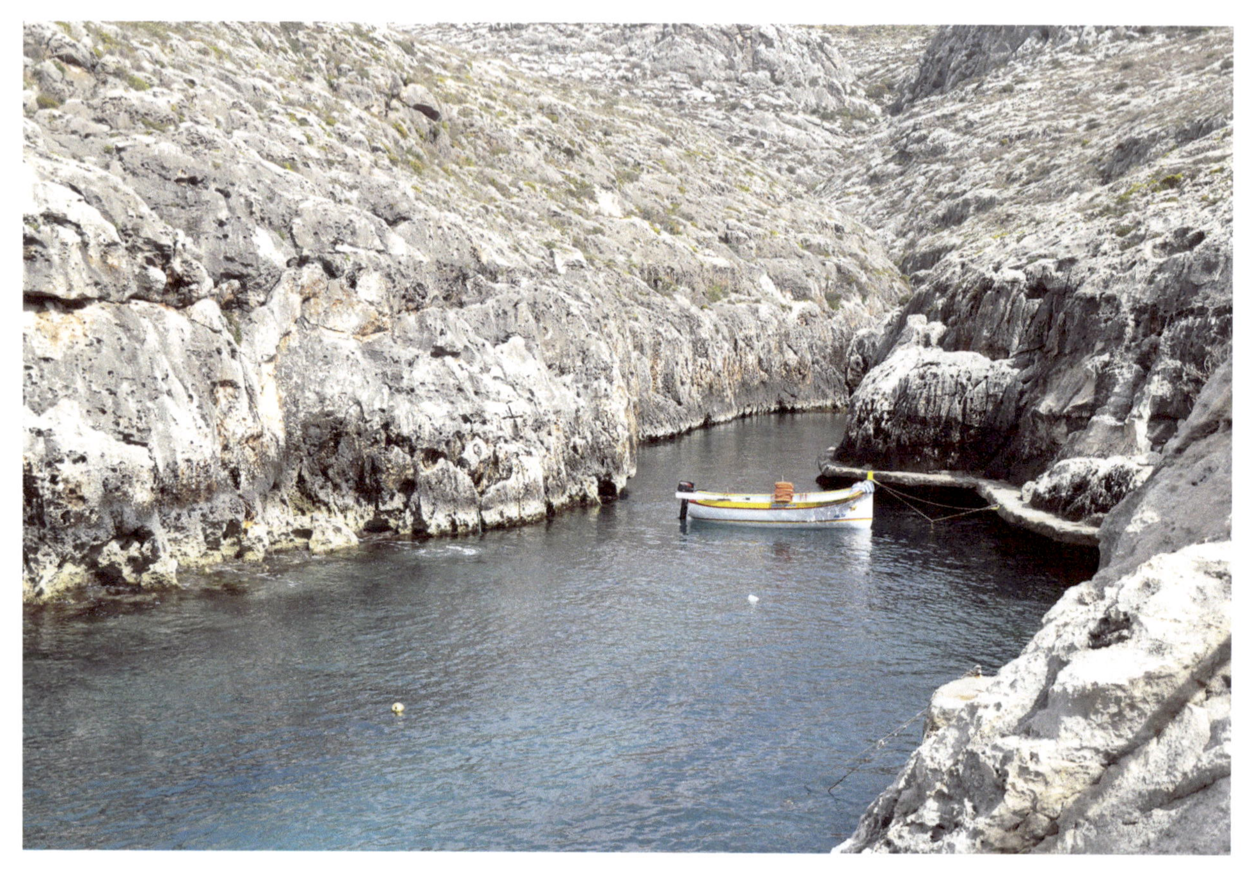

Blue Grotto, Malta

If you believe the noises of the world, rather than the silences of your soul, you will be lost.

--Neale Donald Walsch, 1943-

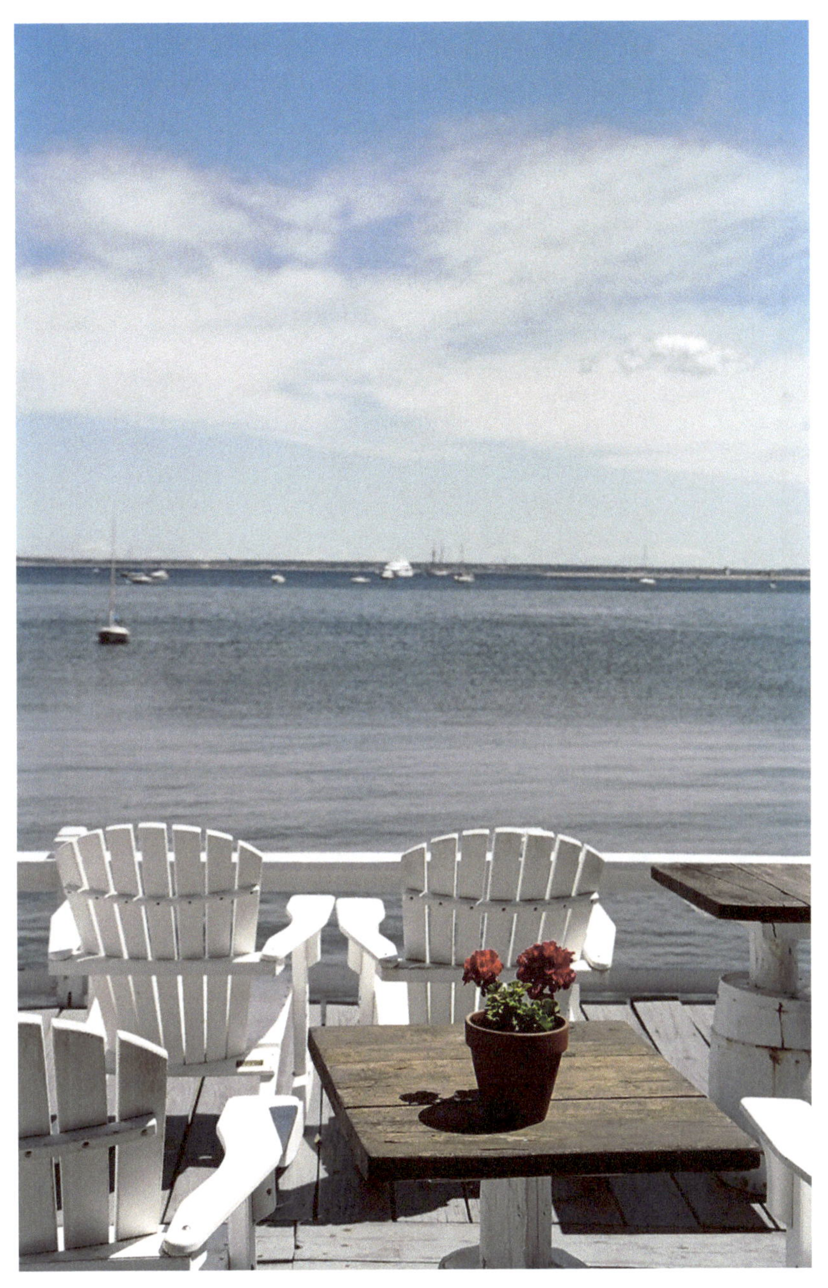

Provincetown, Massachusetts

You pray in your distress and in your need; would that you might also in the fullness of your joy and in your days of abundance.

--Kahlil Gibran, 1883-1931

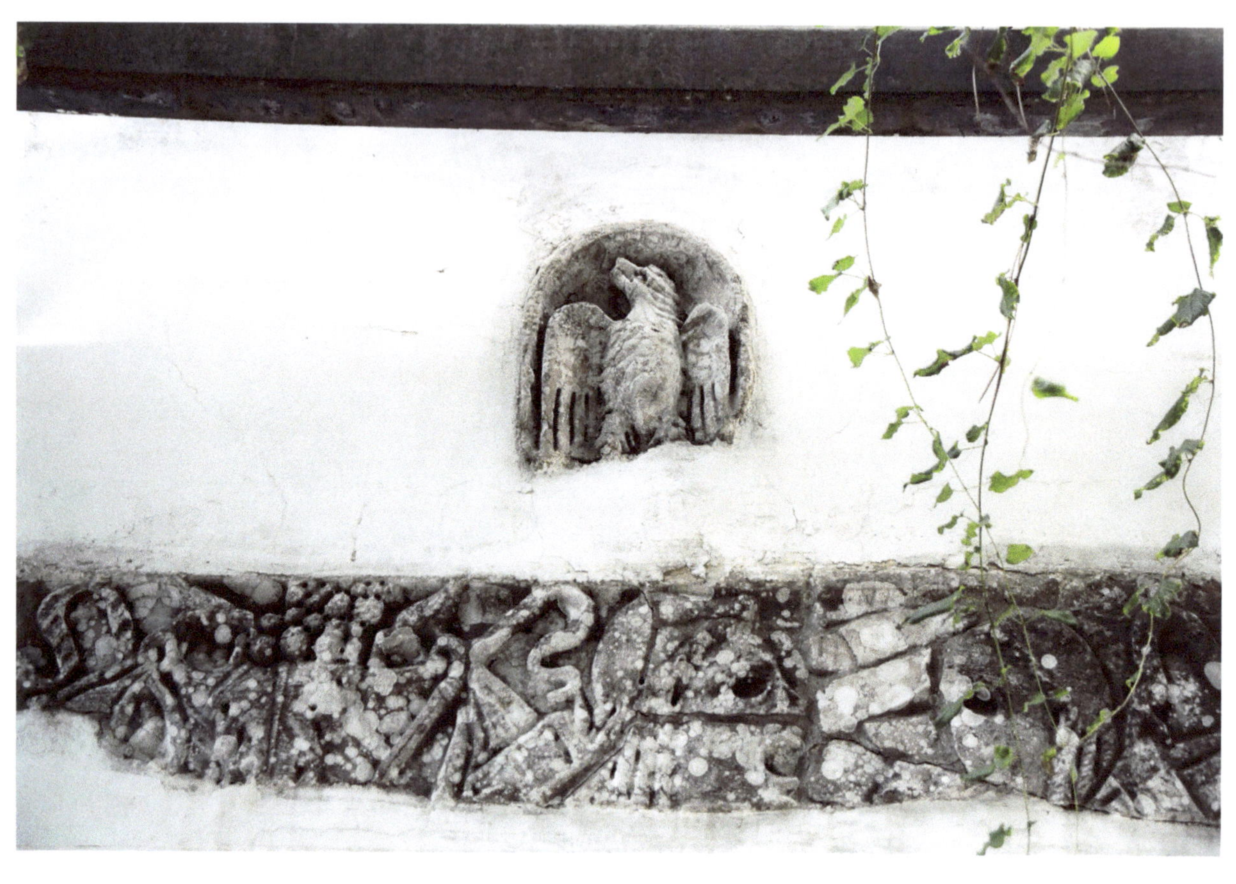

Capri, Italy

For the birds that cannot soar,
God has provided low branches.
--Turkish proverb

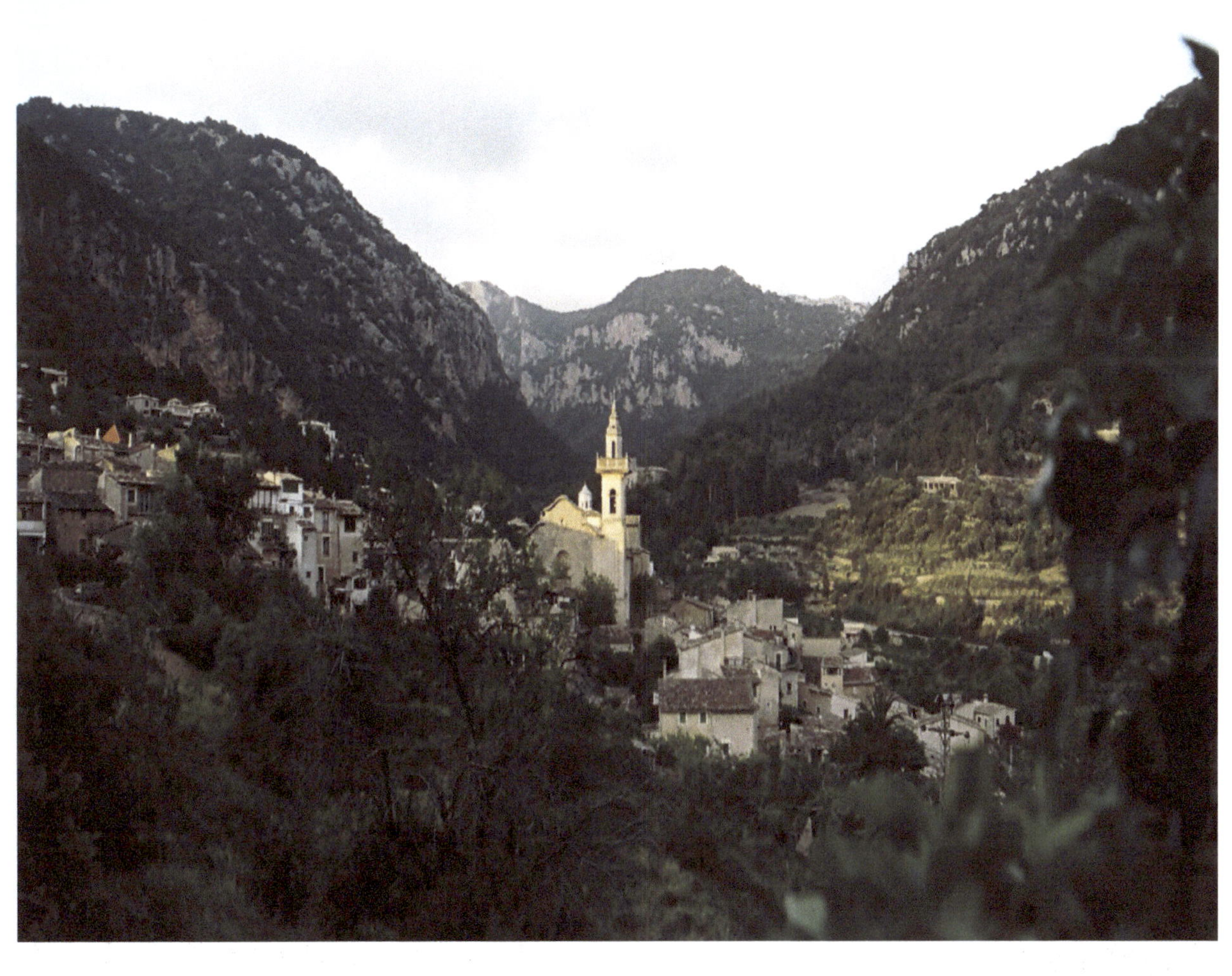

Majorca, Spain

When walking through the "valley of shadows," remember, a shadow is cast by a Light.

– H. K. Barclay

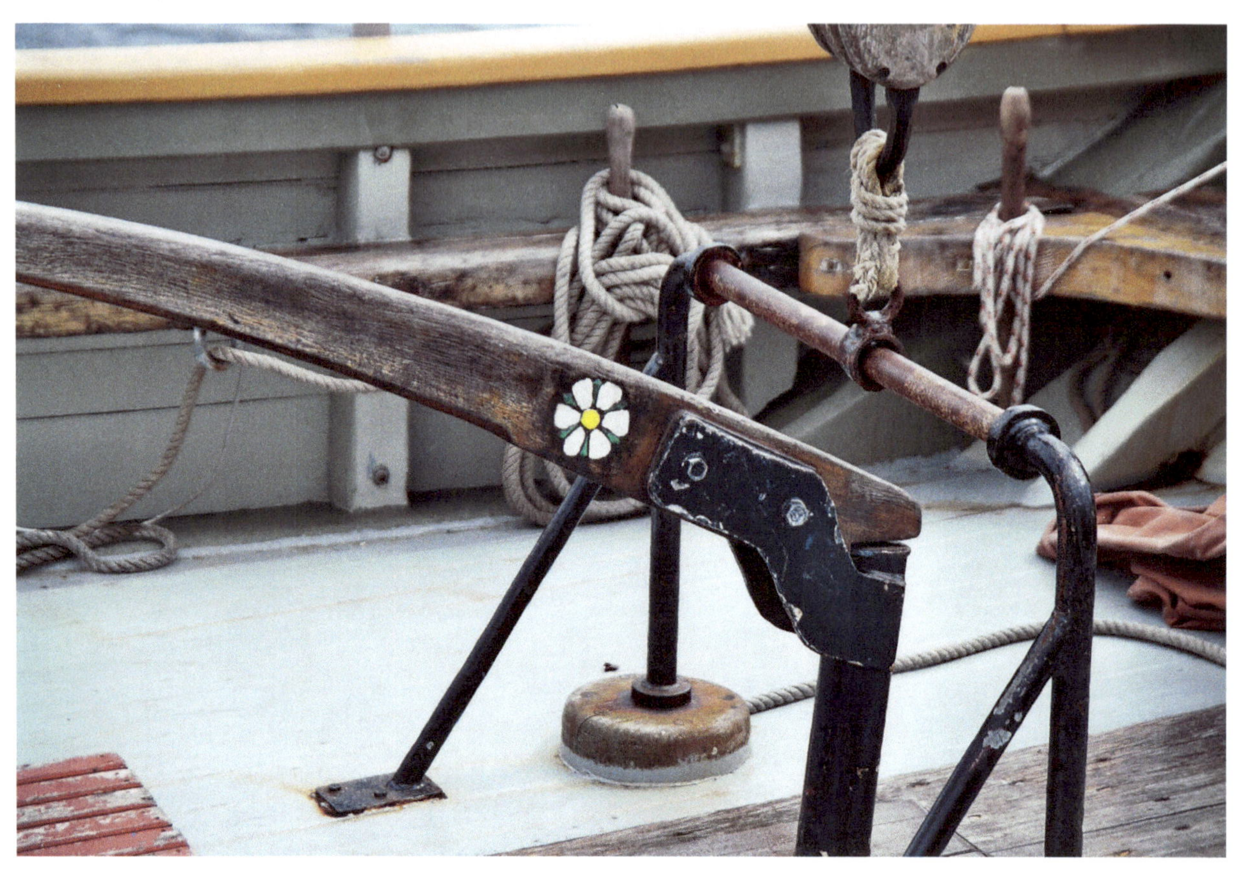

Saint-Malo, France

God's will is not an itinerary, but an attitude.

--Andrew Dhuse

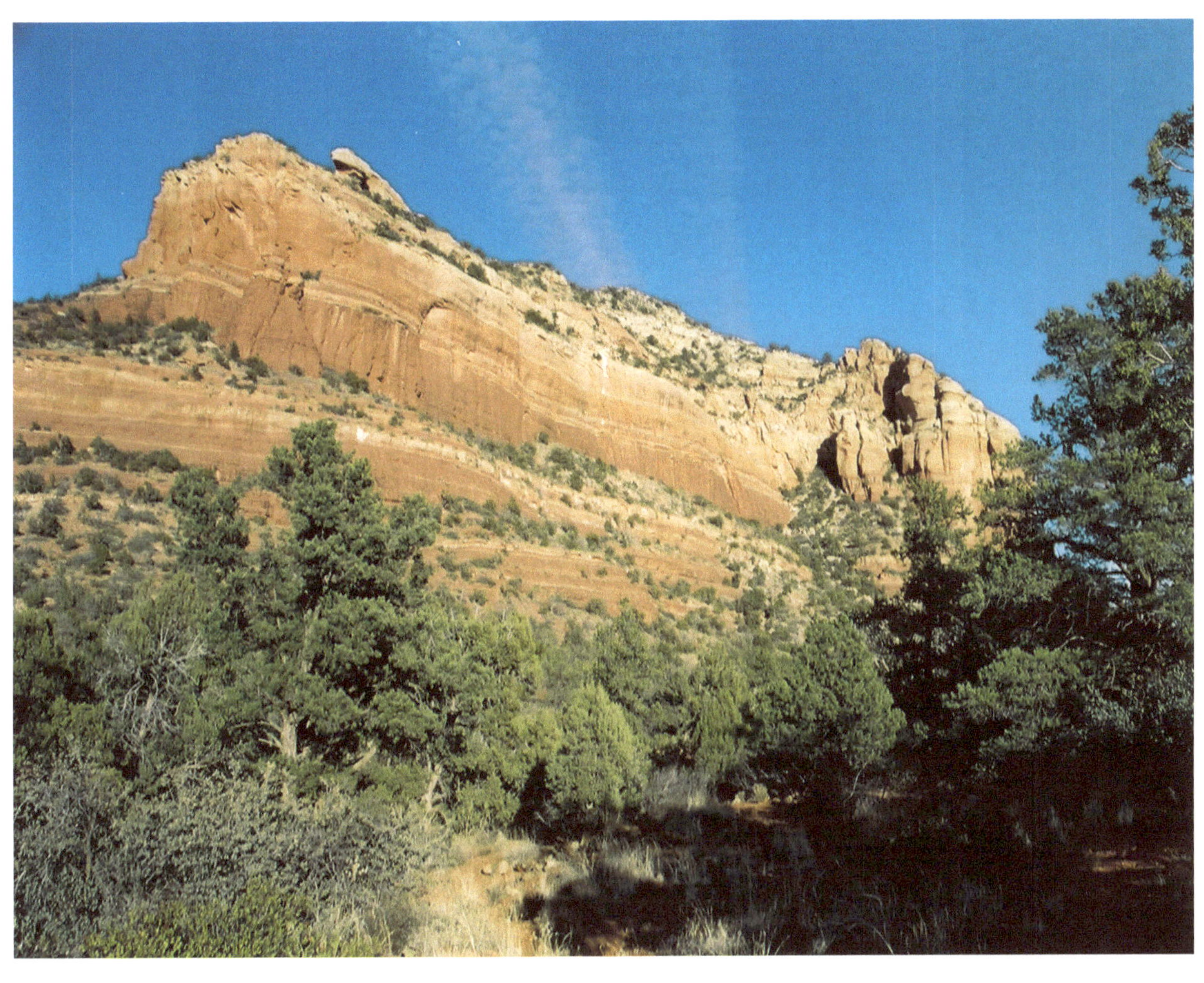

Sedona, Arizona

Because God's gifts put man's best dreams to shame.

– Elizabeth Barrett Browning, 1806-1861

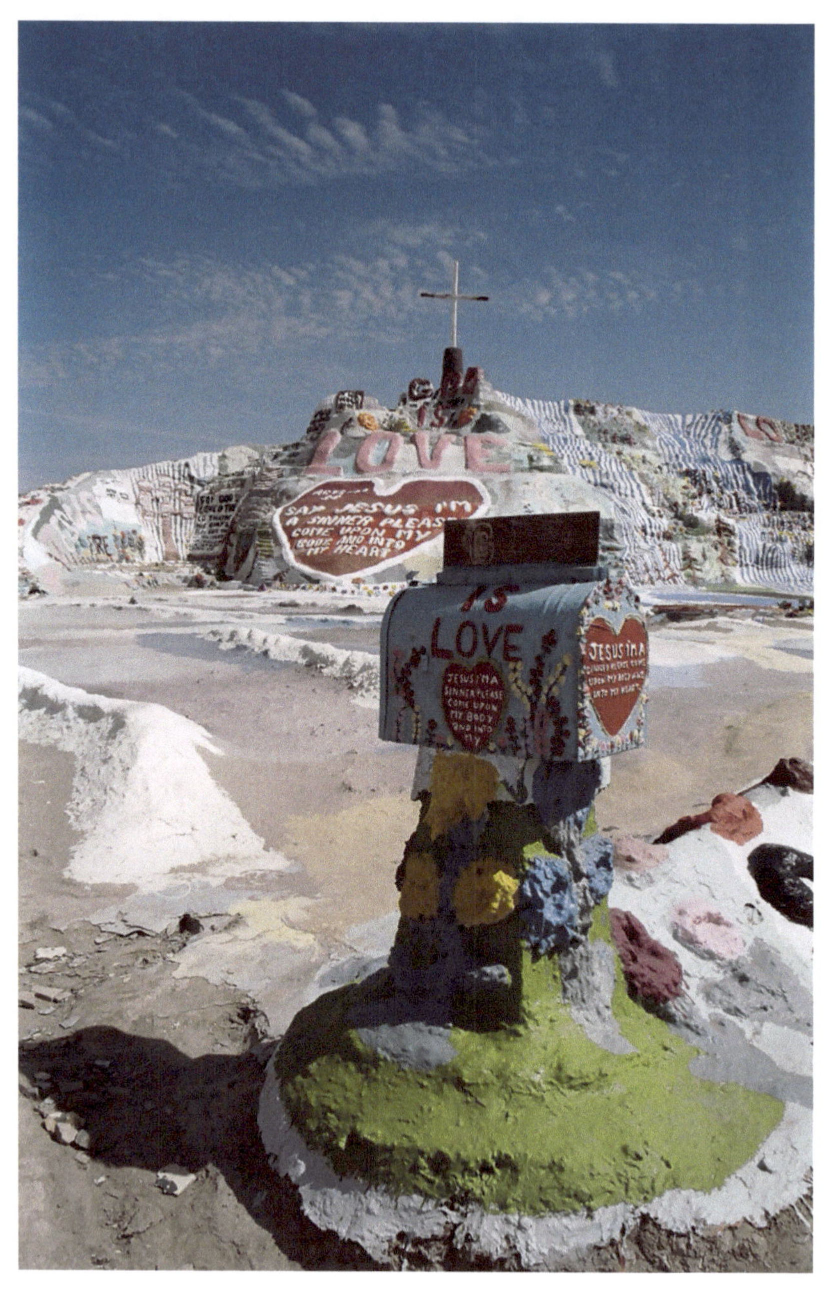


Salvation Mountian, California

I am a little pencil in the hand of a writing God who is sending a love letter to the world.

--Mother Teresa, 1910-1997

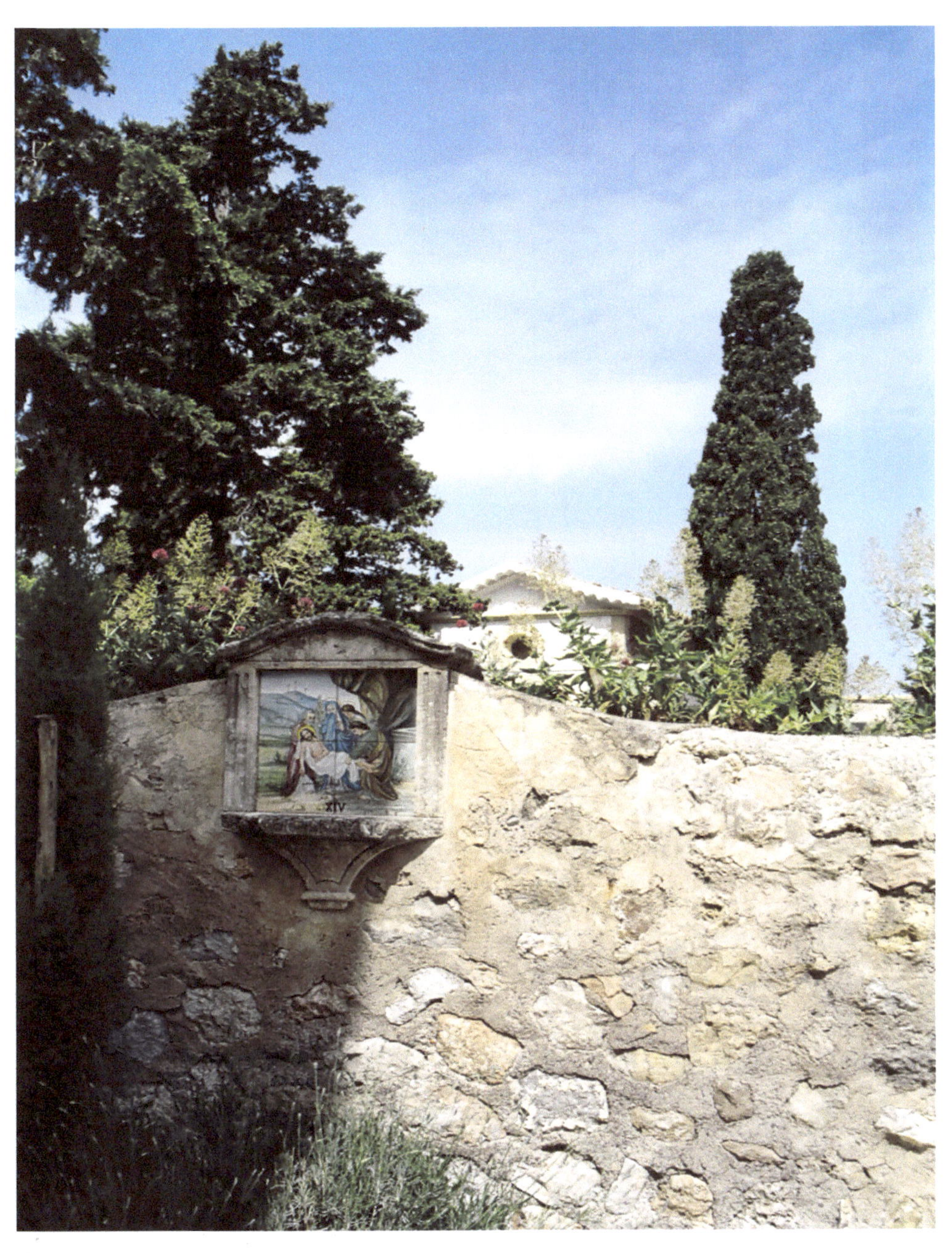

Majorca, Spain

Faith is love taking the form of aspiration.

--William Ellery Channing, 1817-1901

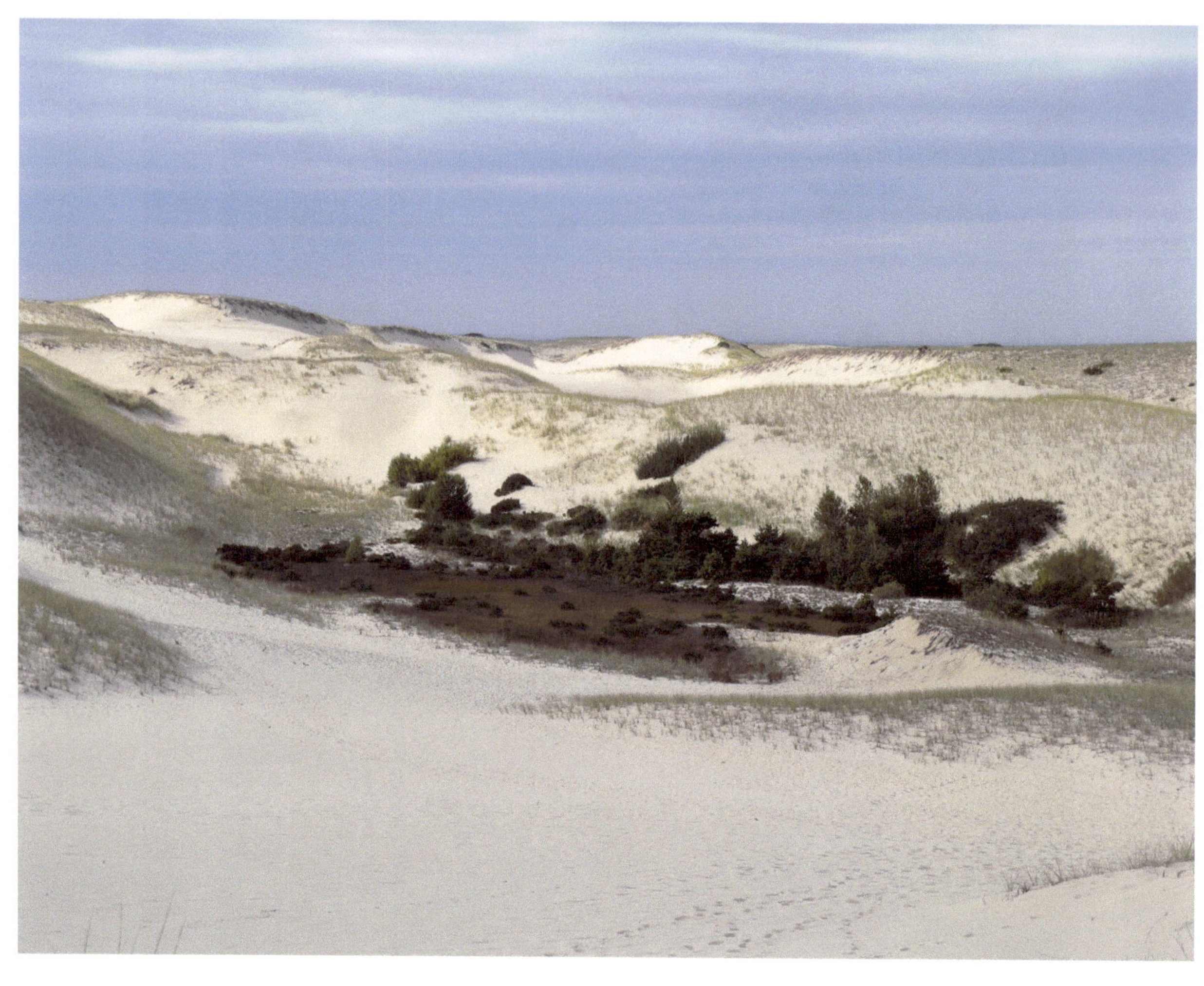

Truro, Massachusetts

Faith is an oasis in the heart which can never be reached by the caravan of thinking.

– Kahlil Gibran, 1883-1931

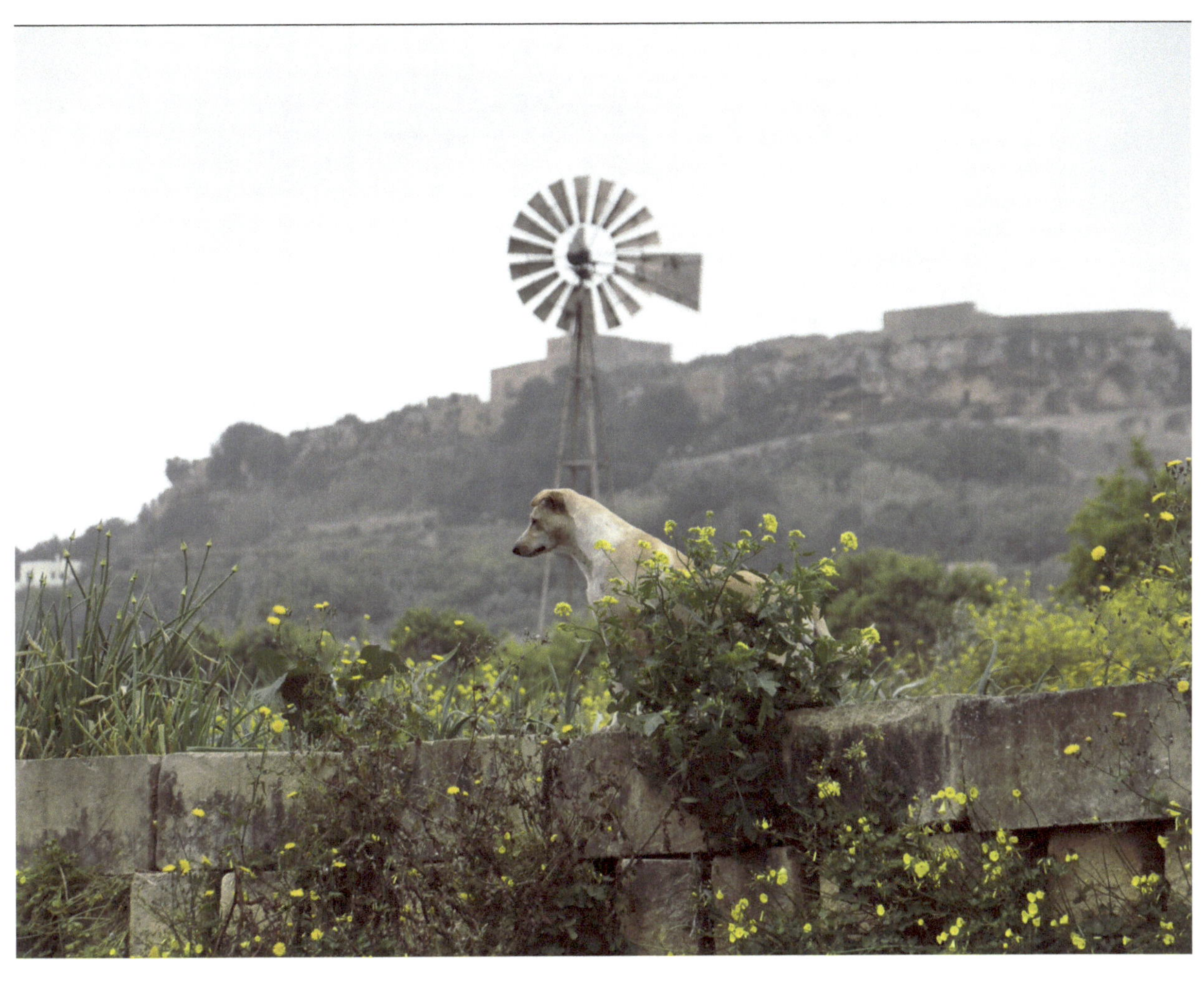

Ramla Bay, Gozo

I will not fear, for you are ever with me,
and you will never leave me to face my perils alone.
--Thomas Merton, 1915 - 1968

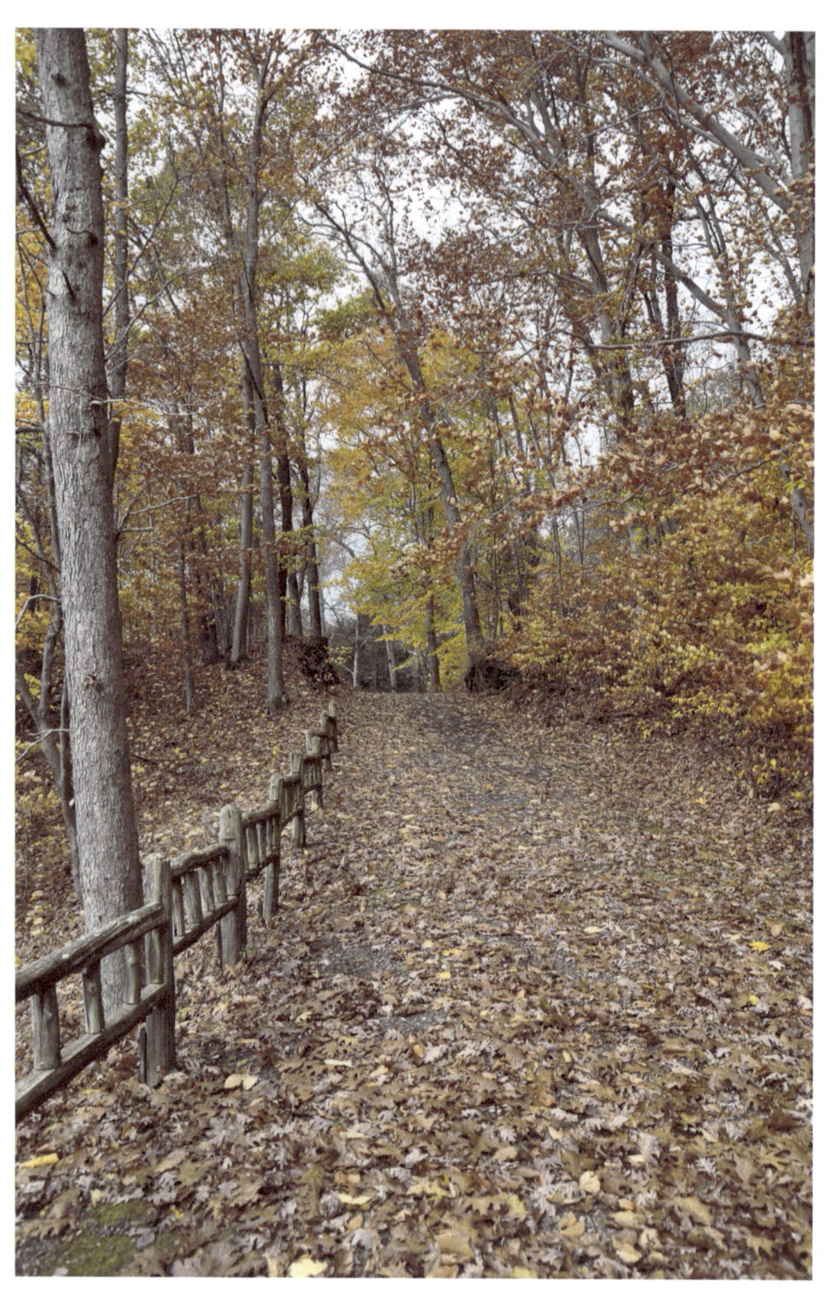

East Haddam, Connecticut

"An agnostic found himself in trouble and a friend suggested he pray.
"How can I pray when I do not know if there is a God?" he asked.
"If you are lost in the forest," his friend replied,
"you do not wait until you find someone before shouting for help."
--Dan Plies

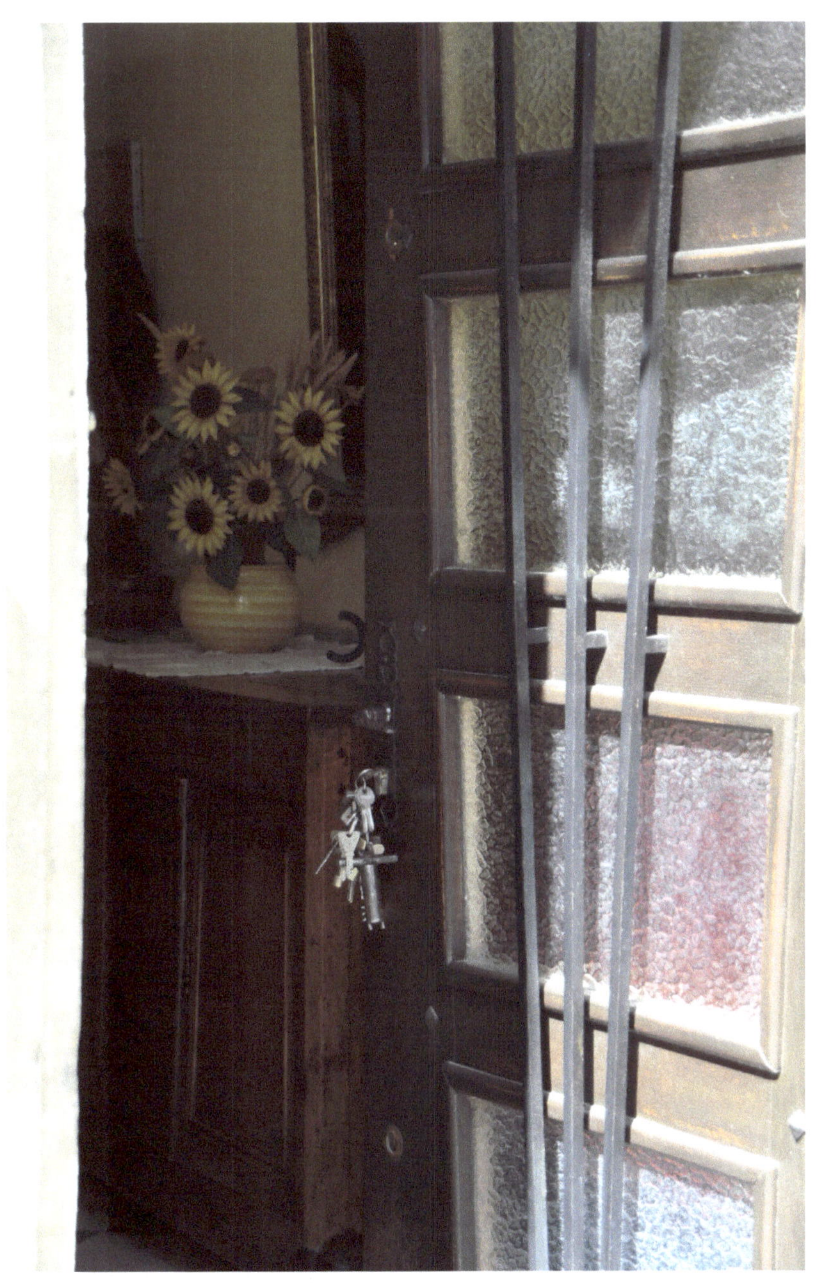

Puivert, France

To me, faith means not worrying.

--John Dewey, 1859 - 1952

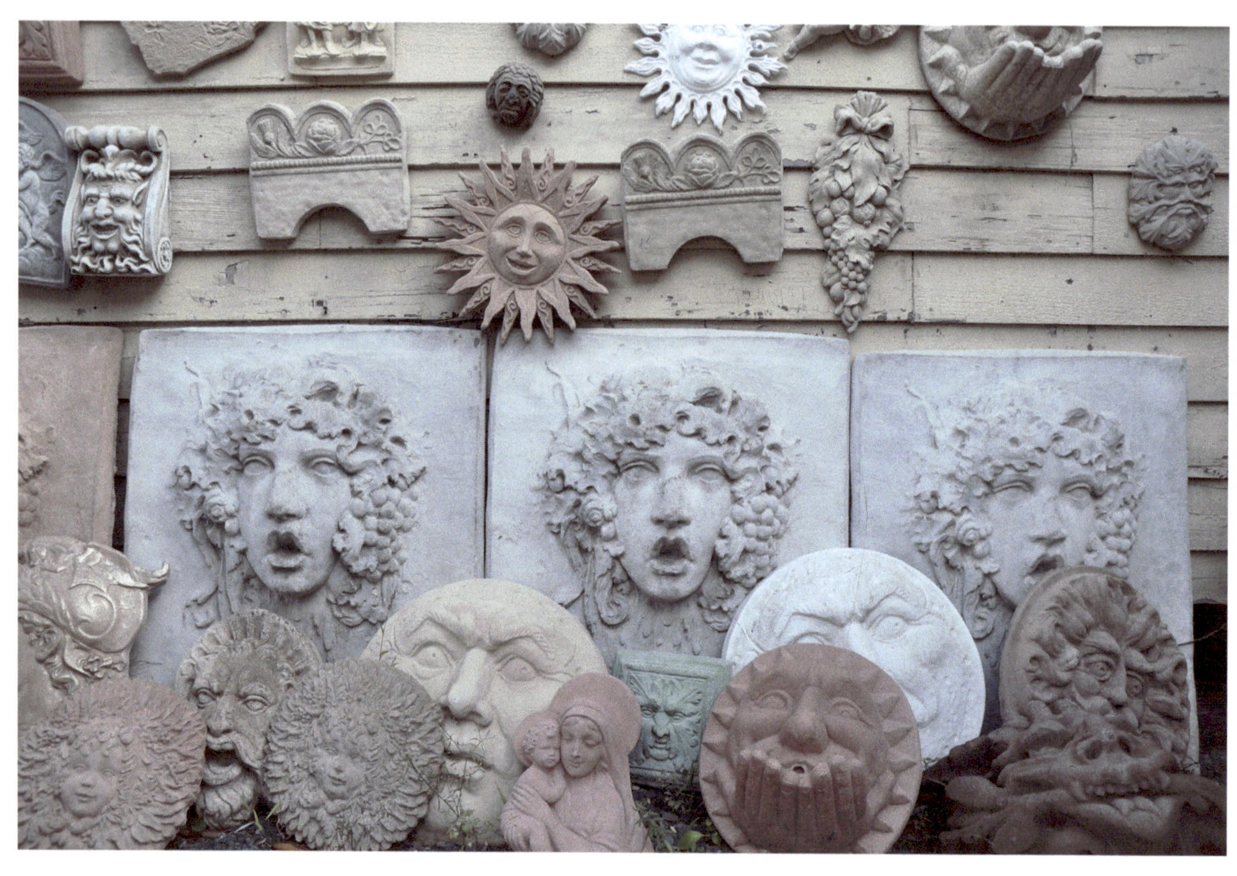

Turners Falls, Massachusetts

Whether we name divine presence synchronicity, serendipity, or graced moments matters little.
What matters is the reality that our hearts have been understood.
Nothing is as real as a healthy dose of magic which restores our spirits.
--Nancy Long

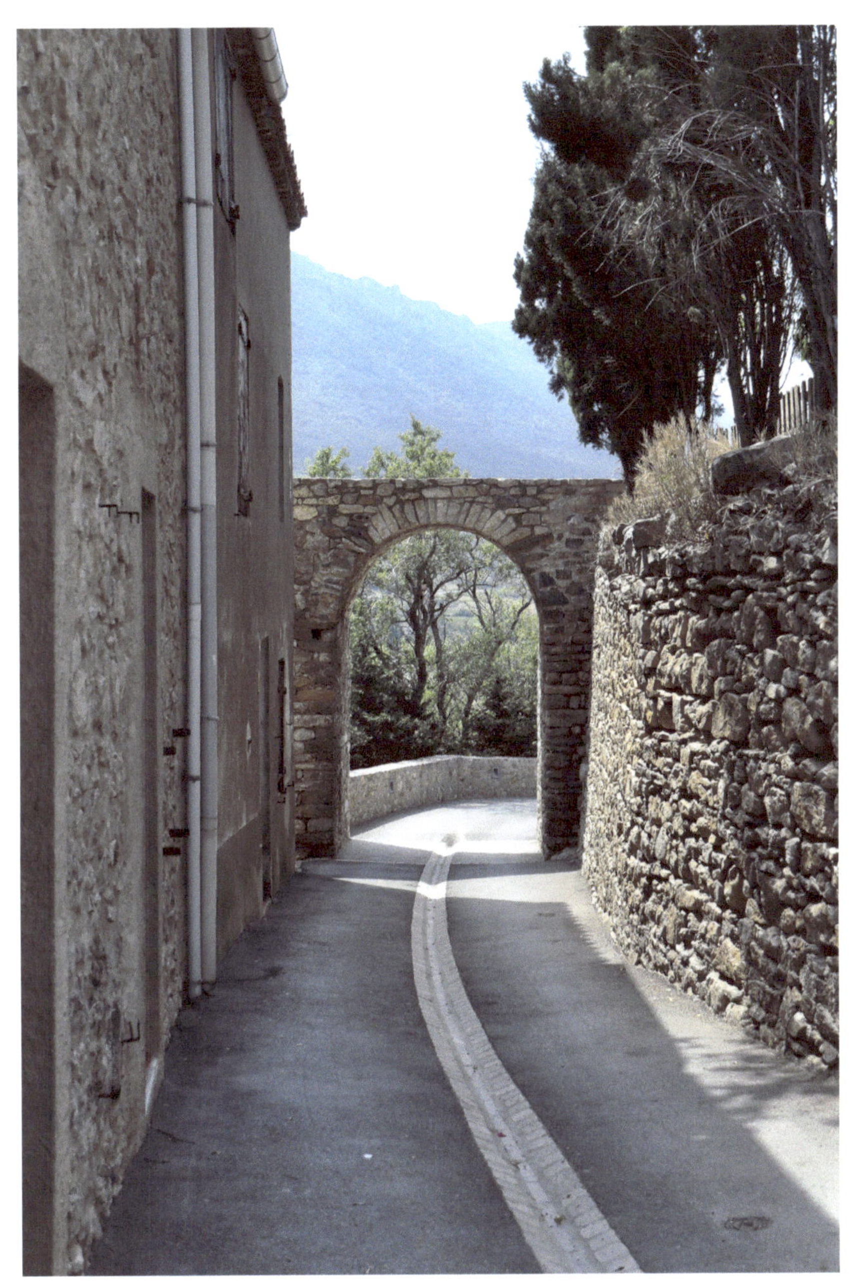

Cucugnan, France

Faith is building on what you know is here, so you can reach what you know is there.

--Cullen Hightower, 1923 -

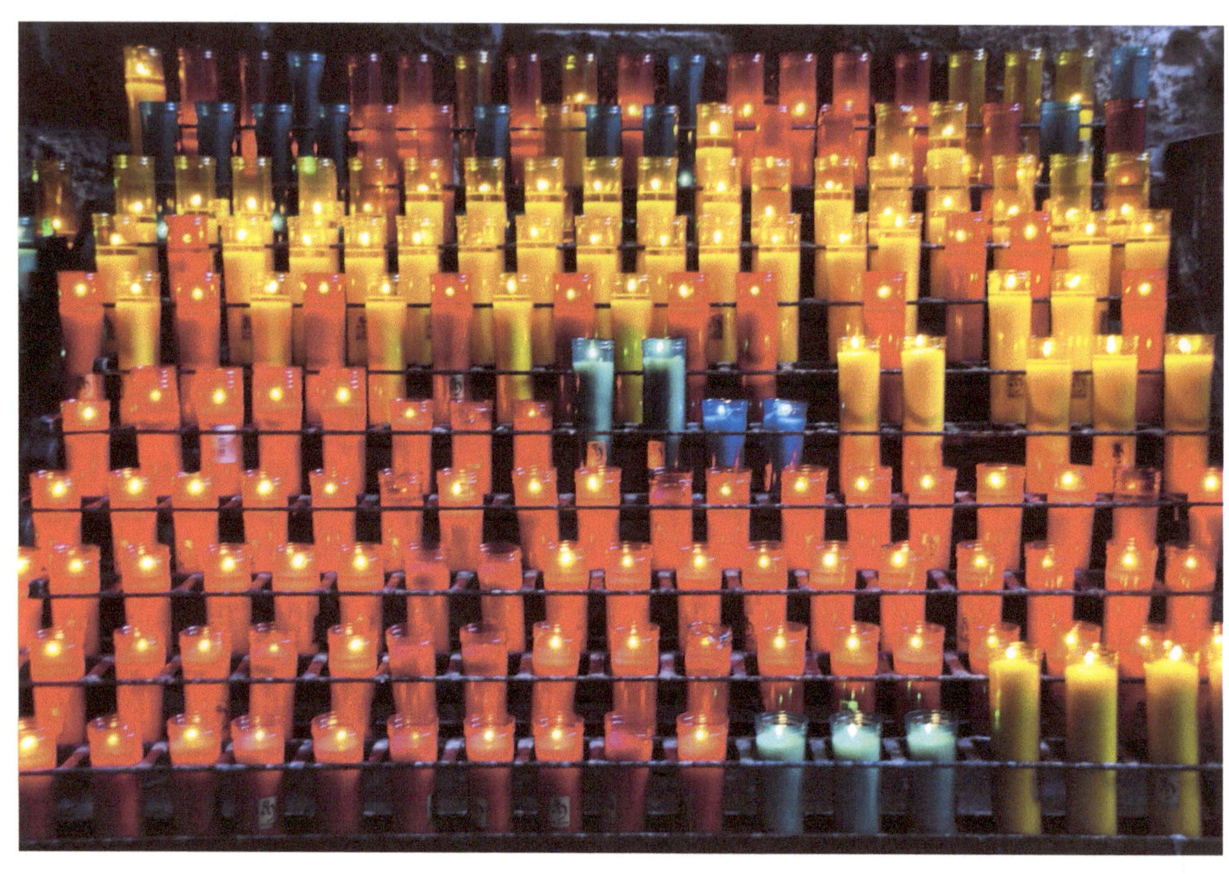

Montserrat, Spain

Patience with others is Love,
Patience with self is Hope,
Patience with God is Faith.
--Adel Bestavros

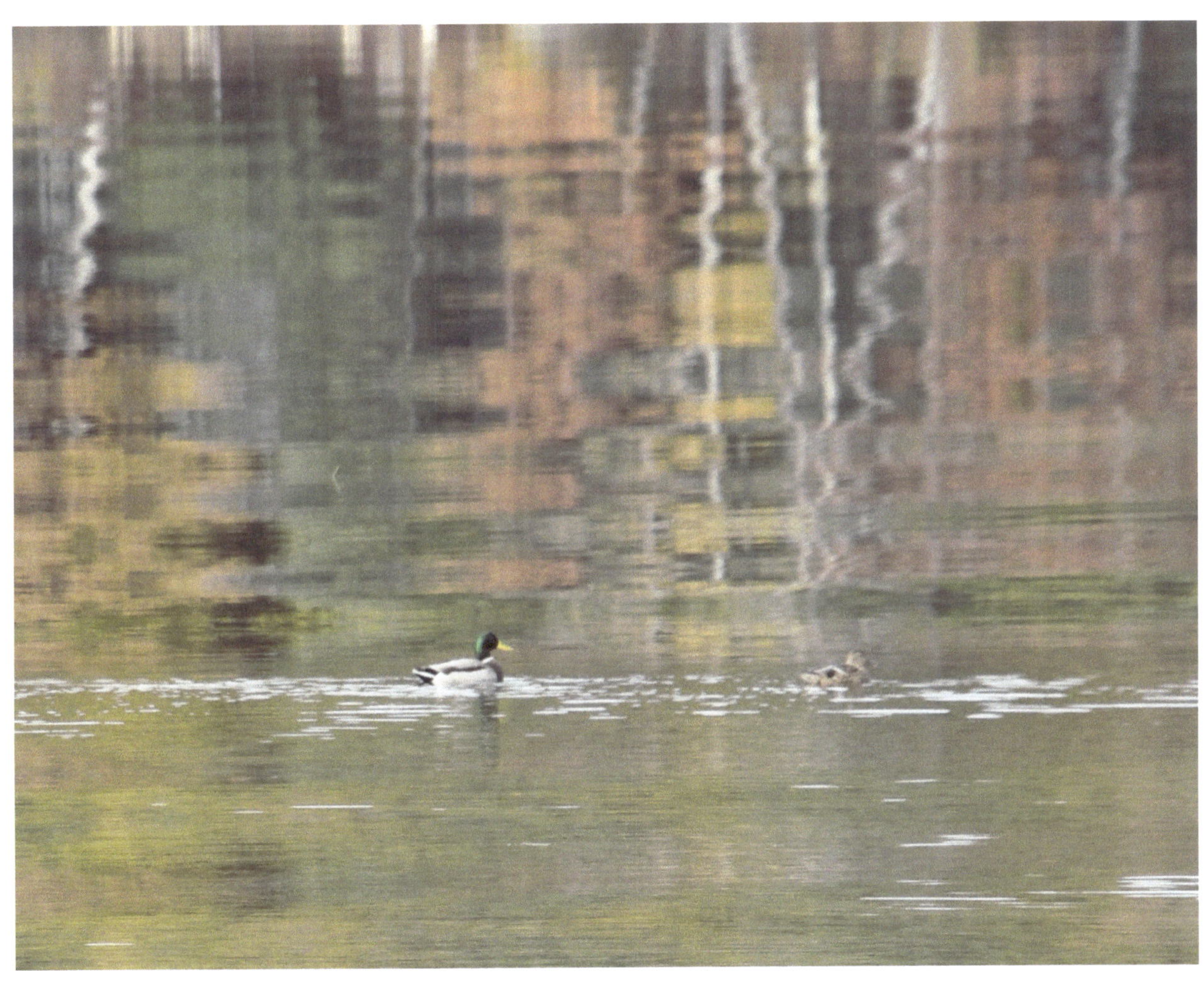

Wolfeboro, New Hampshire

Faith is primarily a process of identification;

the process by which the individual ceases to be himself

and becomes part of something eternal.

--Eric Hoffer, 1902 - 1983

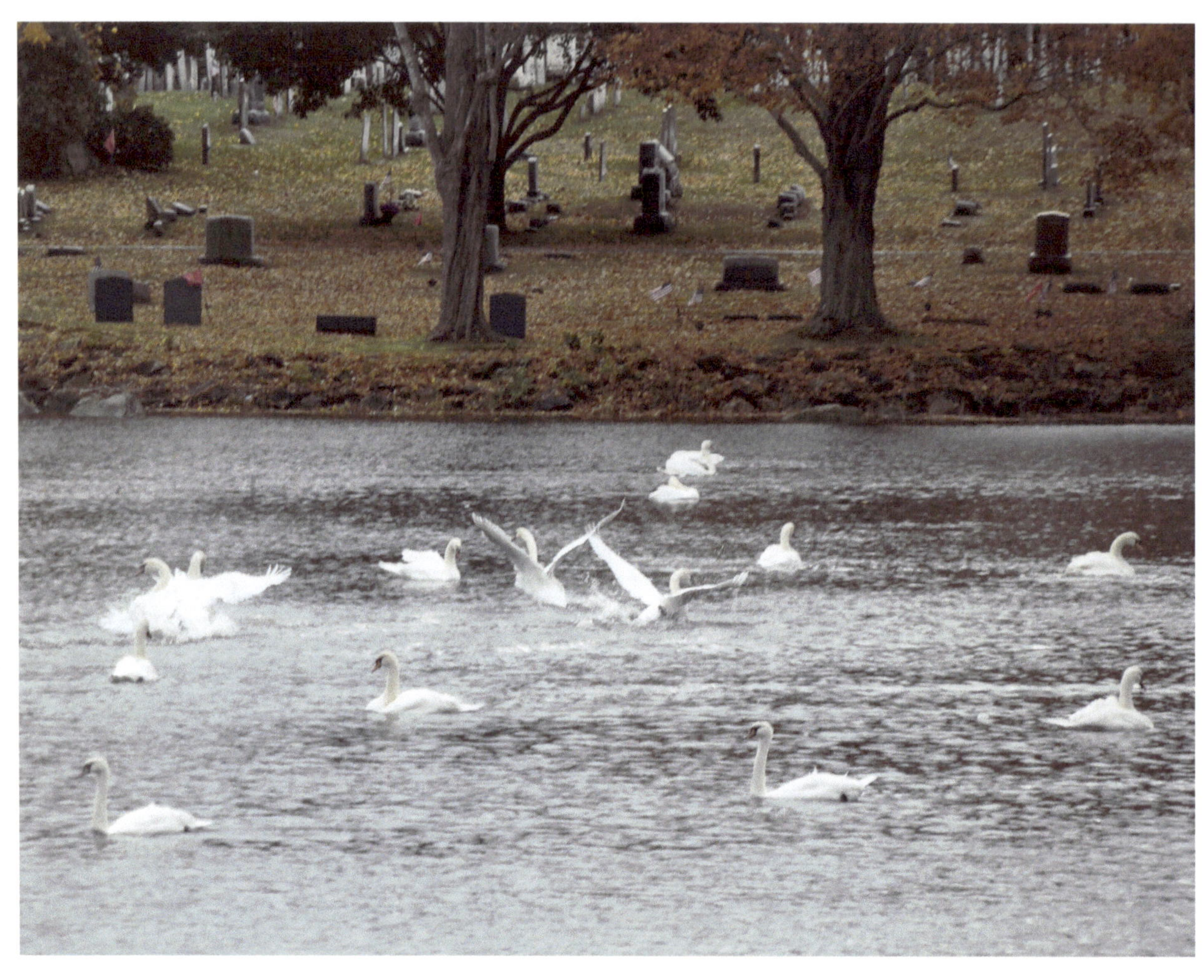

Essex, Connecticut

Faith is an act of a finite being who is grasped by, and turned to, the infinite.

--Paul Tillich, 1886 - 1965

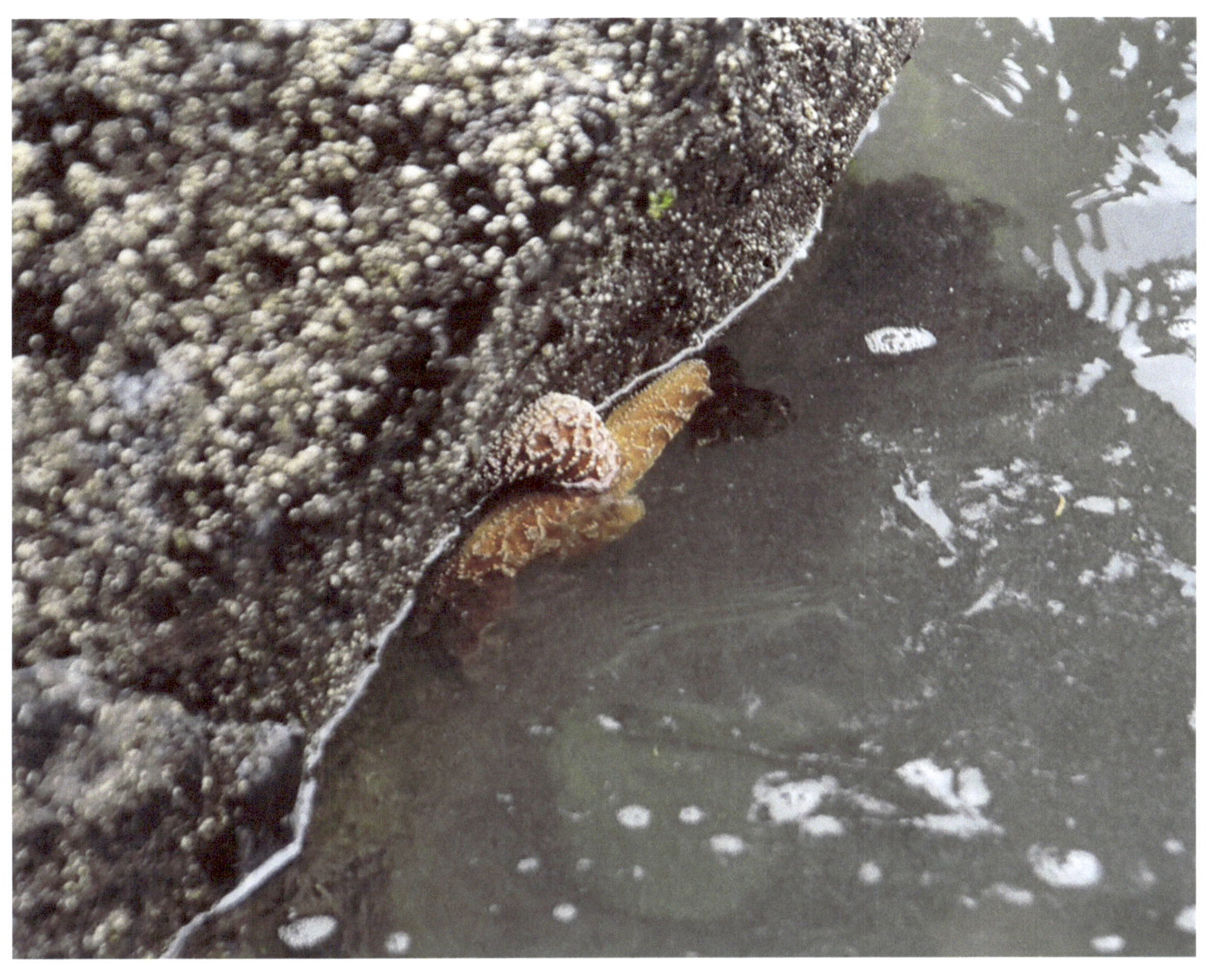

Schooner Bay, British Columbia

Never think that God's delays are God's denials.

Hold on; hold fast, hold out.

Patience is genuis.

--Comte De Buffon, 1707 - 1799

# Bibliography

Dass, Ram, One Liners: A Mini Manual for a Spiritual Life, Bell Tower, Member of Crown Publishing Group, a division of Random House, Inc., 2002.

Deger, Steve and Leslie Anne Gibson, The Little Positive Book of Positive Quotations, Fairfiew Press, 2006.

Fox, Emmet, Around the Year with Emmet Fox, Harper San Franciso, a division of HarperCollins Publishers, 1992.

Ratcliffe, Susan, Little Oxford Dictionary of Quotations, New edition, Oxford University Press, 2005.

Shanahan, John M., The Most Brilliant Thoughts of All Time (in two lines or less), Collins, an imprint of HarperCollins Publishers, 2005.

Toliver, Wendy, The Little Giant Encyclopedia of Inspirational Quotes, Sterling Publishing Co., Inc., 2004.

www.bartleby.com
www.famousquotes.com
www.quotationspage.com
www.quotegarden.com
www.quoteland.com
www.quoteworld.org
www.worldofquotes.com
www.viewfromthepier.com

www.ingramcontent.com/pod-product-compliance
Lightning Source LLC
LaVergne TN
LVHW070129110826
845147LV00002B/221
* 9 7 8 0 9 8 2 2 2 0 2 1 4 *